Birds c
The Solomons,
Vanuatu &
New Caledonia

· Helm Field Guides ·

Birds of The Solomons, Vanuatu & New Caledonia

Chris Doughty
Nicolas Day
Andrew Plant

CHRISTOPHER HELM

A & C Black · London

THE COLOUR PLATES
Nicolas Day: 1–8, 11, 12, 15, 16–23, 34–40, 43–49, 55–61, 74, 79–82, 90, 91
Andrew Plant: 9, 10, 13, 14, 24–33, 41, 42, 50–54, 62–73, 75–78, 83–89

© 1999 Text and maps: Chris Doughty
© 1999 Illustrations: Nicolas Day and Andrew Plant

Christopher Helm (Publishers) Ltd, a subsidiary of A & C Black
(Publishers) Ltd, 35 Bedford Row, London WC1R 4JH

0-7136-4690-X

A CIP catalogue record for this book is available from the
British Library

Printed in Singapore

10 9 8 7 6 5 4 3 2 1

Contents

About the Author and Artists   6

Acknowledgements   7

Introduction   8
  Aims of the Book   8
  The Illustrations   8
  Format of the Species Accounts   9
  Distribution Maps   9
  Taxonomy and Nomenclature   9
  Island Names in the Solomons   10
  Bird Habitats   10
  Abbreviations Used in the Book   12

Family Introductions   13

Glossary of Terms Used in the Guide   23

Parts of a Bird   26

Species Accounts   28

Further Reading   200

Index of Common English Names   201

Index of Scientific Names   204

About the Author and Artists

Author

Chris Doughty is originally from the U.K. and has been living in Australia for the past 25 years, with his wife Christine and children, Curtis, Paul, Adam and Kendal. His interest in birds developed at an early age and before leaving for Australia he was already a keen field ornithologist. Chris is an active member of the Bird Observers Club of Australia and Birds Australia. He has served on the Australian Rarities Committee and is the founding Director of Peregrine Bird Tours. He is acknowledged as one of the world's most experienced bird tour leaders, having led in excess of 100 birding tours to most parts of the world. He is particularly interested in the avifauna of Australia and the South Pacific, and has enjoyed field trips to many South Pacific islands. Chris has field experience with every Australian breeding species, with the exception of two probably extinct species.

Illustrators

Nicolas Day was born in Surrey in the U.K. and emigrated to Australia at the age of ten. He later became a keeper at the Royal Melbourne Zoological Gardens, and began painting professionally in 1977. His work has been exhibited in Canada, the United Kingdom and Japan. Nick has previously illustrated *Field Guide to the Birds of Australia* and *Field Guide to the Birds of the Australian Capital Territory*. He has worked as a naturalist guide on overland safaris in Australia and birded and sketched as far afield as the Outer Hebrides and the Subantarctic. He was recently the artist on the 1997 expedition to Raine Island in the Coral Sea.

Andrew Plant was born in Melbourne and at an early age was introduced to birdwatching by his father. He studied at Melbourne University where he earned a B.Sc. (Hons) in Zoology, majoring in bird behaviour. In 1982 he was awarded the Sam Slater Memorial Award for the best new wildlife artist, by the Wildlife Artists Society of Australasia. Andrew has worked as a freelance commercial artist and illustrator since 1984. In 1992 he became a full-time book illustrator and has illustrated well over 40 books for use in primary, secondary and tertiary education, together with books on medicine and biology and several children's story books. Andrew has birded and sketched in several countries, from the bottom of Ngorongoro Crater to the Everest Base Camp. He also has a keen interest in theatre and works as a choreographer and set designer and painter. Andrew was married to Bronwyn in 1996.

Acknowledgements

We would like to acknowledge the help of the following people and institutions for their assistance in the preparation, reviewing and compilation of this book. The staff of the British Museum (Natural History) at Tring, particularly Mark Adams, for allowing reference to their skin collection and answering queries regarding undescribed plumages; Les Christidis and Rory O'Brien, curators of the Ornithology Department, Museum of Victoria, in Melbourne, for allowing reference to their skin collection; Birds Australia Library, Melbourne; Bird Observers Club of Australia Library, Melbourne, in particular reference librarian, Mrs Virgil Hubregtse, for her kind assistance.

Two people in particular deserve special thanks: David Gibb for supplying bird illustrations from a field trip he undertook to the Solomon Islands in the early 1990s, and Moray Iles who provided valuable information on the status, distribution and calls of Solomon Island birds.

Special thanks to those who helped in the physical preparation of the book, in particular Ellen McCulloch for undertaking the tedious job of proofreading the entire manuscript, and my wife Christine for typing the manuscript.

Among family members, friends, correspondents and field companions a special thanks to Mike Carter, Peter Trusler, Ken Simpson, Jeff Davies, Nick Green, Betty, Harry, Tony and Pat Day, Andrew and Lorraine Wegener, David Plant, Trevor Foon, Robyn Spencer, Lyn and Tristan Roberts, Stephanie, Rod, Anika and Adam Steel, Ann and Phil Westwood and Bronwyn Plant.

Introduction

This is the first comprehensive field guide to the avifauna of this fascinating region of the Southwest Pacific. A few books dealing with some of the birds of the region have been written, but none has been devoted entirely to this region, nor have they provided the reader with a quick and easy way of identifying the many species of colourful and interesting birds that inhabit these beautiful tropical islands.

This book describes and illustrates 362 species of resident and migratory birds, encompassing every species that is known to have occurred in the region, together with several species that are likely to occur as vagrants but as yet have not been officially recorded. These South Pacific islands have been isolated from mainland Australia and New Guinea for many millions of years, and despite rather close proximity to each other, the millennia-long isolation between islands has resulted in the evolution of a highly endemic avifauna. Of the 350 species that have been known to occur here, 117 are endemic, many of them restricted to just one or two islands. Some species are already thought to be extinct. They have been included in the field guide in the very real hope that some of them may yet occur in remote, seldom visited areas, of which there are a great many throughout the region. It is also hoped that by including extinct species, it may bring readers to an awareness of how much may already be lost and just how important it is to preserve what remains.

The geographical area covered by the guide encompasses a host of oceanic islands located between New Guinea and New Zealand and comprises three major groups: (a) The Solomon Islands; (b) Vanuatu, together with Banks Islands and the Santa Cruz Islands; (c) New Caledonia and the Loyalty Islands.

We have included the islands of Bougainville, Buka and Nissan as part of the Solomons, although they are currently regarded as being within the political boundaries of Papua New Guinea. Historically and geographically they have always been part of the Solomons and their avifauna is more closely related to that of the Solomons than to that of New Guinea, so it seems logical to include them in the field guide.

This is without doubt one of the least studied regions of the earth, ornithologically. Over 60 species of birds depicted in this guide have never been illustrated before. Although the author has enjoyed field experience with the vast majority of species included in the book, he is fully aware that there is still a great deal to be learnt regarding the distribution, population densities, and biology of many species occurring in the region.

Aims of the book

The aims of the book are twofold. Firstly, it has been specifically designed for use in the field, with its primary aim to assist birders who are unfamiliar with the avifauna of the region to identify birds quickly and accurately. It makes no pretence to being a handbook or biological reference, indeed, lengthy descriptions of bird behaviour have been deliberately avoided. Instead reliance is placed on accurate, uncluttered illustrations and an informative but concise text which emphasises the essential characteristics and field marks which set one species apart from another. In this guide, the text and distribution map of each species is arranged on the page facing the corresponding illustration, avoiding the frustrating and time-consuming practice of having to search through the book to match-up the illustration and the text; this feature will enable observers to identify birds quickly in the field. Secondly, it is hoped that this book will be used as a catalyst to stimulate interest in the avifauna of the region, and help build upon the present limited knowledge. Once a greater understanding of the avifauna of the region has been gained, it is vitally important to define the most effective means to conserve and protect the avifauna of these beautiful and as yet, largely unspoilt, islands.

The illustrations

As an aid to identification all birds illustrated are in typical, characteristic postures, with similar-looking species placed on the same plate. Where races differ markedly, they also have been illustrated.

Some groups of birds are harder to identify than others, and this is particularly so when they are seen only in flight. For this reason several plates depicting waterfowl, birds of prey and waders in flight are included. For all species, every distinct plumage is illustrated. Breeding plumage, non-breeding plumage, male, female and immature, where the juvenile plumage is sufficiently distinct, have also been illustrated.

Format of the species accounts

The text for each species begins with the bird's common name, followed by its scientific name which is printed in *italic* type and refers to the bird's genus and species in that order. Approximate total body length in centimetres follows the scientific name, and where there is a marked variation in size, as for example in birds of prey, the size range is given. For seabirds, which are usually seen only in flight, the length of the wingspan is also given.

Initial descriptive remarks concern the most important recognition features and any geographical restrictions and are printed in *italic* type. The amount of descriptive text that follows differs; those species which have various colour morphs or are particularly difficult to identify are described in greater detail. The descriptive text complements the illustrations, concentrating mainly upon important field marks which assist in identification. Please refer to the glossary and 'parts of a bird' for definitions of any technical terms used. All birds illustrated should be assumed to be in adult plumage, unless stated otherwise. The sexes should also be assumed to look alike or appear to be similar, unless male and female plumages are described separately. Breeding, non-breeding, immature and juvenile plumages are all described, where they are sufficiently distinct. Differences between races are also described, if they are readily separable in the field. Where two species are similar in appearance, the main distinguishing features are also discussed.

Next follows a short note outlining the preferred habitats of each species. For a precise definition of each habitat, refer to the section **Bird Habitats** on page 10. A brief statement of the bird's known status is then given, including information on abundance, migratory status and geographic range. Finally, there is a brief description of the bird's call, or song. This is written to represent as closely as possible the sound heard, or there is a general description of the type of song given. The songs and calls of a bird not only reveal its presence, but also provide important clues to its identity.

Distribution maps

The maps in the text show the status and distribution of all breeding birds and regular visitors to the region. Rare vagrants do not have a distribution map.

Key to Distribution Maps

| A resident breeding species, which is present throughout the year | A non-breeding visitor | Breeds here but migrates out of the region for a period outside the breeding season |

Taxonomy and nomenclature

In recent times there have been major innovations in methods of taxonomic study and avian classification. The most recent work having the greatest impact on avian taxonomy is Sibley and Ahlquist's (1990) *Phylogeny and Classification of Birds* and its preceding papers, particularly the classification of Sibley and Ahlquist (1985) and Sibley *et al* (1988). The techniques and analytical methods of these studies, based on DNA-DNA hybridisation, is a biochemical method that measures the degree of genetic similarity between the DNA of different species. This is a significant departure from the more traditional method of using morphological differences as the major factor in determining avian speciation and classification.

In this guide, common English names, scientific names and the sequence used follows those in *Birds of the World: A Check List* by James F. Clements (1991). In this check list Clements blends together the results of more recent genetic research with a relatively conservative approach which has enabled him to utilise, wherever possible, well-established more traditional avian classification.

Island names in the Solomons

While reviewing literature for this guide it has become evident that a specific island can be referred to by different names, or in some instances there is more than one way of spelling the name of an island. Some of these are colonial names that have reverted back to their native language names, while others are spelling corrections based on more accurate translations of native names. In the table below, the newly accepted names and newly accepted spellings are set out together with their older equivalents.

New	Old
Santa Isabel	Santa Ysabel
Kulambangra	Kolombangara
Makira	San Cristobal
Nggatokae	Gatukai
Ranongga	Ganongga
Tetepare	Tetepari
Vonavona	Wana Wana

Bird habitats

Birds inhabit every continent and almost every island in the world and have adapted to all ecological environments. Every species of bird has its own preference in habitat, and a bird's distribution is closely linked to habitat preference. Some species are very adaptable and can be found across a wide range of habitats. Another, for example, lives mainly in rainforest, but can be found in smaller numbers in most other habitats within its range. Other species are habitat-specific and are rarely if ever found away from their particular ecological environment.

In the species accounts, habitat preferences are given for each species. The following is a more detailed explanation of the main habitats that occur in the region.

Montane rainforest

Tropical rainforest is often referred to as jungle. It covers most of the region's land surface. The boundary between lowland and montane rainforest is not clearly delineated, but rather one of gradual change. As the altitude increases, lowland tree species are replaced by montane specialties. The lower altitudinal limit of montane rainforest varies from island to island, however, it usually occurs between 700 and 1200 metres. Montane rainforest is sustained by plentiful rainfall throughout the year, much of it from low clouds which envelop and shroud the forest. It is characterised by a variety of evergreen tree species, the crowns of which form two or three layers, creating a closed continuous canopy. The trees, often more than 30 metres tall, comprise many species, some of which bear edible fruits. They are often laden with epiphytes and mosses and it is not uncommon for huge branches to crash to the ground, unable to bear the increasing weight.

Lowland rainforest

Lowland rainforest has a distinctly different and more diverse range of tree species. It also requires regular rainfall, and is often hot and humid. The canopy is usually less dense than that of montane rainforest but the understorey is less open, with a dense covering of climbing palms, tree-ferns, tangled vines and woody saplings. Lowland rainforest varies in altitude between islands, but the upper limits vary between 700 and 1200 metres and it is the dominant habitat throughout the region. Found within its embrace is the greatest diversity of plant, animal and birdlife in the region.

Secondary forest and forest edge

Highly variable habitat; in its early stages it is short scrubby woodland. Older secondary forest can grow quite tall, but differs from uncut forest by having smaller trees and a lower, more open canopy, which lacks emergent trees. Secondary growth along roadsides, clearings and rivers is characterised by thickets, tangled vines and tall shrubs. Increased human activity in forests, clearing of trees, creation of roads etc. has created more habitat for those species of birds that were formally restricted to naturally occurring secondary growth in clearings and along streams.

Savanna

The term 'savanna' refers to natural grasslands with scattered trees and bushes. Most savanna exists on flat or gently rolling country, is often poorly drained, has poor soil and is often subject to periodic burning. Savanna may be dry or, at least seasonally, marshy, and occurs mainly in the lowlands. Extensive clearing of forest has produced pseudo-savannas in many areas. These tend to consist of tangled non-native grasses and are generally referred to as open areas with scattered trees.

Rivers, lakes, swamps and estuaries

Wetlands are non-forested areas that are flooded for much or all of the year. They are of major importance to birds, supporting a large variety of waterbird species. Coastal estuaries and lagoons have extensive mudflats, creating large feeding areas for an array of waterbirds, particularly waders. Rivers and lakes provide areas of open water which also attract a mixture of waterbirds. Swamps support dense cover in the form of reeds, rushes and sedges, often forming dense masses of vegetation such as reedbeds. This habitat is especially attractive to secretive species of birds such as bitterns, crakes, rails, and small warblers.

Gardens and farmland

When the term 'gardens' is used to describe the habitat of a particular species, it does not refer to an ornamental garden of colourful flowers, but the gardens that the native people tend, where they grow taro, yams and sweet potato. These gardens are often far from any villages and are completely surrounded by uncut rainforest, producing artificial clearings and forest edge habitat, within the forest. 'Farmland' refers to commercial agriculture where arable crops such as grains, beans and vegetables are grown. Farmland includes hedges, trees, grassland and weedy areas along fence lines. Many species of birds use farmland for feeding, hunting and nesting.

Mangroves

Mangroves grow mainly in tropical areas, and have a number of specialised adaptations which enable them to survive being inundated permanently or periodically by saline or brackish water. They occur in sheltered inlets and near the mouths of rivers, often in association with areas of extensive intertidal mudflats. Although their total area is small, mangroves are an important habitat for birds that feed on insects, pollen and nectar. Mangroves also provide relatively safe nesting sites for herons and egrets; a number of birds are confined mainly to mangroves.

Seashore

The intertidal zone, where the ocean and the land mass come together, is a narrow strip of sandy beach, rocky outcrop or exposed coral reef. Although the number of species found here is limited, it is of great importance to the substantial numbers of migrant waders and terns which winter in the region after breeding in Siberia and other parts of northern Asia. Sandy beaches also support small numbers of resident breeding birds such as plovers, terns and the endangered Beach Thick-knee.

Ocean

The Southwest Pacific has extensive areas of open sea, and this is home to a diverse and distinctive group of birds known collectively as seabirds. They include albatrosses, petrels, shearwaters, storm-petrels, tropicbirds, frigatebirds, boobies, terns and jaegers.

Abbreviations used in the book

br.	breeding
non-br.	non-breeding
imm.	immature
juv.	juvenile
cm	centimetres
m	metres

Family Introductions

Grebes Family Podicipedidae Page 28–29

Strictly aquatic. Swimming and diving birds with dense, waterproof plumage, thin necks, pointed bills, feet set far back on the body and lobed toes. They are weak fliers and patter along the surface of the water before taking flight. They swim and feed underwater on microscopic aquatic animals and build floating nests of vegetable matter. Two species occur in the region.

Albatrosses Family Diomedeidae Page 30–31

Huge, long-winged seabirds found mainly in the southern oceans. Long, powerful, narrow wings enable them to glide effortlessly under windy conditions. They have a more laboured flapping flight during calm weather. They possess peculiar, raised tubular nostrils, in common with many seabirds. They only come ashore to breed. Two species occur in the region.

Shearwaters and Petrels Family Procellariidae Page 30–37

Giant petrels, petrels, prions and shearwaters. Large to medium-sized seabirds. All have long, narrow, stiffly-held wings and tubular nostrils. Most breed on remote oceanic islands and only come ashore to nest. Many have distinctive flight actions. They feed on small fish, squid and plankton which they pluck from the surface of the ocean. Nineteen species occur in the region, including one endemic.

Storm-Petrels Family Hydrobatidae Page 38–39

Small pelagic seabirds, which only come to land to breed. They have short bills with a hook at the tip and tubular nostrils. Flight erratic and bat-like, they intersperse their gliding with hovering and fluttering over the water, often dabbling their feet while feeding on plankton plucked from the surface of the ocean. Four species occur in the region.

Tropicbirds Family Phaethontidae Page 40–41

Medium-sized seabirds with stout pointed bills, webbed feet, long pointed wings and wedge-shaped tails with greatly elongated central tail feathers in adult plumage. Tropicbirds have a steady pigeon-like flight and plunge-dive for flying-fish and squid. They nest in loose colonies, laying their eggs on open ground under ledges and bushes. Two species occur in the region.

Frigatebirds Family Fregatidae Page 40–41

Large, very long-winged and fork-tailed seabirds. Adapted to an aerial way of life, they rarely perch and never swim or walk and are capable of sustained soaring flight for hours without flapping their wings. They feed on fish and squid plucked from the surface of the ocean or obtained by harassing boobies and terns, forcing them to disgorge their last meal which the frigatebirds then retrieve. They are colonial nesters on remote tropical islands. Two species occur in the region.

Boobies Family Sulidae Page 42–43

Large seabirds with long, pointed wings and wedge-shaped tails, long pointed bills and webbed feet. In flight the cigar-shaped body is distinctive. They feed by spectacular plunge-diving on fish and squid, often pursuing them underwater. They nest colonially on remote tropical islands. Three species occur in the region.

Cormorants Family Phalacrocoracidae   Page 28–29

Medium to large waterbirds which occur on inland waterways and in coastal waters. They have long necks and long, slender bills which are hooked at the tip, fairly long tails and webbed feet. They swim low in the water and the bill is often held slanted upwards. They feed by diving from the surface and swimming and grasping fish underwater. Often seen perched conspicuously in the open with wings held outstretched, allowing them to dry. They roost and nest in colonies, either on the ground or in trees. Three species occur in the region.

Pelicans Family Pelecanidae   Page 28–29

Very large, heavily built waterbirds, with long straight bills and conspicuously distensible throat pouches. Gregarious; flocks are often observed soaring at great heights on rising currents of warm air. Small groups are often observed fishing in a coordinated effort. The fish are caught with a sideways sweeping action of the bill. They nest colonially on the ground. One species occurs in the region.

Waterfowl Family Anatidae   Page 44–49

Gregarious waterbirds, with dense waterproof plumage, short legs, webbed feet and broad, flattened bills adapted for dabbling when feeding on aquatic plants and animals. Most species dive or upend for their food; some graze on plants on land. In some species the sexes differ in plumage, females dull-coloured, while males have colourful breeding plumage. On completion of breeding, some species have an eclipse (non-breeding) plumage, in which males resemble females. Most build simple, down-lined nests on the ground in thick waterside vegetation, while a few nest in holes in trees. Ten species occur in the region, including two which have been introduced.

Herons, Egrets and Bitterns Family Ardeidae   Page 50–53

Long-legged, long-necked wading birds, with sharply pointed bills. Many species have plumes, especially in breeding plumage. They fly slowly, with regular wingbeats, on broad, rounded wings, with head and neck folded close to the body, legs trailing. They frequent the shallows of swamps, lakes, streams and the coast, where they feed on small fish, frogs and crustaceans caught with a lightning-fast stab of the dagger-like bill. Some species are crepuscular or nocturnal. Eleven species occur in the region.

Ibis and Spoonbills Family Threskiornithidae   Page 50–53

Large, wading birds. Ibis have long down-curved bills and spoonbills have straight flat bills with a spatulate tip. They feed on fish, crabs and other small aquatic animals; ibis feed by probing their bills in shallow water and mud, spoonbills feed by sweeping their bills from side-to-side in water, sifting out small aquatic animals. Ibis and spoonbills usually breed colonially, building nests in trees, or on the ground. Three species occur in the region.

Osprey Family Pandionidae   Page 54–55, 64

Medium-sized fish-eating bird of prey, which catches fish by plunge-diving in rivers, lakes, estuaries and shallow coastal waters. Feet are specially adapted for catching fish, having spiny soles and a reversible outer toe. Monotypical (only one species in the family).

Hawks, Eagles and Kites Family Accipitridae   Page 54–61, 64–66

Small to very large birds of prey, with long rounded wings. Typical plumage is a blend of greys and browns, which helps to camouflage them. Many have barred or streaked underparts. They hunt by soaring and diving, or by stealth, seizing their prey in long, hooked talons, evolved for gripping. Most species build their nests in tall trees. Twelve species occur in the region, including four endemics.

Falcons Family Falconidae   Page 62–63, 67

Small to medium-sized birds of prey, mostly swift flying, with long pointed wings. Many species take their prey of small birds and insects while on the wing. Females are often much larger than males. Falcons usually nest in hollow trees, on cliff ledges or in deserted nests of other birds. Three species occur in the region.

Megapodes Family Megapodiidae   Page 68–69

Fairly large fowl-like birds with small heads, plump bodies, strong legs and feet and short tails. These remarkable birds do not incubate their eggs with their own body heat, as other birds do; instead they scratch and scrape soil and decaying vegetation together into a large mound, where the combination of heat from the sun and fermentation maintains the required temperature for the development of the embryo. Their roughly conical mounds can be up to 12 metres across and 3 metres high, making them the largest structures made by birds. On hatching, the young birds dig their way to the surface and are then completely self sufficient, receiving no assistance from the adult birds. Two species occur in the region, one of which is endemic.

Junglefowl Family Phasianidae   Page 68–69

These heavily built ground-dwelling birds have short, rounded wings and strong legs and feet, ideal for scratching and digging. Strongly sexually dimorphic, the male is brilliantly coloured and performs spectacular strutting displays, fanning the tail and whirring the wings. Red Junglefowl is the ancestor of all domestic fowl. Domesticated during the Bronze Age, since that time they have been by far the most important birds in human settlements. One introduced species occurs in the region.

Buttonquail Family Turnicidae   Page 68–69

Small, secretive ground-dwelling birds which superficially resemble true quails, but lack the hind toe. The normal sex roles are reversed; females are larger and more brightly coloured than males and it is the males which incubate the eggs and raise the young. Buttonquails normally inhabit grassland, scrubland and cultivation. Two species occur in the region.

Rails Family Rallidae   Page 70–73

Ground-dwelling wading birds, with long legs and toes. They have a characteristic horizontal body posture, and the short tail is usually held erect and is flicked up and down. They swim well and inhabit dense vegetation in marshes or waterside vegetation in open country or densely wooded areas. Timid and often difficult to observe, flight appears weak, on short rounded wings with legs trailing; in fact most species are strong fliers, many undertaking long-distance, night-time migrations. Some species, particularly those confined to small islands, are flightless, making them vulnerable to introduced predators such as dogs, cats and rats. Ten species occur in the region, four of which are endemic.

Kagu Family Rhynochetidae   Page 68–69

An unusual looking, flightless bird of dense mountain forests. The Kagu's bright red bill and legs contrast strongly with its drab ash-grey plumage. The narrow pointed bill is well adapted for digging in the leaf litter and soil of the forest floor in search of a wide range of animal prey, including insects, grubs, spiders, snails, worms and lizards. Monotypical and endemic.

Sandpipers Family Scolopacidae   Page 74–83, 88–90

Small to medium-sized, long-legged wading birds, with long, slender bills used to probe soft mud searching for marine and freshwater invertebrates. All species which occur in the Southwest Pacific breed in the northern hemisphere and migrate to the Pacific in summer. When here, they are in non-breeding plumage, with intricately mottled upperparts of dull brown, buff and grey. Gregarious in the non-breeding season, they form large roosting and feeding flocks which frequent coastal estuaries and lagoons. Twenty-four species occur in the region.

Thick-knees Family Burhinidae   Page 84–85

Large thickset waders, which superficially resemble small bustards. Thick-knees have swollen knee joints, no hind toes and three front toes with partial webbing at the base. They have stout bills, very large eyes, cryptically coloured plumage, often with a conspicuous wing pattern in flight, and long legs which enable them to run swiftly. Nocturnal and crepuscular, they occur along riverbeds, on ocean beaches and dry inland plains. One species occurs in the region.

Oystercatchers Family Haematopodidae   Page 84–85, 89

Oystercatchers are a distinctive group of large, bulky waders which frequent the seashore. Either black or black and white, they have long, straight orange-red bills, laterally compressed in a wedge-like shape and specially adapted for probing for worms, molluscs and crabs and for opening shellfish. They have stout legs and feet with three toes, which are slightly webbed. One species occurs in the region.

Pratincoles Family Glareolidae   Page 84–85, 89

Small to medium-sized waders of open country. Pratincoles have short bills with wide gapes, long pointed wings and deeply forked tails. Their flight is buoyant and tern-like and they resemble huge swallows. They feed by hawking on the wing and are most active towards dusk. One species occurs in the region.

Plovers and Lapwings Family Charadriidae   Page 84–87, 91

Small to medium-sized waders with large heads, short necks and short bills. Plovers typically run quickly for a few steps, then stop to peck for food from the ground. Lapwings are larger and have broader, more rounded wings. Both nest in shallow, unlined depressions on the ground. Seven species occur in the region.

Gulls and Terns Family Laridae   Page 92–99

Small to large, long-winged, web-footed waterbirds, of coastal waters and inlands swamps and lakes. Most have grey and white plumage. Immature plumage is browner and often makes specific identification difficult. Gulls are large and robust, with broad wings, rounded tails and slightly hooked bills. Terns are smaller and much slimmer with long pointed wings, forked tails and slender, sharply pointed bills and usually feed by plunge-diving. Marsh Terns have only slightly forked tails and a buoyant, fluttering flight, enabling them to pick small food items from the surface of the water. Eighteen species occur in the region.

Jaegers and Skuas Family Stercorariidae   Page 100–101

Medium to large, brown-coloured gull-like seabirds of oceanic and coastal waters. Medium length bill hooked at the tip, long, pointed wings with prominent white flash at the base of the primaries, tail wedge-shaped, with elongated central feathers in some species. Feet are webbed. They obtain much of their food by pirating from gulls and terns, chasing their victims in flight with great agility, forcing them to regurgitate food. Four species occur in the region.

Pigeons and Doves Family Columbidae   Page 102–115

Plump-bodied birds, with small heads, short necks and slender bills, which often thicken towards the tip and usually have a fleshy cere at the base. The plumage is compact, dense and soft. They feed mostly on fruit and seeds, sometimes undertaking long flights to find fruiting trees. The young are fed by regurgitation of a protein rich secretion, produced from glands inside the crop of both parents. Most pigeons and doves nest in trees, building flimsy, stick platforms on which to lay their eggs. Twenty-nine species occur in the region, of which fourteen are endemic and one is introduced.

Parrots Family Psittacidae
Page 116–119

Parrots have a distinctive blunt-headed appearance, strongly hooked bills, with a curved upper mandible fitting neatly over the lower mandible; the tongue is thick. The body is compact, and the tail is normally short. The feet are versatile, able to manipulate food and pass it to the mouth. The bill is often used as a third foot as birds climb about branches of trees. Plumage is often brightly coloured. Most species are gregarious and noisy and have a fast flight. Food consists mainly of seeds, fruit, pollen and nectar. Parrots nest in unlined holes and tree hollows and the eggs are always white. In the region six species occur, one of which is endemic.

Cockatoos Family Cacatuidae
Page 116–117

Cockatoos are large, thickset, short-tailed birds, usually simply coloured. All have a movable crest which is raised immediately after alighting or when the bird is alarmed or excited. Cockatoos have powerful bills for tearing wood, opening seed-capsules and digging. The feet are particularly strong, with two toes forward pointing and two back, perfectly adapted for efficient climbing and grasping. All species have loud, raucous calls. One endemic species occurs in the region.

Lories and Lorikeets Family Loriidae
Page 118–121

Lories and lorikeets have powerful hooked bills, slender bodies, long, pointed wings and usually long, pointed tails. Often brilliantly coloured, exhibiting bright reds, blues, yellows and greens. These gregarious birds move in highly energetic, noisy, swiftly flying flocks, moving from one stand of flowering trees to the next. Their brush-tipped tongues and simple digestive systems are adapted for feeding on pollen, nectar and fruit. They attract attention with loud, piercing shrieks. In the region eight species occur, five of which are endemic.

Old World Cuckoos Family Cuculidae
Page 122–125

Small to medium-sized birds with slightly down-curved bills, long slender bodies, long, graduated tails and long, pointed wings. They are brood parasites, laying their eggs in the nests of other species of birds. Generally solitary and arboreal, they keep to the canopy, where they can be difficult to observe. They call monotonously during the breeding season, making identification easy. There are rare hepatic (reddish-brown) morph females in some species. Six species occur in the region.

Coucals Family Centropodidae
Page 124–125

Large, long and broad-tailed, ground-foraging birds which live in rank vegetation close to the ground and have a distinctive walking gait. Normally found in pairs or in small family groups. Unlike the closely related cuckoos, they build their own round nests of grass, which has a side entrance, and raise their own young. They feed mainly on small terrestrial vertebrates and insects but also prey on eggs and nestlings of other birds. One endemic species occurs in the region.

Barn Owls Family Tytonidae
Page 126–127

Differ from other owls by their well-defined heart-shaped facial discs of pale, stiff feathers, surrounding small, uniformly dark eyes. They have relatively slender bodies, long legs, long rounded wings and short tails. Plumage is soft and fluffy with brown, buff and grey colouring. Only the female incubates the eggs, but both parents cooperate to rear the young. Two species occur in the region.

Owls Family Strigidae
Page 126–127

Small to large nocturnal birds of prey with large heads, short necks and large forward-looking eyes set in a flattened, broad facial disc, which serves to focus sound into the ear openings, an adaptation to enable the owl to pin-point the slightest sound, making it relatively straightforward to locate prey in the dark. They have short, hooked bills, curved talons, broad, rounded wings and short tails. The feathering is very soft, enabling owls to fly silently. They spend the daylight hours roosting in tree hollows or in thick cover. Two species occur, both of which are endemic.

Frogmouths Family Podargidae   Page 128–129

Large nocturnal birds, with broad flat strongly-hooked bills, very wide gapes, large heads, short thick necks, long tails and cryptically coloured plumage. The wings are short and rounded and feathers are soft, enabling them to fly silently. When disturbed during the day the birds close their eyes, stretch out the neck and bill and stay motionless. With the aid of cryptically coloured plumage, a bird appears to be a jagged dead branch. One species occurs in the region.

Owlet-Nightjars Family Aegothelidae   Page 128–129

Small to medium-sized nocturnal birds. The bill is small and wide, with a very wide gape and is surrounded by prominent bristles. Eyes are very large, wings long and rounded, and the tail is moderately long. Legs and feet are small and rather feeble. The plumage is cryptically coloured. At night, owlet-nightjars capture insects both in the air and on the ground. One endemic species occurs in the region.

Eared-nightjars Family Eurostopodidae   Page 128–129

Medium-sized nocturnal birds, with tiny bills but an extremely wide gape, adapted for capturing flying insects at night. They have large eyes, short necks, relatively long, narrow wings and long tails. Plumage is very soft and cryptically coloured. During the day they perch either on the ground or lengthwise along horizontal tree branches. When hawking for food at night, they fly quietly with deep, stiff and irregular wingbeats. They nest on the bare ground and lay cryptically-coloured eggs, which blend with the background. One species occurs in the region.

Treeswifts Family Hemiprocnidae   Page 130–131

Differ from true swifts by having more colourful plumage and being less strictly aerial in habits, often hawking insects from a perch. When perched, have long, slender appearance with long narrow wings crossed. In flight, have long crescent-shaped wings, similar to true swifts, but have a much longer tail and distinctive rapid wingbeats interspersed with glides. Treeswifts build very small, shallow, cup-shaped nests, attached with the bird's own saliva to the branch of a tree. One species occurs in the region.

Swifts Family Apodidae   Page 130–133

Small to medium-sized aerial birds, with small bills, large gapes, compact, streamlined bodies and long, narrow, scythe-like wings. Swifts appear to fly effortlessly with rapid, shallow wingbeats interspersed with long glides. They are insectivorous and catch all their food on the wing. Strictly aerial, they never perch in trees or on telephone wires as swallows often do. They rest by clinging to cliffs with strong feet; the hind toe is reversible, enabling all four toes to be placed forwards for clinging. They have the ability to feed, groom and copulate in flight and some species even sleep on the wing. The cup-shaped nest is made from a salivary secretion and vegetable matter, and is placed in a hollow or under a cliff. Six species occur in the region.

Kingfishers Family Alcedinidae   Page 134–137

Small to medium-sized birds with long, pointed bills, large heads, short necks, stocky bodies, short rounded wings and usually short tails. Many species sit on an exposed perch or hover over water and feed by plunge-diving for fish. Forest-inhabiting species pounce on insects or small vertebrates on the ground, often far from water. Most species of kingfishers nest in horizontal tunnels which they dig into steep earth banks, while others nest in termite mounds or utilise tree hollows. In the region ten species occur of which three are endemic.

Bee-eaters Family Meropidae   Page 138–139

Bee-eaters have long, slender, slightly curved bills, slender bodies, long pointed wings and fairly long tails, usually with elongated central tail feathers. Often brightly coloured, bee-eaters perch conspicuously in the open and feed entirely on flying insects such as bees, hornets and dragonflies which they catch in mid-air before returning to the same perch, where they beat the insect before swallowing it. Bee-eaters excavate nest burrows in steep earth banks or even slight hummocks in the ground. Two species occur in the region.

Rollers Family Coraciidae   Page 138–139

Rollers are medium-sized robust birds with wide, slightly hooked bills, large heads, stocky bodies and medium-length tails. Many species are brightly coloured. They spend long periods sitting motionless on high, exposed perches, looking for large insects, lizards and other small animals, which they catch on the ground, or by making aerial sorties. Usually solitary or in pairs. Their flight is powerful and during the breeding season they perform spectacular acrobatic, rolling display flights. One species occurs in the region.

Hornbills Family Bucerotidae   Page 138–139

Medium-sized to very large, broad-winged forest birds with long tails and huge bills, often with a casque on the upper mandible. Most species nest in tree hollows, and while incubating the eggs, the female is sealed inside the nest cavity by the male and is completely dependent upon him providing her with food. During this period she moults her flight feathers. Hornbills feed mainly on fruit and berries, but also take small animals such as snakes, lizards and the nestlings of other birds. One species occurs in the region.

Pittas Family Pittidae   Page 138–139

Pittas are ground-dwelling forest birds with plump bodies, short tails and long legs and are amongst the most brightly coloured birds in the world. They are often shy, secretive and difficult to observe, and are best detected by their loud, whistling calls. They have an erect stance and a characteristic bounding gait. One endemic species occurs in the region.

Australo-Papuan Warblers Family Pardalotidae   Page 146–147

Small, active, insectivorous birds, usually with short straight bills and sombre brown, olive, green or yellow plumage. They typically forage by hovering close to the outer foliage of trees, catching small leaf insects or flying insects with an audible snap of the bill. Most have pleasant, melodious songs. All build domed nests of interwoven vegetable fibre. Some nests are suspended from tree branches while others are concealed in natural hollows. One endemic species occurs in the region.

Honeyeaters Family Meliphagidae   Page 140–145

A diverse group of small to moderately large birds. Active and pugnacious, they feed on nectar, insects and fruit. The distinctive family characteristic is a long, tubular, brush-tipped tongue, an adaptation for extracting nectar from flowers. Plumage is variable: can be dull and nondescript or brightly coloured. Green, brown, yellow and red are common colours in honeyeaters. Some species have coloured bare skin and wattles on the head, others have tufts of feathers on the sides of the head, or on the throat. With few exceptions the nest is cup-shaped and concealed within the outer foliage of trees. In the region sixteen species occur of which fourteen are endemic, plus one which is introduced.

Australasian Robins Family Eopsaltriidae   Page 146–147

Australasian robins look plump and round-headed. Some perch upright, others perch sideways on the trunks of trees, and all have the characteristic habit of flicking their wingtips. They feed by catching insects in flight or by dropping from a perch to secure insects on the ground. Most species prefer rainforest but will visit partially cleared areas. They are usually tame and confiding. In the region two species occur, one of which is endemic.

Whistlers Family Pachycephalidae   Page 148–149

The whistlers are medium-sized, robust birds and have short stout bills which are slightly hooked at the tip. They are usually found in the lower canopy of the forest where they methodically glean insects and their larvae from leaves and twigs or drag them out from under the bark of trees. Whistlers are usually observed singly, in pairs or in small family parties and can sometimes be found in mixed-species foraging flocks. All build cup-shaped nests and lay spotted eggs. In the region five species occur, two of which are endemic.

Monarch Flycatchers Family Monarchidae   Page 150–163

Small to medium-sized insectivorous birds which have flattened bills, with bristles at each side of a broad gape to help them snare food. They are often sexually dimorphic. Most species glean insects from foliage in the middle or lower part of the canopy. Fantails have long, broad tails, which are often held cocked and fanned and they have short, rounded wings. They inhabit the undergrowth and lower parts of the canopy. Monarch flycatchers build cup-shaped, neatly constructed nests, usually placed in a tree or bush; fantails build nests shaped like a wine glass, without the base. Twenty-six species occur in the region, of which eighteen are endemic.

Drongos Family Dicruridae   Page 164–165

Drongos typically have black plumage, glossed with blue, green or purple. They have stout bills with arched culmens and hooked tips and usually have diagnostic deeply forked tails. Arboreal and conspicuous, they usually hunt from exposed perches and catch insects on the wing. They are normally pugnacious and give a variety of harsh scolding notes, which alternate with musical whistles; they often mimic other species. They build frail saucer-shaped nests which are usually placed in the fork of a tree. One endemic species occurs in the region.

Crows Family Corvidae   Page 164–165

Crows are noisy gregarious, robust birds with stout bills and strong feet. Most crows are wholly black in plumage. Crows are adaptable and intelligent. Most species are omnivorous and many will rob the nests of other birds. Most build untidy, cup-shaped nests, usually placed in a tree. In the region three species occur, all endemic.

Woodswallows Family Artamidae   Page 166–167

Woodswallows are stocky, aerial-feeding birds with thick-based pointed bills. They glide on stiff, broad-based, triangular-shaped wings and have short square tails. They spend long periods perched conspicuously on bare tree limbs and telegraph wires. Nests are flimsy and cup-shaped. Woodswallows are gregarious and often gather in groups of 12 or more to roost at night, pressing against each other in tight, compact bunches on bare tree limbs or telegraph wires. One species occurs in the region.

Bellmagpies Family Cracticidae   Page 166–167

Large, robust, boldly patterned black-and-white birds, which resemble the shape of a crow. Mainly ground-dwelling birds, they feed on insects, lizards, small rodents and smaller birds. Magpies are unusual in holding permanent territories defended by small family parties. They have rich, mellow, organ-like calls, often given in unison. They build compact shallow stick nests, normally placed in the fork of a tree. One introduced species occurs in the region.

Cuckoo-shrikes Family Campephagidae   Page 166–171

Medium-sized to moderately large birds with elongated bodies, long pointed wings and moderately long tails, the shape superficially resembling cuckoos. Most species are various shades of grey with some black markings, which is why in some parts of the world they are referred to as 'Grey-birds'. They have a characteristic habit of resettling their wings after alighting and have a strongly undulating flight. They feed mainly on insects. Flimsy cup-shaped nests are bound together with bark and cobwebs, and normally placed in the horizontal fork of a tree. In the region nine species occur, three of which are endemic.

Thrushes Family Turdidae   Page 172–173

Medium-sized plumpish songbirds, usually found in forested areas. They spend much time foraging on the ground feeding primarily on insects, grubs, snails, worms and fallen fruit. Most species build well-formed cup-shaped nests of twigs, grasses and leaves, often strengthened with mud. Thrushes usually maintain pair bonds throughout the year, in sedentary species from year to year. They are amongst the finest songsters in the bird world. In the region five species occur, one of which is endemic.

Starlings Family Sturnidae   Page 174–179

Stocky, medium-sized birds, with slightly down-curved, medium-length bills, and strong legs and feet. Many species of starling have black plumage, which is glossed with blue, green or purple. Some starlings are arboreal woodland species, others are more terrestrial and prefer relatively open country. The ranges of this latter group are steadily increasing, due to continued deforestation. Starlings tend to be gregarious, noisy birds and often nest and roost together. They have a large repertoire of calls and some are accomplished mimics. In the region fourteen species occur, seven of which are endemic and one is introduced.

Swallows Family Hirundinidae   Page 180–181

Small, aerial-feeding, insectivorous birds. Their long, pointed wings, streamlined bodies, short necks and wide gaping bills are adaptations which enable them to feed on a wide variety of flying insects, whilst on the wing. Most species are gregarious, some nesting in colonies. Swallows nest in natural hollows in trees or rocks, excavate their own burrows in earth banks, or build nests constructed of mud pellets, under cliff ledges, bridges or buildings. Three species occur in the region.

Bulbuls Family Pycnonotidae   Page 182–183

Restless, agile birds, bulbuls are mainly arboreal fruit and insect eaters. They are common and noisy inhabitants of gardens, cultivation and secondary growth. Bulbuls build flimsy, shallow, cap-shaped nests of grass and leaves, normally placed in bushes or low trees. One introduced species occurs in the region.

White-eyes Family Zosteropidae   Page 184–189

Small, active, warbler-like birds, white-eyes are noisy and gregarious. They obtain nectar from blossoms and eat insects, soft fruit and berries. Predominantly yellowish-green above and yellowish-white below, most species have a narrow ring of white feathers around the eyes. They build small cup-shaped nests which are usually placed in the fork of horizontal branches. Eighteen species occur in the region, of which sixteen are endemic.

Old World Warblers Family Sylviidae   Page 190–193

Small to medium-sized, active, insectivorous songbirds, with thin pointed bills. Many are fairly sombrely coloured birds, predominantly brown or green and yellow. Some species are arboreal, preferring to glean insects from the lower canopy, others prefer the dense understorey where they creep around in the undergrowth, occasionally giving short glimpses of themselves. Most have eyeline stripes and some have crown stripes. Most species of old world warblers breed in cold temperate areas of the northern hemisphere and are migratory, wintering further south. Nine species occur in the region, of which six are endemic.

Old World Sparrows Family Passeridae   Page 196–197

Small to medium-sized birds with compact bodies and short conical bills adapted to feeding on seeds and grain. Many species are gregarious and often nest and roost in colonies. Most species are sexually dimorphic. They build large, untidy, dome-shaped nests crammed into holes and crevices in trees or buildings. One introduced species occurs in the region.

Waxbills and Allies Family Estrildidae   Page 194–197

Small to medium-sized birds with compact bodies and thick conical bills. They fly in tight, closely packed flocks. They feed almost exclusively on seeds and make local movements to areas of greatest food abundance, which enables them to breed all year round. They build rather untidy domed nests with a side entrance, usually placed near the ground in low cover. Nine species occur in the region, of which two are endemic and three are introduced.

Wagtails Family Motacillidae Page 182–183

Small, ground-dwelling birds of open country. They have slender bills, slender bodies and long legs and tails, and the tails are frequently wagged up and down. They feed on insects which are usually caught on the ground or occasionally snatched from the air. They inhabit mainly grassy areas often in the vicinity of water. Flight is strong and deeply undulating. Two species occur in the region.

Flowerpeckers Family Dicaeidae Page 198–199

Very small, active, dumpy, arboreal birds with short bills and short tails. Males are usually more brightly coloured than females and immatures. Most species eat berries (particularly mistletoe) and figs plus insects, and some species take nectar. They build deep, hanging, purse-like nests, suspended from twigs, usually placed high in a tree. In the region two species occur, both of which are endemic.

Sunbirds Family Nectariniidae Page 198–199

Small, active, arboreal, nectar- and insect-eating birds with long, thin, curved bills. Their tongues are specially adapted for feeding on nectar and are even more tubular than those of honeyeaters. Nectar is taken while the bird is perched or when hovering. Males usually have bright iridescent plumage while the females are usually rather drab. They build pendulous domed nests with a side entrance, usually hung from low branches. One species occurs in the region.

Finches Family Fringillidae Page 196–197

Small to medium-sized birds, with thick conical bills and notched tails. Males are often more brightly coloured than females. Finches are gregarious and are often found in large flocks. Most species feed mainly on seeds, but insects and fruit also make up their diet. They build small, cup-shaped nests which are usually placed in low cover. One introduced species occurs in the region.

Glossary of Terms Used in the Guide

abdomen: the rear section of the body.
adult: a bird which has reached the stage where it no longer changes physically because of age.
arboreal: tree dwelling.
axillaries: feathers covering the 'armpit' area, where the underwing joins the body.
belly: the lowest part of the undersurface of a bird.
bib: a contrasting, usually dark area, on the throat and upperbreast.
bifurcate: feathers which are divided at the tip into two prongs.
brackish: fresh water which has mixed with salt water.
breeding plumage: plumage worn during breeding season; frequently more brightly coloured than non-breeding plumage.
carpal bar: prominent dark bar on the bend of the wing, often prominent in immature terns.
carpal joint: the 'wrist', forming the bend of the wing.
cere: a bare, leathery patch of skin at the base of the upper beak into which the nostrils open, particularly evident in raptors and pigeons.
chin: the part of a bird's exterior immediately below the bill and above the throat.
collar: a band of contrasting colour around the neck.
colonial: roosting, feeding or nesting in groups.
colour morph: when some members of the same species are of one colour and others another, they are known as colour morphs; the colour being genetically determined and permanent, as in the case of reef egrets.
coverts: feathers that cover, and thus protect; for example, secondary coverts cover the bases of the secondaries, ear-coverts cover the ear region.
crepuscular: active at dawn and dusk.
crest: a tuft of feathers on the upper part of the head; in some species can be raised or lowered.
crown: top of the head.
cryptic: having camouflaged protective colouring.
culmen: the ridge along the top of the upper mandible on a bird's bill.
diagnostic: a distinctive feature that accurately indicates the species of a bird. It could be related to build, colours, markings, calls or behaviour.
dihedral: indicates that the bird's wings are held raised in a V shape; a slight dihedral refers to the wings raised only slightly above the horizontal.
distensible: capable of being stretched or inflated.
diurnal: active during daylight hours.
duetting: when male and female of a breeding pair sing in response to each other, usually producing different songs.
ear-coverts: short feathers covering the ear opening, situated behind and slightly below the eyes; often distinctly coloured.
eclipse plumage: dull plumage acquired by the drakes of most species of ducks during a transitional moult, usually following the breeding season and before they acquire the next brightly coloured breeding plumage.
endangered: a species which is likely to become extinct if its population continues to decline.
endemic: a species whose breeding and non-breeding ranges are confined to a particular region.
erectile: capable of being raised, usually referring to the crest of a bird.
extinct: no longer in existence.
eyebrow stripe: a prominent curving streak above a bird's eye.
eyeline: a contrasting, usually dark, narrow line from the base of the bill through the eye.
flank: the side of a bird's breast and belly, adjacent to and below the closed wing.
flight feathers: the longest, most well-developed feathers of wings and tail, used for flight; on the wings these feathers are divided into primaries, secondaries and tertials.
forehead: the front part of the crown, extending down to the base of the bill.
foreneck: the lower throat.
frontal shield: bare leathery skin on the forehead, often distinctively coloured as in the white frontal shield of the coot.

gape: the mouth, from one corner of the bill to the other, usually brightly coloured in nestlings.

graduated: refers to long tails which narrow at regular intervals.

gregarious: living in groups.

gular pouch: an expandable pouch of bare skin on the throat of pelicans, cormorants etc., used for short-term storage of food.

habitat: the kind of place where a bird lives, for example rainforest, mangroves etc.

hepatic: brown colour morph found in some cuckoos.

hindneck: part of a bird's upperparts, between the nape and the mantle.

immature: a bird that has moulted from juvenile plumage but has not attained adult plumage; can also include juvenile plumage, when not sufficiently distinct.

introduced: a species brought into an area where it is not indigenous, by human agency.

iridescence: the effect of changing colours, caused by reflected light, rather than pigmentation, for example on hummingbirds.

irruption: an irregular movement whereby large numbers of birds move into areas where they are not usually found; can be triggered by drought, high rainfall or an abundance of food.

jowl: loose skin below the jawbone.

juvenile: the first full-feathered plumage of a young bird, having replaced the natal down.

lanceolate: lanced-shaped; slender and pointed.

leading edge: forward edge of wing.

lobes: stiff flap of skin outgrowths around the toes, which aid swimming, in grebes, for example.

local: found only in certain confined areas.

lores: the area between the base of the bill and the eye, sometimes distinctively coloured.

M pattern: a contrasting, M-shaped dark pattern visible on the upper surface of certain birds in flight, formed by the outer primaries, primary coverts and carpal bar.

mandible: one of the two parts of a bird's bill; respectively the upper and lower mandibles.

mangroves: small trees that have adapted to live in salt water; they protect large expanses of mud in shallow coastal areas and estuaries.

mantle: the central back, lying between the nape and the rump.

mask: dark patch around the eye extending to the base of the bill.

melanistic: having excessive black pigmentation, an aberrant condition producing darker individuals than normal.

migration: regular, usually seasonal flights, between a bird's breeding grounds to winter quarters, and return.

mirror: white spots on the otherwise black primaries of certain species of gulls.

montane: pertaining to mountains.

moustachial streak: a contrasting streak extending backwards and downwards from the base of the bill.

nape: the back of a bird's head between the crown and the hindneck.

nuchal: pertaining to the nape.

oceanic: found mainly at sea, only coming to land to breed.

plumage: the covering of feathers over a bird's body which may vary with age, sex or time of year.

plume: elongated, decorative, ornamental feather, often used in display.

polymorphic: having more than two distinct plumage morphs within a species.

posterior: towards the back.

primaries: the outermost and longest flight feathers on a bird's wing.

race: a geographical population of a species.

resident: remaining in the same area all year; non-migratory.

rump: area of a bird's body between the back and the uppertail-coverts, often distinctively coloured, for example in waders.

saddle: the mantle, the term used where the colour of the upper surface of the wings continues across the back without a break.

scapulars: the shoulder feathers of a bird, covering the gap between the folded wing and the body.

secondaries: the inner flight feathers of a bird's wing, immediately inward from the primaries.

sedentary: not moving far throughout the year.

sexually dimorphic: when males and females of the same species differ in size, structure or plumage, for example buttonquails.

shaft: the central horny portion of a feather, its lower end, the quill point, buried in the skin.

shoulder-patch: a contrasting area of colour where the wing meets the body.

skulking: creeping about in an unobtrusive manner close to the ground, usually within dense cover.

soaring: flying on still, outstretched wings, without flapping, using thermals or updraughts to gain height.

spatulate: spoon-shaped, a description of the bill of the spoonbill.
speculum: iridescent patch on the wing of a duck.
subterminal: second from the end.
suffusion: tinged with colour.
terminal: at the end.
terrestrial: ground dwelling.
tertials: the innermost flight feathers on a bird's wing.
tibia: one of the bones of the shin.
trailing edge: hind edge of wing.
vagrant: rare or accidental to the region.
vent: area surrounding cloaca.
vermiculations: fine, often wavy, lines that create an overall effect, rather than standing out as distinct markings.
wingbar: a usually pale line across the wing, formed by pale tips to the wing-coverts.
wing-coverts: the small feathers which cover the bases of the primaries, secondaries and tertials.
wingspan: the measurement between wingtips, when the wings are fully spread.

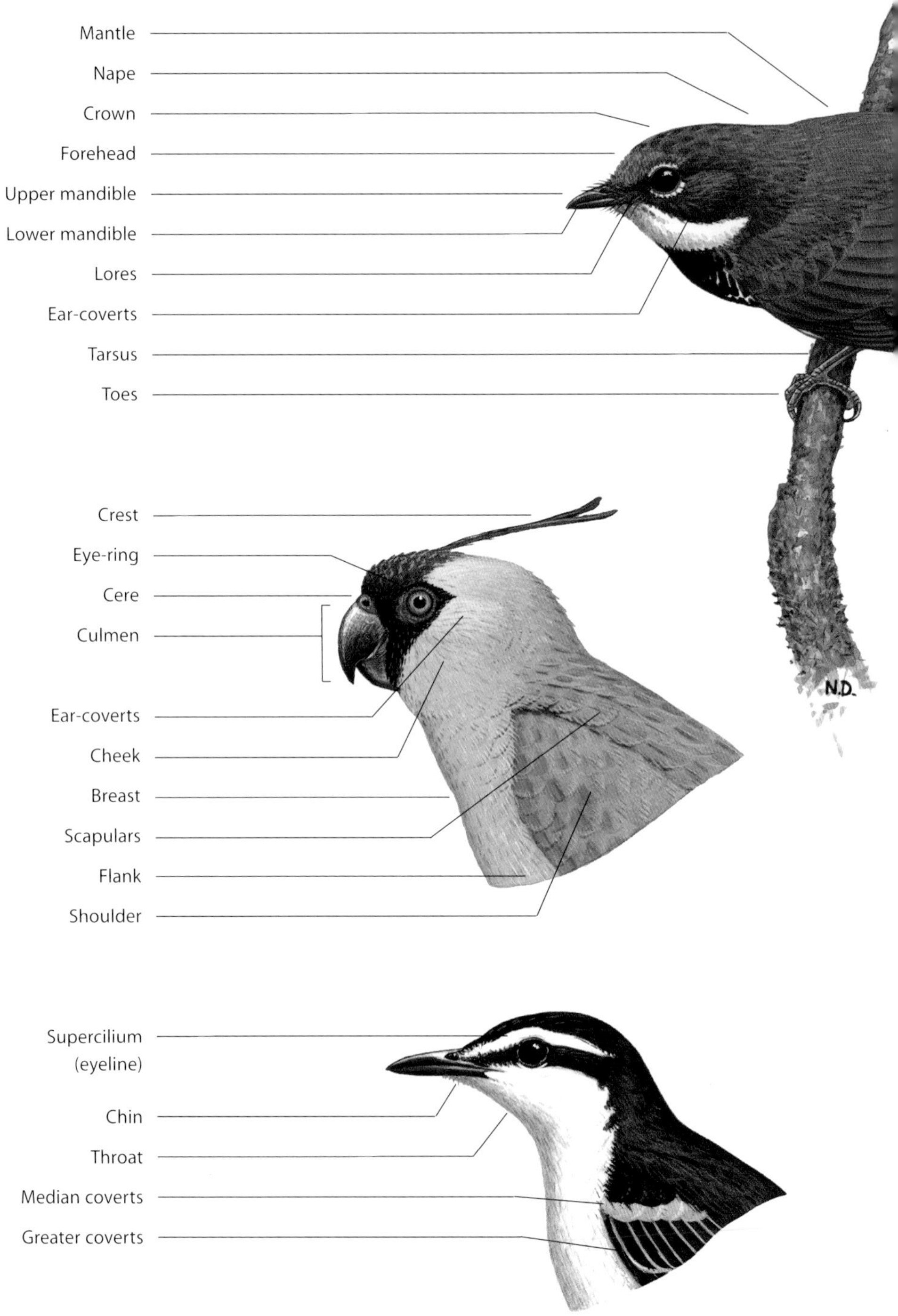

Mantle

Nape

Crown

Forehead

Upper mandible

Lower mandible

Lores

Ear-coverts

Tarsus

Toes

Crest

Eye-ring

Cere

Culmen

Ear-coverts

Cheek

Breast

Scapulars

Flank

Shoulder

Supercilium
(eyeline)

Chin

Throat

Median coverts

Greater coverts

N.D.

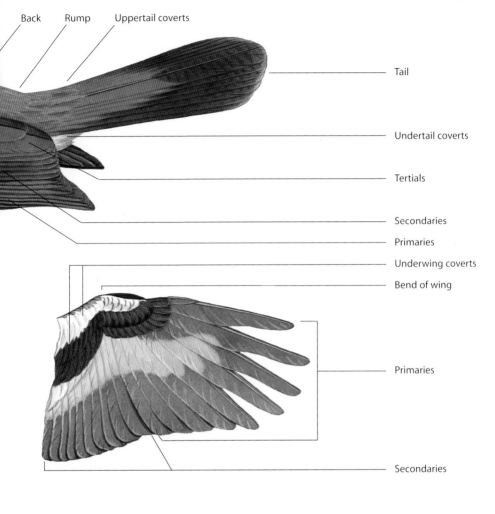

Back

Rump

Uppertail coverts

Tail

Undertail coverts

Tertials

Secondaries

Primaries

Underwing coverts

Bend of wing

Primaries

Secondaries

Lesser coverts

Alula

Greater coverts

Leading edge

Trailing edge

Tertials

Speculum

LITTLE GREBE *Tachybaptus ruficollis* 25 cm

In breeding plumage, has dark brown upper body, paler brown below, black crown extending down back of neck, with conspicuous chestnut sides to face, throat and neck and a conspicuous bright yellow gape-patch. In non-breeding plumage chestnut is replaced by brown, has pale buff throat and no yellow gape-patch. Similar to Australasian Grebe but has dark red iris, chestnut throat and the white wingbar is confined to the secondaries.
SEXES Alike. **IMM** Similar to non-breeding adult. **HABITAT** Freshwater lakes and ponds. **STATUS** Now very rare on Bouganville Island in the Solomons. **CALL** A distinctive whinnying trill.

AUSTRALASIAN GREBE *Tachybaptus novaehollandiae* 25 cm

In breeding plumage, has dark grey-brown upper body, pale brown below, black of crown extending down back of neck; chin and throat also black, narrow chestnut stripe from the eye, which broadens down to the mid neck, and has a conspicuous bright yellow gape-patch. In non-breeding plumage chestnut is replaced by grey-brown, has white throat and off white gape-patch. Similar to Little Grebe but has yellow iris, black throat and the broad white wing patch extends almost the full length of the wing.
SEXES Alike. **IMM** Similar to non-breeding adult. **HABITAT** Freshwater lakes and ponds. **STATUS** Common breeding bird in New Caledonia and Lake Tengano, on Rennell Island in the Solomons. **CALL** A distinctive rapid trill, similar to Little Grebe, but less harsh.

LITTLE PIED CORMORANT *Phalacrocorax melanoleucos* 55–65 cm

The only black and white cormorant of the region. Adult black with white face and underparts, short, yellow bill, a hint of a crest on the crown.
SEXES Alike. **IMM** Black of cap extends below eye; thighs black. **HABITAT** Swamps, lakes, mangroves and rivers. **STATUS** Uncommon and local resident in New Caledonia. Sporadic irruptions, presumably from Australia into Vanuatu, and Bougainville and Santa Ana Islands in the Solomons. **CALL** Normally silent except at breeding colony, where it produces a small range of cooing and clicking sounds.

GREAT CORMORANT *Phalacrocorax carbo* 80–85 cm

The largest cormorant of the region. Adult in breeding plumage is glossy black with yellow facial skin, white gular patch at base of bill and white flank patches. Flank patches not present in non-breeding plumage.
SEXES Alike. **IMM** mottled dark and light brown with varying amounts of white on foreneck, breast and abdomen. **HABITAT** Lakes. **STATUS** A recent coloniser of Lake Tengano, on Rennell Island in the Solomons, where it is thriving and increasing rapidly in numbers. **CALL** Normally silent except at breeding colony, where birds produce harsh croaks, grunts and hisses.

LITTLE BLACK CORMORANT *Phalacrocorax sulcirostris* 55–65 cm

The only all-black cormorant of the region. A slender, all dark black cormorant; in good light there is a glossy green sheen to the back. Slender lead-grey bill. Adults become dull brown-black after breeding.
SEXES Alike. **HABITAT** Lakes and rivers. **STATUS** Periodic irruptions into New Caledonia, from Australia. **CALL** Normally silent except at breeding colony, where males make hoarse barking croaks, whistles and ticking calls.

AUSTRALIAN PELICAN *Pelecanus conspicillatus* 160–180 cm

A very large black and white bird with short legs and tail and a huge pink bill with a distensible throat pouch. In flight, black primaries and secondaries contrast with the predominantly white wing-coverts. In breeding plumage eyering becomes orange-yellow, the bill becomes bright pink and the throat pouch scarlet.
SEXES Alike. **IMM** Brownish wings. **HABITAT** Inland waters and occasionally coastal mudflats. **STATUS** Periodic occurrence throughout the region, presumably birds from Australia. **CALL** Soft grunts.

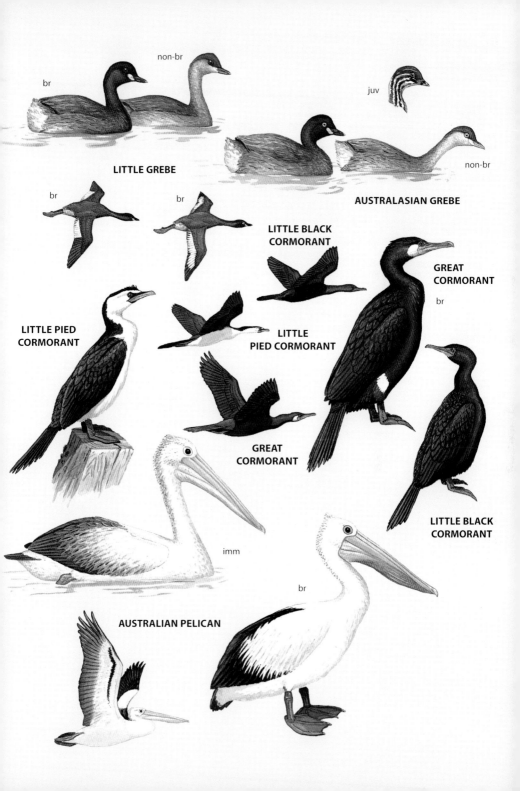

br   non-br

LITTLE GREBE

juv

non-br

AUSTRALASIAN GREBE

br   br

LITTLE BLACK
CORMORANT

GREAT
CORMORANT

br

LITTLE PIED
CORMORANT

LITTLE
PIED CORMORANT

GREAT
CORMORANT

LITTLE BLACK
CORMORANT

imm

AUSTRALIAN PELICAN

br

WANDERING ALBATROSS *Diomedea exulans* 110–135 cm Wingspan 250–350 cm

Gigantic, the only albatross in these waters with a white back. Plumage variable, there are several mottled stages as the bird progressively whitens with age. In adult plumage the head and body are white, the upperwing is predominantly white with black primaries and trailing edge, the white tail usually retains black margins. Underwing, white with black trailing edge and wingtip. This feature remains constant throughout all stages of plumage, together with a huge pink bill.

SEXES Alike. **JUV:** Completely chocolate-brown except for conspicuous white mask and underwing. **IMM** As juvenile on head and upperparts but with white feather tips appearing on saddle, rump and centre of upperwing. Underparts; belly and flanks mainly white, with brown breast band and undertail-coverts. **HABITAT** Oceanic. **STATUS** Vagrant. **CALL** Harsh croaks and braying.

BLACK-BROWED ALBATROSS *Diomedea melanophris* 80–95 cm Wingspan 210–250 cm

The only black-backed albatross recorded from the region. A medium-sized albatross, the adult has a white head, with a black brow and a bright yellow-orange bill. The wings, mantle, back and scapulars are black, the rump and uppertail-coverts are white, and the tail grey-black. The underwing is white with a broad black leading edge, broadest behind carpel joint, with a narrower black trailing edge and wingtip.

SEXES Alike. **IMM** Blackish-brown bill with dull yellow base and black tip; varying amounts of grey on head and sides of neck, sometimes forming a distinct collar. Underwing all dark with a pale grey centre. **HABITAT** Oceanic and coastal waters. **STATUS** Vagrant. **CALL** Harsh cackling croaks and low grunts.

ANTARCTIC GIANT PETREL *Macronectes giganteus* 85–100 cm Wingspan 150–210 cm

Albatross size, with a huge horn-coloured bill with green tip and a distinctive stiff-winged, flapping motion in flight. Dimorphic. Dark morph, irregularly mottled grey-brown all over, apart from whitish head and neck. White morph, which is far less common, is pure white with scattered black feathers on body and wings. No change with age.

SEXES Alike. **IMM** Dark morph only, brownish-black all over, back and wings slightly greyer. **HABITAT** Oceanic and coastal waters. **STATUS** Vagrant. **CALL** Harsh growling and braying.

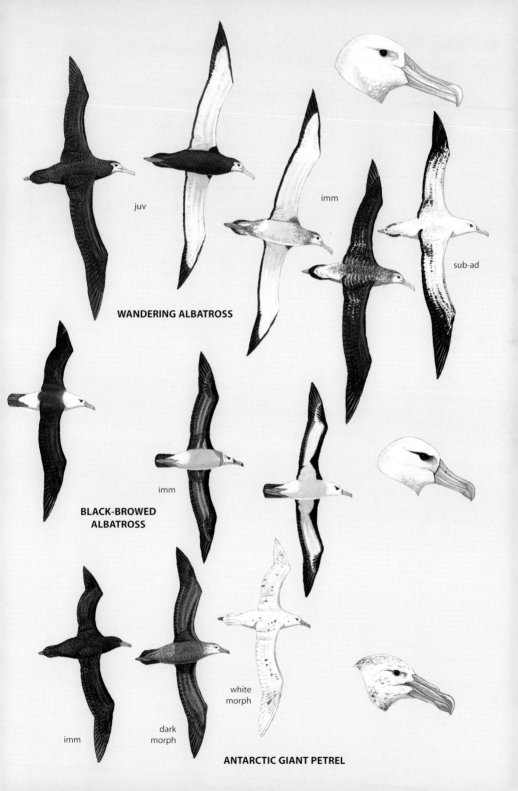

WANDERING ALBATROSS

juv

imm

sub-ad

BLACK-BROWED ALBATROSS

imm

imm

white morph

dark morph

ANTARCTIC GIANT PETREL

BECK'S PETREL *Pseudobulweria becki* 29 cm Wingspan 76 cm

Almost identical in plumage to Tahiti Petrel, but only three-quarters the size and with a less robust bill.
SEXES Alike. **HABITAT** Oceanic and coastal waters. **STATUS** Known from only two specimens taken at sea in 1928 in the Solomons: one taken north of Buka Island, Bougainville and the other northwest of Rendova Island.

TAHITI PETREL *Pseudobulweria rostrata* 38–40 cm Wingspan 84 cm

Almost identical in plumage to Beck's Petrel, but 25% larger. A large, stocky petrel with a large black bill and wedge-shaped tail. Entirely sooty brown except for sharply defined white lower breast, belly and undertail-coverts. Uppertail-coverts normally contrastingly paler brown. Underwing paler brown than upperparts with a lighter area along the middle of the wing, formed by paler bases to the primaries.
SEXES Alike. **HABITAT** Oceanic and coastal waters. **STATUS** Common breeding bird in New Caledonia, vagrant to the Solomons and Vanuatu. **CALL** Silent at sea.

HERALD PETREL *Pterodroma heraldica* 34–39 cm Wingspan 88–102 cm

Polymorphic, two main colour morphs, dark and pale, with varying intermediate morphs. A medium to large pterodroma with typical long narrow wings and wedge-shaped tail. Dark morph, head and body, slaty brown with faint 'M' pattern on upperwing, from wingtip to wingtip, discernible in good light. Underwing shows dull silvery flash across base of primaries, greater coverts and secondaries, forming tapering line extending inwards towards body. Pale line on leading edge of innerwing. Pale morph, head and chest pale brownish with white throat patch, underbody white. Upperparts dark greyish-brown with faint 'M' pattern, from wingtip to wingtip. Underwing dark with prominent white patch across base of primaries, greater coverts and secondaries as in dark morph.
SEXES Alike. **HABITAT** Oceanic and coastal waters. **STATUS** Vagrant. **CALL** Silent at sea.

PROVIDENCE PETREL *Pterodroma solandri* 40 cm Wingspan 95–105 cm

A medium to large pterodroma with long narrow wings and long slightly wedge-shaped tail. A mainly greyish-brown petrel with brown head and a scaly white face and forehead. Has a conspicuous white triangular patch in the central section of the underwing, formed by white bases to the primaries.
SEXES Alike. **HABITAT** Oceanic. **STATUS** Vagrant. **CALL** Loud screaming rapidly repeated 'kik-kik-kik'.

BULWER'S PETREL *Bulweria bulwerii* 26–28 cm Wingspan 68–73 cm

A small, distinctive, uniformly dark brown petrel, not much larger than a storm-petrel. Has a long wedge-shaped tail, which is normally carried folded into a diagnostic long narrow point, wedge shape only apparent when tail is spread briefly while manoeuvring. In good light a pale buff diagonal bar is evident across the upperwing.
SEXES Alike. **HABITAT** Oceanic. **STATUS** Vagrant. **CALL** Silent at sea.

KERMADEC PETREL *Pterodroma neglecta* 38 cm Wingspan 92 cm

Polymorphic, two main colour morphs, dark and pale, with a greater variation of intermediate morphs than any other petrel. A medium to large pterodroma with long, fairly broad wings and relatively short squarish tail. Dark morph, entirely blackish-brown, underbody slightly paler. Whitish primary shafts show as skua-like flash on upperwing. Underwing dark with bold, skua-like, prominent white flashes across base of primaries and narrow white crescent on outer greater coverts, not extending onto secondaries as in Herald and Providence Petrels. Pale morph, head and breast band greyish-white, with white underparts contrasting with greyish-brown upperparts and underwings. Wing markings as dark morph with additional white line on leading edge of innerwing. Intermediate morphs vary from birds with dark head and chest, with white throat and underbody, to all-dark birds with white mottling on underbody.
SEXES Alike. **HABITAT** Oceanic. **STATUS** Vagrant. **CALL** Silent at sea.

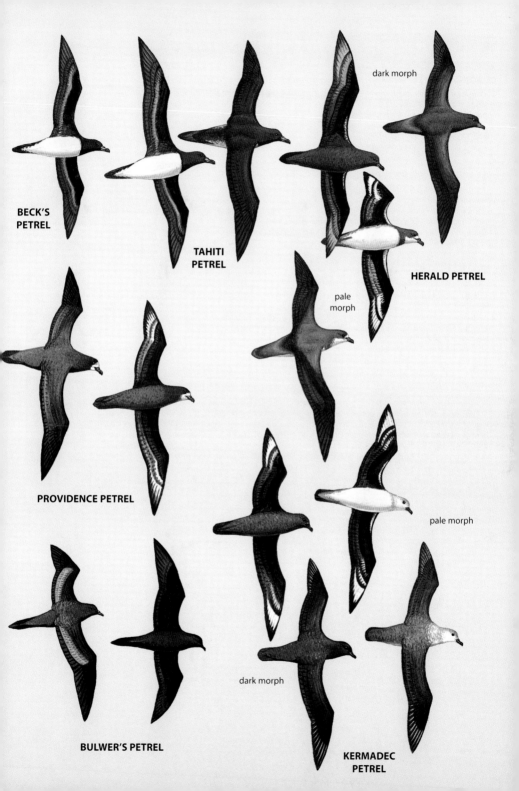

BECK'S PETREL

TAHITI PETREL

dark morph

HERALD PETREL

pale morph

PROVIDENCE PETREL

pale morph

BULWER'S PETREL

dark morph

KERMADEC PETREL

BLACK-WINGED PETREL *Pterodroma nigripennis* 28–30 cm Wingspan 63–71 cm

Small grey and white gadfly petrel with diagnostic underwing pattern. Upperbody and wings pale grey, with black eye patch and dusky tail tip, which becomes blacker and more contrasting with wear. Black 'M' pattern from wingtip to wingtip. Underbody white with pale grey collar. Underwing white, with a conspicuous black leading margin extending diagonally across to a point midway between the carpal joint and axillaries.
SEXES Alike. **HABITAT** Oceanic and coastal waters. **STATUS** Common breeding bird in New Caledonia, vagrant elsewhere in the region. **CALL** A high-pitched rapidly repeated, 'peet'.

WHITE-NECKED PETREL *Pterodroma cervicalis* 43 cm Wingspan 100 cm

A large grey and white gadfly petrel with conspicuous black cap and white nape collar. Upperparts medium grey with a darker grey 'M' marking, extending from wingtip to wingtip; forehead white; top of head black with a conspicuous white nape collar. Underparts white, except for a black leading margin extending from the carpal joint diagonally for a short distance over the white inner underwing-coverts.
SEXES Alike. **HABITAT** Oceanic and coastal waters. **STATUS** Possibly breeds in small numbers in the Vanuatu archipelago. **CALL** Silent at sea.

GOULD'S PETREL *Pterodroma leucoptera* 30 cm Wingspan 70 cm

Head darker than any other small pterodroma. A small grey and white gadfly petrel with dark grey upperparts with a black 'M' marking, extending from wingtip to wingtip. Forehead white freckled with black, lores and cheeks conspicuously white contrasting sharply with the black eye patch, crown and sides of neck. Underparts white except for a black leading margin extending from the carpal joint diagonally for a short distance over the white inner underwing-coverts.
SEXES Alike. **HABITAT** Oceanic and coastal waters. **STATUS** Common breeding bird in New Caledonia, with occasional offshore sightings from Vanuatu. **CALL** Silent at sea.

COLLARED PETREL *Pterodroma brevipes* 30 cm Wingspan 70 cm

A small grey and white gadfly petrel with grey upperparts and a black 'M' marking, extending from wingtip to wingtip. Black of crown shades gradually into grey of upper back; forehead and throat patch white, rest of underparts highly variable. Most individuals have a grey breast-band, with white throat, belly and undertail, but others, except for a white throat have completely grey underbodies. Underwing white except for a black leading margin extending from the carpal joint diagonally for a short distance over the white inner underwing-coverts.
SEXES Alike. **HABITAT** Oceanic and coastal waters. **STATUS** Breeds in small numbers in New Caledonia, Vanuatu and possibly the Solomons. **CALL** Silent at sea.

ANTARCTIC PRION *Pachyptila desolata* 27 cm Wingspan 61–66 cm

The only species of prion which has so far been recorded from the region. A small petrel with pale blue-grey upperparts, a greyish-black mark through and behind the eye, a black 'M' marking, extending from wingtip to wingtip, tail grey with a narrow black terminal band. Underparts wholly white except for the blue-grey of the hindneck which extends down sides of neck and upperbreast, forming a conspicuous half-collar.
SEXES Alike. **HABITAT** Oceanic and coastal waters. **STATUS** Occasionally recorded at sea from New Caledonia and Vanuatu. **CALL** Silent at sea.

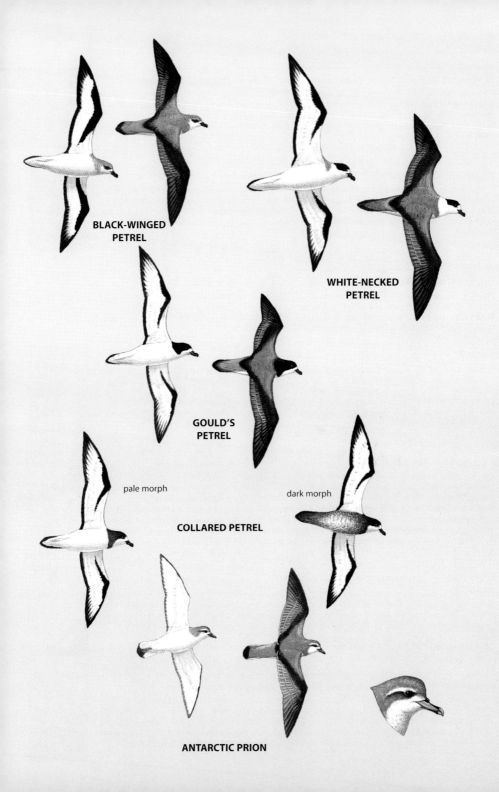

BLACK-WINGED PETREL

WHITE-NECKED PETREL

GOULD'S PETREL

pale morph

dark morph

COLLARED PETREL

ANTARCTIC PRION

STREAKED SHEARWATER *Calonectris leucomelas* 48 cm Wingspan 122 cm

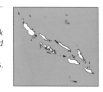

White face with streaked hindcrown diagnostic. Very large shearwater with white face and head with dark streaks to hindcrown; upperparts brown with pale scalloping, underparts white. Bill pale with dark tip, legs and feet pink.
SEXES Alike. **HABITAT** Oceanic and coastal waters. **STATUS** Uncommon summer visitor to the Solomons. **CALL** Silent at sea.

WEDGE-TAILED SHEARWATER *Puffinus pacificus* 38–46 cm Wingspan 97–105 cm

All dark with conspicuous wedge-shaped tail. A large dark brown, slender-bodied shearwater with long wedge-shaped tail, dark bill and flesh-coloured feet. Races with white underparts not yet recorded from the region.
SEXES Alike. **HABITAT** Oceanic and coastal waters. **STATUS** Abundant breeding bird in New Caledonia and Vanuatu, casual visitor to the Solomons. **CALL** Silent at sea.

FLESH-FOOTED SHEARWATER *Puffinus carneipes* 40–45 cm Wingspan 99–107 cm

Diagnostic pale pink bill, legs and feet. A large uniformly dark chocolate-brown shearwater, larger and darker than Wedge-tailed Shearwater and with a rounded tail.
SEXES Alike. **HABITAT** Oceanic and coastal waters. **STATUS** Not officially recorded from the region, but small numbers likely to pass through on migration. **CALL** Silent at sea.

SHORT-TAILED SHEARWATER *Puffinus tenuirostris* 40–45 cm Wingspan 95–100 cm

Only shearwater in the region whose feet extend beyond the tail, in flight. A medium-sized dark shearwater with a short, fan-shaped tail. Underwing grey-brown; primaries can be reflective in strong sunlight, causing them to appear silvery. Bill blackish-grey; legs and feet dark grey.
SEXES Alike. **HABITAT** Oceanic and coastal waters. **STATUS** Large numbers pass through the region, mainly on the return leg of their migration, during the months of September to November. **CALL** Silent at sea.

HEINROTH'S SHEARWATER *Puffinus heinrothi* 23–27 cm Wingspan 58–60 cm

Combination of small size, white on underwing and sometimes on belly, distinguishes this extremely rare shearwater. Small all-dark shearwater, except for white centre to underwing, centre of abdomen and chin. The amount of white on the abdomen varies and is difficult to observe at sea. Bill dark, feet flesh-coloured.
SEXES Alike. **HABITAT** Coastal waters. **STATUS** There are only a handful of specimens of this species and until recently, just a few sight records from New Britain and Bougainville. Recent sightings from the central Solomons, in the New Georgia group, (Moray Isles), and in the Indispensable Strait off the Florida Islands, by the author. Breeding grounds almost certainly in the mountains of New Britain, Bougainville and other islands in the Solomons.

FLUTTERING SHEARWATER *Puffinus gavia* 32–37 cm Wingspan 76 cm

White underwing, body and undertail diagnostic. A small, stocky, short-winged shearwater, with uniformly dark brown upperparts. Grey-brown sides of face extend below the eye and grey-brown of hindneck extends broadly downwards and forwards to form a distinct half-collar. Underbody including undertail-coverts white, except for brown thigh patch, and tip of tail. Underwing mostly greyish-white, trailing edge brown, axillaries dusky-grey.
SEXES Alike. **HABITAT** Oceanic and coastal waters. **STATUS** Breeds on Banks Island and possibly in New Caledonia. Vagrant to Vanuatu and the Solomons. **CALL** Silent at sea.

AUDUBON'S SHEARWATER *Puffinus lherminieri* 30–31 cm Wingspan 69 cm

Black undertail-coverts and underside of tail diagnostic. A small stocky, short-winged shearwater with uniformly sooty black upperparts and clean cut white underparts. Dark upperparts extend below the eye and onto sides of breast. Wing linings white, contrasting sharply with dark flight feathers. Legs and feet flesh-coloured.
SEXES Alike. **HABITAT** Oceanic and coastal waters. **STATUS** Fairly common breeding bird in Vanuatu, may breed in small numbers in New Caledonia and sight records from the Solomons. **CALL** Silent at sea.

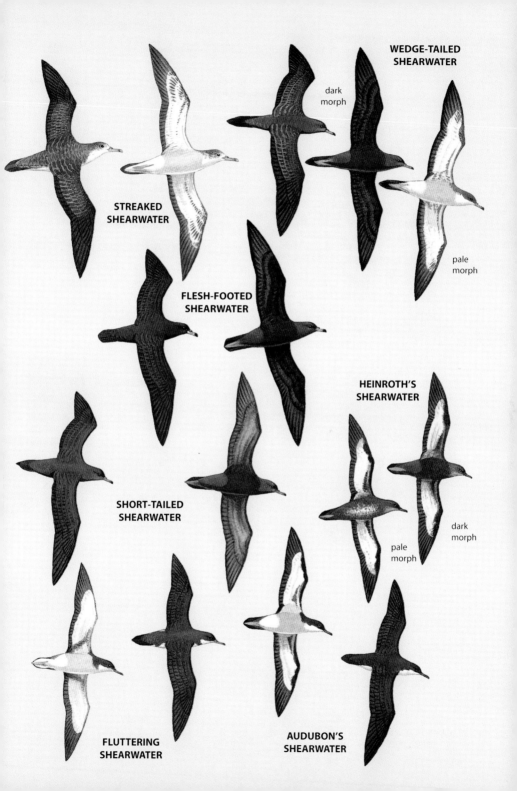

WEDGE-TAILED
SHEARWATER

dark
morph

STREAKED
SHEARWATER

pale
morph

FLESH-FOOTED
SHEARWATER

HEINROTH'S
SHEARWATER

SHORT-TAILED
SHEARWATER

pale
morph

dark
morph

FLUTTERING
SHEARWATER

AUDUBON'S
SHEARWATER

WILSON'S STORM-PETREL *Oceanites oceanicus* 15–19 cm Wingspan 38–42 cm

Only storm-petrel in the region with all dark underwings. A small, dainty petrel, with broad rounded wings and a square tail. All sooty-black except for prominent U-shaped white band across rump and white outer undertail-coverts. Pronounced pale greyish-brown crescent across the upperwing-coverts. Bill black, legs and feet black, with yellow webs discernible at close range.
SEXES Alike. **HABITAT** Oceanic. **STATUS** Small numbers present, mainly during winter months from April to October. **CALL** Silent at sea.

BLACK-BELLIED STORM-PETREL *Fregetta tropica* 20 cm Wingspan 45–46 cm

Diagnostic black central belly stripe from breast to undertail. A small, dainty petrel with broad rounded wings and a square tail. All sooty black except for prominent U-shaped white band across rump, white flanks and centre of underwing. The black belly stripe is variable and can be greatly reduced or occasionally, absent altogether. Bill, legs and feet black.
SEXES Alike. **HABITAT** Oceanic. **STATUS** A few birds present during winter months, from May to September. **CALL** Silent at sea.

WHITE-BELLIED STORM-PETREL *Fregetta grallaria* 18–22 cm Wingspan 46–48 cm

Square tail and totally white belly diagnostic. Size and shape as for Black-bellied Storm-Petrel, to which it is very similar. All blackish except for prominent U-shaped white band across rump, white belly and centre of underwing. Rare dark morph breeds on Lord Howe Island, not recorded from the region. Bill, legs and feet black.
SEXES Alike. **HABITAT** Oceanic. **STATUS** Vagrant. **CALL** Silent at sea.

POLYNESIAN STORM-PETREL *Nesofregetta fuliginosa* 24–26 cm Wingspan 54–58 cm

Large size and deeply forked tail with broad rounded wings diagnostic. Polymorphic; the common pale morph is all sooty black except for narrow U-shaped white band across rump, white throat patch, belly and centre of underwing. Rare dark morph breeds in Samoa, and has not occurred in the region. Intermediate morphs show variable amounts of white below, streaked with black. Bill, legs and feet black.
SEXES Alike. **HABITAT** Oceanic. **STATUS** Breeds in small numbers in Vanuatu, occasional wanderer to the Solomons and New Caledonia. **CALL** Silent at sea.

WILSON'S STORM-PETREL

BLACK-BELLIED STORM-PETREL

WHITE-BELLIED STORM-PETREL

pale morph

intermediate morph

POLYNESIAN STORM-PETREL

RED-TAILED TROPICBIRD *Phaethon rubricauda* 56–65 cm plus 28–39 cm central tail feathers

Stout, pigeon-like all silky white bird, often with a pink suffusion to the plumage. Bill bright red, pointed, stout and tern-like. Conspicuous black eyestripe beginning at the base of the bill, curving upwards and passing through and behind the eye; wings white, with narrow black primary shafts and broad black shaft streaks on tertials. White tail with long bright red, stiff central tail feathers.
SEXES Alike. **IMM** Bill dark grey. Lacks elongated central tail feathers. Upperparts white with heavy black vermiculations and mottling giving a barred effect; more heavily barred and more black on the wings than immature White-tailed Tropicbird. **HABITAT** Oceanic and coastal waters. **STATUS** Occasional wanderer throughout the region. **CALL** Silent at sea.

WHITE-TAILED TROPICBIRD *Phaethon lepturus* 40–45 cm plus 30–40 cm central tail feathers

A smaller, more slender tropicbird, all brilliant white; some birds show a peach suffusion to the plumage. Bill bright yellow, pointed, stout and tern-like. Conspicuous black eyestripe beginning at the base of the bill, curving upwards and passing through and well beyond the eye; wings white, with thick black primary shafts and a prominent broad diagonal black bar across the inner upperwing. White tail with long white stiff central tail feathers.
SEXES Alike. **IMM** Bill dull yellowish with black tip. Lacks elongated central tail feathers. Upperparts white with heavy black vermiculations and mottling, giving a barred effect; less heavily barred and less black on the wings than immature Red-tailed Tropicbird. **HABITAT** Oceanic and coastal waters. **STATUS** Breeds in small numbers in Vanuatu and New Caledonia, occasional wanderer to the Solomons. **CALL** Silent at sea.

GREAT FRIGATEBIRD *Fregata minor* 85–105 cm

Very large, mainly black bird with long pointed wings and deeply forked tail. Most often seen soaring high on motionless wings.
ADULT MALE Black with metallic green and purple gloss on the mantle and a diagonal brownish bar across the inner upperwing. Bright red inflatable throat pouch and lacks white axillaries of Lesser Frigatebird. Iris dark brown, eyering is blue. Bill grey. Legs and feet dull pink. **ADULT FEMALE** Black with a diagonal scaly buff bar across the inner upperwing; grey chin and white throat and breast. **IMM** Rusty brown head and white breast. **HABITAT** Oceanic and coastal waters. **STATUS** Breeds in small numbers in New Caledonia, regular wanderer to Vanuatu and the Solomons. **CALL** Silent at sea.

LESSER FRIGATEBIRD *Fregata ariel* 70–80 cm

Similar to Great Frigatebird, but smaller and readily identifiable by presence of white axillaries.
ADULT MALE Black with metallic green and purple gloss on the mantle and an indistinct diagonal pale brown bar across the inner upperwing. Bright red inflatable throat pouch and prominent white axillaries. Iris, eyering, bill, legs and feet as in Great Frigatebird. **ADULT FEMALE** As Great Frigatebird but with black throat forming dark hood, with narrow white collar on hindneck and prominent white axillaries. **IMM** As Great Frigatebird but with indistinct white axillaries. **HABITAT** Oceanic and coastal waters. **STATUS** Breeds in good numbers in New Caledonia. Present throughout the year in Vanuatu and the Solomons, but breeding there has yet to be confirmed. **CALL** Silent at sea.

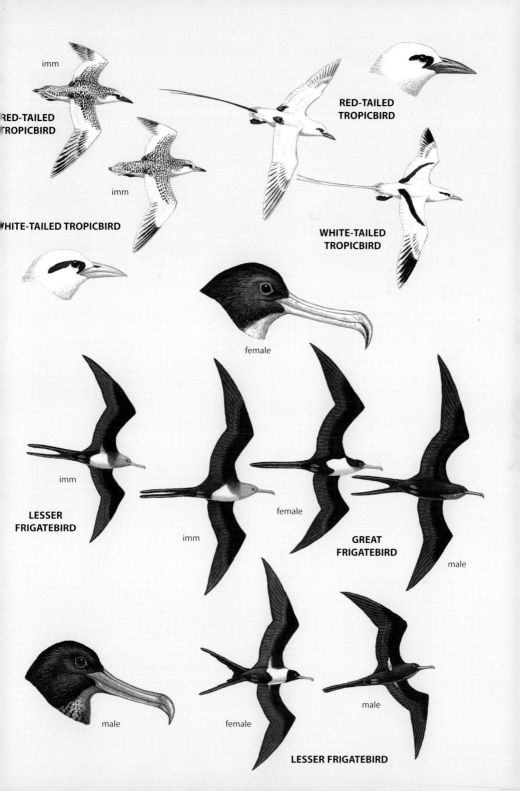

imm

RED-TAILED
TROPICBIRD

RED-TAILED
TROPICBIRD

imm

WHITE-TAILED TROPICBIRD

WHITE-TAILED
TROPICBIRD

female

imm

LESSER
FRIGATEBIRD

imm

female

GREAT
FRIGATEBIRD

male

male

female

male

LESSER FRIGATEBIRD

MASKED BOOBY *Sula dactylatra* 75–85 cm

The largest booby. All species have long, cigar-shaped bodies, pointed bills and tails, and long, narrow pointed wings. Adult Masked Booby is a brilliant black and white bird, all white with black primaries, secondaries, tips of longer scapulars and tail. Bill yellow, facial skin blue-black giving a masked appearance. Feet normally grey, but colour is variable.
SEXES Alike. **IMM** Mottled brown head, obvious white nuchal collar, heavily mottled back, rump and upperwing. Breast and abdomen white, tail dark. Underwing-coverts white with central dark line on median coverts. **HABITAT** Oceanic and coastal waters. **STATUS** Breeds in New Caledonia, occasional wanderer to Vanuatu and the Solomons. **CALL** Silent at sea.

RED-FOOTED BOOBY *Sula sula* 66–75 cm

The smallest booby, but with typical booby shape. Polymorphic with three main colour morphs: white, the commonest colour morph in the region, white-tailed brown morph, which is fairly common, and the very uncommon dark morph. White morph: all white except for black primaries and secondaries and a distinctive black patch at the carpal joint of the underwing; pale blue bill with bright pink face and blue skin around the eye; legs and feet bright red. White-tailed brown morph: head, neck, wings, mantle and upper back, pale brown, lower back, rump and tail white. Dark morph completely chocolate-brown, sometimes with golden suffusion on head and nape.
SEXES Alike. **IMM** Brown with paler underparts, black bill and grey legs and feet. **HABITAT** Oceanic and coastal waters. **STATUS** Breeds throughout the region. **CALL** Silent at sea.

BROWN BOOBY *Sula leucogaster* 70–76 cm

Medium-sized booby, with typical booby shape.
ADULT MALE Dark chocolate-brown except for white belly, undertail-coverts and centre of the inner underwing. Bill bluish-grey with deep blue base. Legs and feet greenish-yellow. **ADULT FEMALE** Plumage as for male. Bare skin of face, eyering and base of bill yellow, rest of bill yellowish. **IMM** A paler version of the adult with greyish belly mottled brown; white underwing is also mottled brown. Bill and facial skin dark greyish-blue. **HABITAT** Oceanic and coastal waters. **STATUS** Breeds throughout the region. **CALL** Silent at sea.

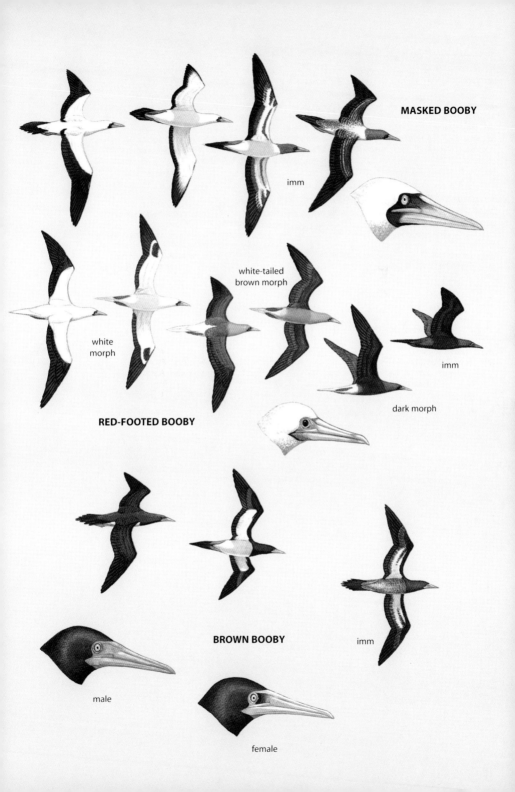

MASKED BOOBY

imm

white-tailed
brown morph

white
morph

imm

dark morph

RED-FOOTED BOOBY

BROWN BOOBY

imm

male

female

WHITE-EYED DUCK *Aythya australis* 45–60 cm

A chocolate-brown duck. In flight, shows a distinctive white wingbar, the full length of the upperwing.
ADULT MALE Fairly uniform chocolate-brown plumage, with distinct white undertail-coverts visible when swimming; has very noticeable pale blue-grey subterminal band on dark grey bill and prominent white eye. White patch on lower breast and abdomen. **ADULT FEMALE** Like male but paler on head, neck and upperparts, slight mottling on lower breast and abdomen. **IMM** Like adult female but slightly paler, particularly on chin and throat. **HABITAT** Deep inland waters. **STATUS** Breeds in small numbers in Vanuatu, sporadic irruptions occur in the Solomons and New Caledonia, presumably birds from Australia. **CALL** Soft whistle.

PLUMED WHISTLING-DUCK *Dendrocygna eytoni* 40–60 cm

Diagnostic elongated buff flank-plumes project above bodyline. Head, neck and upper breast pale brown, pale cinnamon breast with black barring; back and tail dark brown, separated by a narrow, pale horseshoe-shaped rump band. Bill pink with some black mottling; legs and feet pink. Like Wandering Whistling-Duck it has a very erect stance and is highly gregarious.
SEXES Alike. **IMM** Slightly paler and duller than adult with indistinct barring on breast and short flank-plumes. **HABITAT** Inland waters. **STATUS** One recent sighting from Makira Island in the Solomons. **CALL** Distinctive high-pitched whistle.

WANDERING WHISTLING-DUCK *Dendrocygna arcuata* 55–60 cm

Similar in shape to Plumed Whistling-Duck, flank-plumes cream coloured and very short. Upperparts blackish-brown with rich chestnut margins to feathers of back, white uppertail-coverts and horseshoe-shaped rump band. Throat pale brown, underparts rich chestnut, short, cream- coloured flank-plumes with chestnut edges. Bill, legs and feet black.
SEXES Alike. **IMM** Duller, with pale centre to abdomen. **HABITAT** Inland waters. **STATUS** Small numbers have bred in New Caledonia, but no sightings since late 1970s. **CALL** Loud constant twittering interspersed with high-pitched whistles.

CANADA GOOSE *Branta canadensis* 64–100 cm

Large size and black head and neck with distinctive white chin-strap, diagnostic. Brown mantle, back and wings, feathers edged with buff. Uppertail-coverts white, forming U-shaped rump band; tail black. Breast pale grey-brown, feathers edged with brown, giving a barred appearance. Abdomen and undertail-coverts white contrasting with black undertail. Bill, legs and feet grey.
SEXES Alike. **HABITAT** Inland waters. **STATUS** Occasional wanderers reach New Caledonia, presumably from New Zealand, where it has been introduced from North America. **CALL** Loud honk.

WHITE-EYED DUCK

male

female

PLUMED WHISTLING-DUCK

WANDERING WHISTLING-DUCK

CANADA GOOSE

GREY TEAL Anas gracilis 42–44 cm

The palest duck of the region. A small, uniformly grey duck with pale edging to most body feathers, producing an overall scaly or mottled appearance. In good light, a white throat and paler face distinguish it from darker female Brown Teal. Bill, legs and feet grey. In flight shows a dark greenish speculum surrounded by white.
SEXES Alike **HABITAT** Inland waters. **STATUS** Sporadic irruptions, during drought conditions in Australia, to New Caledonia and Vanuatu. A small resident population on Lake Tengano, on Rennell Island in the Solomons; now severely threatened by the introduction of *Tilapia* into the lake. Small numbers still survive at the western end of the lake. **CALL** Loud penetrating quack repeated rapidly up to 20 times, falling in pitch.

BROWN TEAL Anas aucklandica 48 cm

A small, dark brown duck with a diagnostic white collar and eyering.
ADULT MALE Dark brown head with green iridescence on the nape. Back uniformly dark brown, feathers edged paler. Reddish-brown breast finely mottled and barred; white patch at base of tail. Bill, legs and feet grey. In flight shows dark green speculum. **ADULT FEMALE** Uniformly brown, with narrow white eyering. **IMM** Similar to female. **HABITAT** Coastal wetlands and island shores. **STATUS** This endangered and sedentary New Zealand duck has, surprisingly, been observed in New Caledonia on more than one occasion. **CALL** A high-pitched whistle.

MALLARD Anas platyrhynchos 50–76 cm

Male is unmistakable, with a yellow bill, glossy green head, white collar and rich purple-brown breast. Back grey-brown and abdomen and flanks silvery-grey, with fine vermiculations. Legs and feet orange. When in eclipse plumage resembles female. In flight, shows glossy purplish-blue speculum.
ADULT FEMALE Mottled brown with paler head and face, bill orange-brown with dark saddle, legs and feet dull orange. **IMM** Similar to female. **HABITAT** Any stretch of open water. **STATUS** Introduced to New Caledonia in the early 1970s, now possibly extirpated. Vagrant in Vanuatu (one record). **CALL** Loud resonant quack.

PACIFIC BLACK DUCK Anas superciliosa 47–60 cm

Striking facial pattern diagnostic. A large, heavily built, uniformly brown duck. Top of head and nape black, back dark brown, feathers edged paler. Sides of face and throat off-white, marked by two bold black stripes, one through the eye, the other below it. Bill grey, legs and feet grey-green. In flight shows bright green speculum.
SEXES Alike. **HABITAT** Inland waters. **STATUS** A common breeding bird throughout the region. **CALL** Long drawn-out quack.

NORTHERN PINTAIL Anas acuta 50–76 cm

Male is grey with distinctive chocolate-brown head, upper foreneck and hindneck, a conspicuous white line runs down the side of the neck to the white breast and underparts, very long pointed tail. Bill, legs and feet grey. When in eclipse plumage resembles female but the bill is grey edged with black. In flight, shows dark bronzy-green speculum with buff leading edge and white trailing edge.
ADULT FEMALE Uniformly mottled grey-brown, with short, pointed tail. **IMM** Resembles female. **HABITAT** Inland waters. **STATUS** Vagrant, two records from Bougainville Island in the Solomons. **CALL** Low quack.

AUSTRALIAN SHOVELER Anas rhynchotis 45–55 cm

Easily identified by large, spatulate bill and low sloping forehead.
ADULT MALE Head and neck bluish-grey with turquoise gloss and vertical white crescent in front of yellow eye. Back dark brown, breast freckled dark-brown and white, abdomen and flanks bright chestnut spotted with black; prominent white patch on posterior flanks. Bill dark grey, legs and feet orange. In flight, shows conspicuous pale blue-grey upperwing-coverts and green speculum edged with white. Eclipse plumage duller version of breeding plumage. **ADULT FEMALE** Uniformly mottled dark brown, wing markings as male. **IMM** Resembles female. **HABITAT** Inland waters. **STATUS** Vagrant to New Caledonia, probably from New Zealand. **CALL** Rapid series of quacks.

GREY TEAL

BROWN TEAL

female

male

MALLARD

male

female

PACIFIC BLACK DUCK

NORTHERN PINTAIL

male

male

AUSTRALIAN SHOVELER

female

female

female

**PLUMED
WHISTLING-DUCK**

**WANDERING
WHISTLING-DUCK**

CANADA GOOSE

female

BROWN TEAL

GREY TEAL

male

MALLARD

male

female

PACIFIC BLACK DUCK

NORTHERN PINTAIL

male

female

AUSTRALIAN SHOVELER

male

female

WHITE-EYED DUCK

male

female

LITTLE EGRET *Egretta garzetta* 55–65 cm

The black legs and yellow soles to the feet readily identify this species. This small egret's slender bill is always black, contrasting with the yellow facial skin. In breeding plumage plumes on nape, breast and back.
SEXES Alike. **HABITAT** Marshes, inland waters and shoreline. **STATUS** Rare vagrant to Bougainville Island in the Solomons. **CALL** Harsh croak.

PACIFIC REEF-EGRET *Egretta sacra* 60–65 cm

The combination of a long thick bill and short thick dull grey-yellow legs, distinguish this species from other egrets and herons in the region. A medium-sized polymorphic egret. Dark morph uniform slate grey. White morph wholly white. Mottled morph, which is rather rare, is white variably mottled with slate grey.
SEXES Alike. **HABITAT** Reefs, rocky coasts, mangroves and lakes and rivers, sometimes far inland. **STATUS** Common breeding species throughout the region. **CALL** Loud guttural croak.

INTERMEDIATE EGRET *Egretta intermedia* 56–70 cm

Intermediate in size between Cattle and Great Egrets. Differs from Great Egret by shorter bill, higher forehead and noticeably shorter neck, not held in such a pronounced 'S' shape. Breeding plumage: red bill with bright green facial skin, red tibia and long plumes on the back and breast. Non-breeding plumage: yellow bill and facial skin, black legs and lacks plumes.
SEXES Alike. **HABITAT** Marshes and inland waters. **STATUS** Rare vagrant to Bougainville Island in the Solomons. **CALL** Soft croaking.

GREAT EGRET *Casmerodius albus* 83–103 cm

The largest egret of the region. Differs from Intermediate Egret by its larger size, longer bill, flat crown, the gape extending beyond the eye, proportionally longer neck, often held in pronounced 'S' shape. Breeding plumage: black bill with olive-green facial skin, red-brown tibia and long elaborate plumes, only on the back. Non-breeding plumage: yellow bill and facial skin, black legs and lacks plumes.
SEXES Alike. **HABITAT** Rivers, lakes, marshes and tidal flats. **STATUS** Small numbers breed on Lake Tengano, on Rennell Island in the Solomons. Rare vagrant to Bougainville Island in the Solomons and New Caledonia. Not recorded from Vanuatu. **CALL** A range of harsh guttural croaks.

CATTLE EGRET *Bubulcus ibis* 54–70 cm

This small egret has a distinctive stocky, short-necked, hunched-up posture, a very high forehead and noticeably large jowl. Breeding plumage: head, neck, breast and back tinged with orange-buff, bill bright red with yellow tip, legs pale red. Non-breeding plumage: wholly white, with yellow bill and black legs.
SEXES Alike. **HABITAT** Usually in small flocks in pasture, often accompanies livestock, occasionally in wetlands. **STATUS** Sporadic irruptions into New Caledonia, presumably from Australia. **CALL** Low-pitched 'kwark'.

AUSTRALIAN IBIS *Threskiornis molucca* 65–75 cm

A plump-bodied mainly white bird, with very long, down-curved black bill, unfeathered black head and neck and black plumes over tail.
SEXES Alike. **HABITAT** Marshes, agricultural land and tidal flats. **STATUS** Abundant breeding bird on Rennell and Bellona islands in the Solomons. **CALL** Harsh guttural croak.

ROYAL SPOONBILL *Platalea regia* 74–81 cm

A white heron-like bird with a diagnostic black spoon-shaped bill and black legs. In breeding plumage has a white drooping crest on the nape.
SEXES Alike. **HABITAT** Shallow wetlands and tidal flats. **STATUS** Sporadic irruptions into New Caledonia and Rennell Island in the Solomons. **CALL** Soft grunts, groans and hisses.

non-br

dark morph

white morph

**PACIFIC
REEF-EGRET**

br

**LITTLE
EGRET**

br

non-br

non-br

**INTERMEDIATE
EGRET**

br

**GREAT
EGRET**

non-br

**CATTLE
EGRET**

br

br

**AUSTRALIAN
IBIS**

non-br

**ROYAL
SPOONBILL**

WHITE-FACED HERON *Egretta novaehollandiae* **66–68 cm**

Medium-sized heron easily identified by overall blue-grey plumage, conspicuous white face and throat and yellow legs. In breeding plumage has pinkish-brown plumes on lower foreneck and breast and long grey plumes on back.
SEXES Alike. **IMM** As non-breeding adult, with brown wash to plumage, lacks white face. **HABITAT** Wetlands, rivers, farm dams, pasture and tidal flats. **STATUS** Common breeding bird in New Caledonia, rare vagrant to Vanuatu and the Solomons. **CALL** Guttural 'graaw'.

STRIATED HERON *Butorides striatus* **38–48 cm**

Distinctive, small stocky heron with heavy dark bill, short neck and thick short legs. Plumage varies greatly throughout the region. All show glossy black crown, with either dark grey-green above and light grey below, or rufous-brown above and rufous below.
SEXES Alike. **IMM** White streaks on crown and heavily streaked underparts. **HABITAT** Tidal flats, mangroves, lakes and rivers. **STATUS** Local and uncommon throughout the region. **CALL** Harsh 'tch-aah' and explosive 'hoo'.

YELLOW BITTERN *Ixobrychus sinensis* **30–40 cm**

Small size and black wings with sharply contrasting buff patches on secondary coverts readily identify this species.
ADULT MALE Yellowish-brown back, yellowish-buff below with black crown, tail and primaries. Bill, legs and feet yellow. **ADULT FEMALE** Similar to male but chin, throat and breast white, broadly striped with cinnamon. **IMM** Browner and heavily streaked above and below. **HABITAT** Dense waterside vegetation and reedbeds fringing inland wetlands. **STATUS** Uncommon breeding bird on Bougainville Island, rare winter visitor elsewhere in the Solomons. **CALL** Deep croaks.

RUFOUS NIGHT-HERON *Nycticorax caledonicus* **55–65 cm**

A distinctive, short-necked, stocky heron. Two races occur; both have black crowns, N. c mandibularis, has chestnut-brown back and wings, dull chestnut underparts and black nuchal plumes. N. c. caledonicus, has rufous-cinnamon back and wings, is white below with a cinnamon wash to the neck and upper breast and white nuchal plumes.
SEXES Alike. **IMM** Drab brown, darker above with pale streaks on head and breast and pale spots on back and wings. **HABITAT** Swamps, rivers and tidal flats. **STATUS** *N. c. mandibularis* breeds in the Solomons and New Caledonia. *N. c. caledonicus* is an occasional wanderer throughout the region. **CALL** Hoarse croak-like 'qu-ock'.

BLACK BITTERN *Ixobrychus flavicollis* **54–66 cm**

A slender, long-necked, medium-sized bittern.
ADULT MALE Black with conspicuous buffy-yellow neck patches and streaks on breast. **ADULT FEMALE** Like male, but browner and paler. **IMM** Upperparts dark brown scalloped buff, pale yellow neck patches and fine streaking on breast. **HABITAT** Mangroves, tall grass and reeds along river edge and beside inland waters. **STATUS** Uncommon breeding bird in the Solomons. **CALL** Loud booming during breeding season.

AUSTRALASIAN BITTERN *Botaurus poiciloptilus* **66–76 cm**

Large, stocky, long-necked bittern with cryptic plumage. Upperparts brown, mottled with buff, especially on wings. Foreneck yellowish-brown with black-brown streaked stripes, pale yellow belly and thighs.
SEXES Alike. **HABITAT** Wetland with tall dense vegetation. **STATUS** Uncommon breeding bird in New Caledonia. **CALL** Deep resonant booms during breeding season, particularly at night.

GLOSSY IBIS *Plegadis falcinellus* **55–65 cm**

The only dark coloured ibis of the region. At a distance appears brownish-black, but at close range shows the head, neck and body to be dark chestnut, with wing and tail glossy green with bronze and purple iridescence.
SEXES Alike. **IMM** Dull brown, with white streaking on face, throat and neck. **HABITAT** Wet grasslands and inland waters. **STATUS** Uncommon wanderer to Bougainville Island in the Solomons. **CALL** Guttural grunts.

WHITE-FACED HERON

non-br

br

rufous morph

grey morph

STRIATED HERON

imm

YELLOW BITTERN

female

male

imm

imm

RUFOUS NIGHT-HERON

mandibularis

caledonicus

imm

GLOSSY IBIS

female

imm

BLACK BITTERN

male

AUSTRALASIAN BITTERN

OSPREY *Pandion haliaetus* 50–65 cm

A medium-sized, distinctive, fish-eating raptor, intermediate in size between Brahminy Kite and White-bellied Sea-Eagle, has distinctive bowed wings. Dark brown above, head and underparts white with a distinctive bold dark brown stripe through and behind the eye, merging with brown nape; variable brown breast band. Long narrow wings, underwing white with barred flight feathers and a conspicuous black patch on the carpal joint. **SEXES** Alike. **HABITAT** Inland rivers and wetlands, mangroves, estuaries, tidal flats and offshore islands. **STATUS** Common breeding bird in the Solomons and New Caledonia. Not recorded from Vanuatu. **CALL** A repeated reedy whistle.

PACIFIC BAZA *Aviceda subcristata* 35–45 cm

Prominent erectile crest diagnostic of this species. A medium-sized hawk with broad, rounded, deeply fingered wings. Silvery-grey mantle and back, tinged dark brown on scapulars and tertials, with blue-grey wings. Head, neck and breast grey, belly and flanks white with bold rufous-brown bars, vent and undertail-coverts apricot. Wings below silvery-grey with heavy black barring and prominent apricot underwing-coverts, tail silvery-grey with broad black terminal band. **SEXES** Alike. **IMM** Dark grey-brown upperparts, scalloped with rufous-brown, chin and throat white, fore-neck and upper breast uniform buff, lower breast, belly and flanks creamy-white with narrow brown bars. **HABITAT** Forest, secondary growth and gardens. **STATUS** Fairly common breeding bird throughout the Solomons. **CALL** Mellow whistle, repeated several times.

WHISTLING KITE *Haliastur sphenurus* 50–60 cm

A medium-sized, sandy-brown, rather untidy kite, with distinctive, long rounded pale, unbarred tail and diagnostic pale open 'M' on underwing. Soars and glides on characteristically slightly arched wings. Brown plumage mottled and streaked with buff, paler on the head and underparts. Long, rounded, unbarred tail separates it from immature Brahminy Kite. **SEXES** Alike. **IMM** As adult but with bolder streaking on underparts and pale tips to feathers of upperparts, giving a spotted appearance. **HABITAT** Secondary growth, farmland, wetlands, lakes and rivers. **STATUS** Common breeding bird in New Caledonia. **CALL** Loud, distinctive, descending whistle.

BRAHMINY KITE *Haliastur indus* 45–50 cm

The adult is unmistakable with its white head, mantle, breast, upper belly and tail tip, contrasting sharply with chestnut back, wings, lower breast and undertail. **SEXES** Alike. **IMM** Dark brown, heavily mottled with buff on the upperparts and boldly streaked on head and breast. Similar in plumage to immature Whistling Kite, but easily separated by shorter wings and much shorter tail. **HABITAT** Found mainly along the coast, in open lowlands and forest edge, often over lakes, rivers and estuaries. **STATUS** Common breeding bird throughout the Solomons, scarce wanderer to Vanuatu. **CALL** Drawn out 'ker-ree ker-ree ker-ree'.

OSPREY

PACIFIC BAZA

WHISTLING KITE

imm

BRAHMINY KITE

WHITE-BELLIED SEA-EAGLE   *Haliaeetus leucogaster* 75–85 cm

Large dark grey and white eagle, with very broad wings and very short rounded tail. Wings held in a prominent dihedral when gliding and soaring. Adults unmistakable: head, neck, underparts and terminal half of tail pure white, back, upperwing-coverts and base of tail dark grey; black primaries to both upper and underwing.
SEXES Alike. **IMM** Upperparts pale brown mottled with darker brown, many feathers edged with fulvous, whitish 'bulls-eye' on underwing and almost white tail. **HABITAT** Coastal wetlands, larger rivers and off-shore islands. **STATUS** In this region occurs only on Nissan Island, the most northerly of the Solomon Islands, replaced elsewhere in the Solomons by *H. sanfordi*. **CALL** Loud, nasal, 'cank-cank-cank'.

SOLOMON SEA-EAGLE   *Haliaeetus sanfordi* 70–90 cm

Very large uniformly dark brown eagle, similar to White-bellied Sea-Eagle in size and shape, with very broad wings and slightly wedge-shaped tail. Wings held in a prominent dihedral when gliding and soaring. Upperparts blackish-brown, shading to black on primaries and tail. Underparts dull rufous-brown, with conspicuous pale buff head with lanceolate feathers and a dark eyeline.
SEXES Alike. **IMM** Dark brown mottled with buff and heavily streaked below with greyish-white, similar to immature Brahminy Kite, but much larger. Has a more pronounced wedge-shaped tail than adult. **HABITAT** Occurs from inshore waters and tidal flats to montane rainforest, but is most frequently encountered in coastal areas. **STATUS** Moderately common locally, where not persecuted; endemic to the Solomons. **CALL** A high-pitched 'eh-eh-eh' grating chatter.

SWAMP HARRIER   *Circus approximans* 50–60 cm

The only species of harrier in the region; readily identified by slim-bodied appearance and long narrow wings and tail. Habitually glides over the ground with head down and wings held in a shallow 'V'.
ADULT MALE Dark brown above, mottled with black and buff. White uppertail-coverts form prominent pale patch at the base of the tail, which is faintly barred. Underparts pale buff, streaked dark brown. **ADULT FEMALE** Greyer upperparts and tail, with more pale streaking on underbody. **IMM** Distinctive, uniform blackish-brown above, uppertail-coverts and tail rich brownish-orange, tinged grey and faintly barred. Creamy streaks on nape form prominent pale patch. Underbody uniform dark chestnut. **HABITAT** Marshes, reedbeds, open meadows and farmland. **STATUS** A common breeding bird in Vanuatu and New Caledonia. **CALL** High-pitched, rattling 'cheet', when alarmed.

WHITE-BELLIED SEA-EAGLE

imm

SOLOMON SEA-EAGLE

male

imm

SWAMP HARRIER

VARIABLE GOSHAWK *Accipiter hiogaster* 38–55 cm

Unmistakable, medium-sized goshawk. Only goshawk in the region with grey upperparts and rufous under-parts. Uniformly dark slate grey above, including wings and tail, slightly darker wingtips. Throat and sides of head pale grey, rest of underparts rufous.
SEXES Alike, except in size, female larger. **IMM** Upperparts brown, tail heavily barred, with 15 or 16 bars, underparts whitish, heavily mottled with large roundish dark brown spots, thighs and lower abdomen rufous. **HABITAT** Occurs in open cleared country and heavily forested areas, from the lowlands up to 1000 m. **STATUS** A common breeding bird throughout most of the Solomons, not found on Makira and Rennell islands. **CALL** Rapid 'ki-ki-ki-ki'.

BROWN GOSHAWK *Accipiter fasciatus* 38–45 cm

A medium-sized goshawk, easily separated from others in the region by dull grey-brown upperparts, barred cin-namon underparts and long, rounded tail. Upperparts dull grey-brown, tinged blue, with rufous collar across the nape; head and throat pale grey. Entire underparts, including undertail and wing-coverts, finely banded cin-namon and white. Slight barring on undertail.
SEXES Alike, except in size, female larger. **JUV**: Upperparts dark brown, feathers edged with rufous. Underparts white, chin and throat narrowly streaked dark brown, large dark brown spots on foreneck and breast; rest of underparts heavily barred cream and dark chestnut-brown. **IMM** More like adult, but head is darker, upperparts browner, pale streaks on face, bars on underparts are darker and broader. **HABITAT** Woodland, forest edge and trees fringing watercourses. **STATUS** Common breeding bird in Vanuatu, New Caledonia, and Rennell Island in the Solomons. **CALL** Fast chattering 'se-se-se'.

WHITE-BELLIED GOSHAWK *Accipiter haplochrous* 32–36 cm

Blue-grey and white plumage and restricted range make this medium-sized goshawk unmistakable. Uniformly dark blue-grey above including wings and tail, wingtips noticeably darker, almost black. Head and throat dark blue-grey, as the upperparts, contrasting with a much paler blue-grey bib on the chest, extending down to the upper breast, rest of underparts pure white. Eye bright crimson.
SEXES Alike, except in size, female larger. **IMM** Similar to Brown Goshawk, but noticeably smaller and usu-ally found in different habitat. Upperparts, brownish-black, feathers edged with pale rufous. Underparts creamy-white, chin and throat narrowly streaked with brown, large dark brown spots on foreneck and breast; rest of underparts heavily barred cream and dark brown. **HABITAT** Dense rainforest and forest edge. **STATUS** Found only on mainland New Caledonia, where it is still fairly common in heavily forested areas. **CALL** High-pitched, rapid 'tseee-tseee-tseee'.

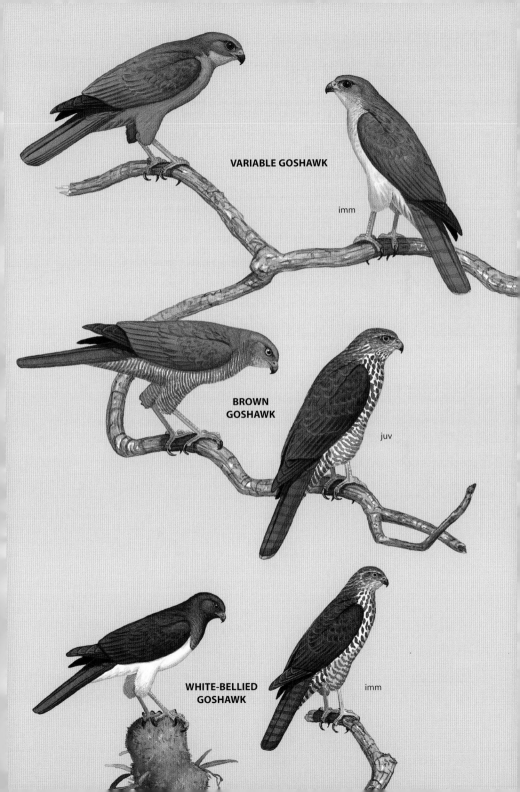

VARIABLE GOSHAWK

imm

BROWN
GOSHAWK

juv

WHITE-BELLIED
GOSHAWK

imm

PIED GOSHAWK *Accipiter albogularis* 35–40 cm

A medium-sized polymorphic goshawk. Separated from Imitator Sparrowhawk by larger size, paler upperparts and, when present, a chestnut collar. Slate-grey morph: slate-grey above including sides of head, the entire underparts and underwing-coverts are pure white. May have a chestnut collar on the hindneck ending in a rufous patch either side of the throat, others have a less defined collar or none at all. Pied morph: upperparts slaty-black with off-white underparts and underwing-coverts. Melanistic morph: uniformly black above and below.
SEXES Alike, except in size, female larger. **IMM** Two colour morphs. Brown morph: blackish-brown above, feathers narrowly edged with rufous, an indistinct white collar on the hindneck.; underparts creamy or pale buff, chin and throat narrowly streaked with brown, large rufous drop-shaped spots on the breast and heart-shaped bars on the abdomen. Tawny morph similar, but ground colour throughout is deep, rich tawny or chestnut. **HABITAT** Rainforest, forest edge, secondary growth, clearings, gardens and the edge of villages. **STATUS** Fairly common endemic bird in the Solomon and Santa Cruz islands. **CALL** A loud, rapidly repeated 'ku-ku-ku'.

IMITATOR SPARROWHAWK *Accipiter imitator* 28–33 cm

A small polymorphic accipiter. Separated from Pied Goshawk, by smaller size, uniformly jet-black upperparts and tail, lacks chestnut collar and does not have a melanistic colour morph. Black-breasted morph: uniformly jet-black upperparts, throat and breast, the remainder of the underparts are white. White-breasted morph is similar, but throat and breast white.
SEXES Alike, except in size, female larger. **IMM** Upperparts barred brownish-black and dull rufous, some white on the crown and a rufous collar. Underparts buffy with slight streaking on the throat, breast finely barred with rufous. Barring on abdomen reduced or totally lacking. **HABITAT** Rainforest and tall secondary forest. **STATUS** Uncommon endemic bird on the islands of Choiseul and Santa Isabel in the Solomons. Vagrant to Bougainville Island. **CALL** A loud, high-pitched raspy 'reo' call, repeated at approximately 5-second intervals.

MEYER'S GOSHAWK *Accipiter meyerianus* 48–56 cm

A very large polymorphic goshawk, by far the largest accipiter in the region. Very distinct pied morph has upperparts and sides of head and neck black, narrow greyish eyebrow and bases of nape feathers white; tail has narrow white tip and four fairly distinct grey bars. Throat and underparts white with faint narrow, wavy, greyish barring on breast, becoming less distinct on thighs and lower abdomen. The much rarer melanistic morph is entirely black, except for the white bases of the nape feathers and four grey bars and narrow white tail tip.
SEXES Alike, except in size, female larger. **IMM** Upperparts blackish-brown, with tawny to buff bars and edges to feathers, eye-brows, nape and rump particularly tawny. The underparts are rich tawny, conspicuously streaked with black. **HABITAT** Hill and montane rainforest, forest edge and adjacent gardens. **STATUS** A scarce bird throughout its entire range, occurring as a rare breeding species on Kulambangra and Guadalcanal Islands in the Solomons. **CALL** Slightly hoarse, rapidly repeated 'ka-ah-ka-ah-ka-ah'.

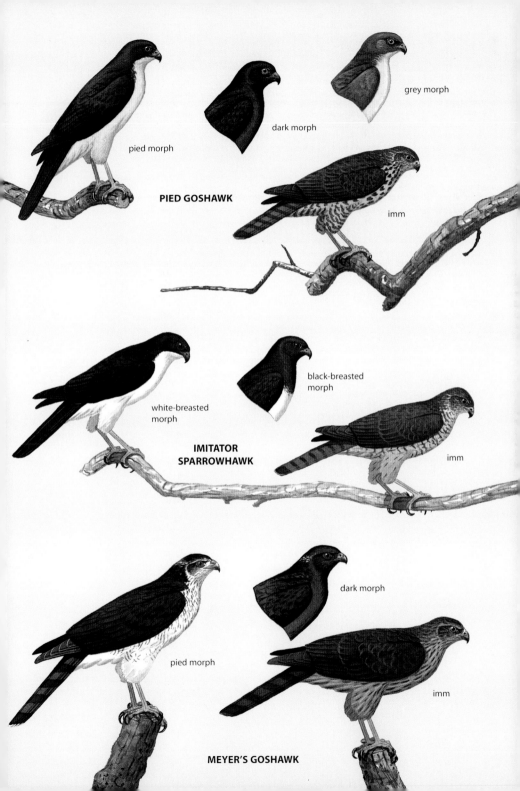

pied morph

dark morph

grey morph

PIED GOSHAWK

imm

white-breasted
morph

black-breasted
morph

**IMITATOR
SPARROWHAWK**

imm

pied morph

dark morph

imm

MEYER'S GOSHAWK

AUSTRALIAN KESTREL *Falco cenchroides* 30–35 cm

The chestnut upperparts and distinctive hovering flight make this small falcon unmistakable.
ADULT MALE Saddle and innerwing-coverts chestnut, streaked with black, contrasting sharply with black outerwing. Crown, nape and hindneck blue-grey finely streaked black. Face whitish with distinct moustachial streak. Tail pale grey with prominent black subterminal band. Underparts white, with faint buff wash across foreneck and breast, finely streaked black. **ADULT FEMALE** Similar to male but head pale rufous, with fine black streaks and tail pale rufous with fine black barring. **IMM** Similar to adult female. **HABITAT** Most open country areas, especially farmland, grasslands and coastal heath. **STATUS** Scarce non-breeding visitor to New Caledonia. **CALL** Repeated high-pitched chattering 'kee-kee-kee'.

ORIENTAL HOBBY *Falco severus* 24–30 cm

A very small, extremely fast-flying falcon, which catches prey in the air. A small, slender bird with narrow, scythe-like, sharply pointed wings and short tail, giving a swift-like appearance. The upperparts including the sides of the head and face are very dark grey, almost black, the tail is completely unbarred. Chin, throat and upper breast buff coloured, lower breast and abdomen dark rufous. Yellow eyering, legs and feet.
SEXES Alike, except in size, female larger. **IMM** Similar to adult, but underparts heavily streaked with black. **HABITAT** Woodland, forest and forest edge. **STATUS** Uncommon winter visitor to the Solomons. **CALL** A rapid 'chi-chi-chi-chi-chi'.

PEREGRINE FALCON *Falco peregrinus* 35–50 cm

Similar in shape, but much larger than Oriental Hobby, with distinctive thickset, deep-chested appearance, with broad-based pointed wings. Crown, nape and lower neck black, rest of upperparts including tail slightly paler, faintly barred blackish. Black cap and broad triangular shaped moustachial patch form blackish hood contrasting with white chin, throat and upper breast. There is a very pale rufous wash to the upper breast and a small number of black streaks and spots; lower breast and abdomen completely covered in narrow black bars.
SEXES Alike, except in size, female much larger. **IMM** Dark brown above with rufous edges to most feathers; greyish to rufous underparts, paler on throat and breast and heavily streaked blackish-brown. **HABITAT** Forested areas, open lowlands, wetlands, cliffs and offshore islands. **STATUS** Uncommon breeding bird in Vanuatu and New Caledonia, rare wanderer to the Solomons. **CALL** Loud, high-pitched and repetitive 'hek-hek-hek'.

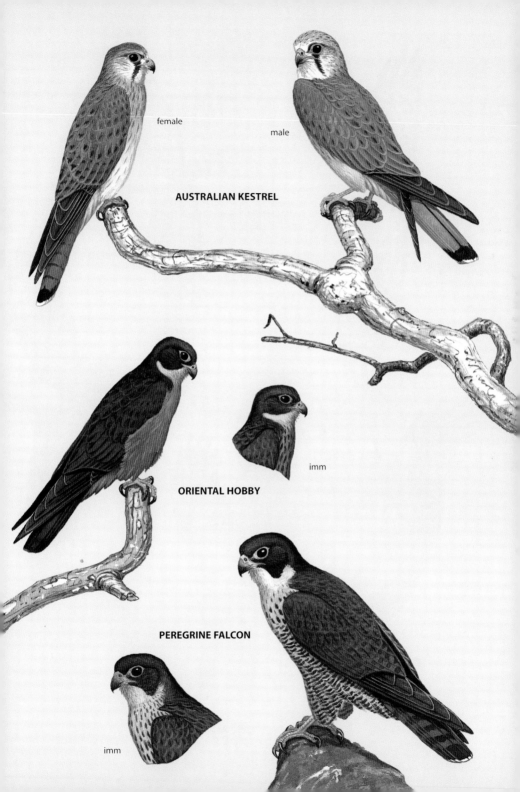

AUSTRALIAN KESTREL

female

male

ORIENTAL HOBBY

imm

PEREGRINE FALCON

imm

OSPREY

PACIFIC BAZA

WHISTLING KITE

BRAHMINY KITE

imm

WHITE-BELLIED SEA-EAGLE

imm

SOLOMON SEA-EAGLE

male

SWAMP HARRIER

imm

VARIABLE GOSHAWK

BROWN GOSHAWK

imm

juv

WHITE-BELLIED GOSHAWK

imm

imm

imm

grey morph

PIED GOSHAWK

pied morph

dark morph

IMITATOR SPARROWHAWK

imm

white-breasted morph

dark-breasted morph

pied morph

dark morph

imm

MEYER'S GOSHAWK

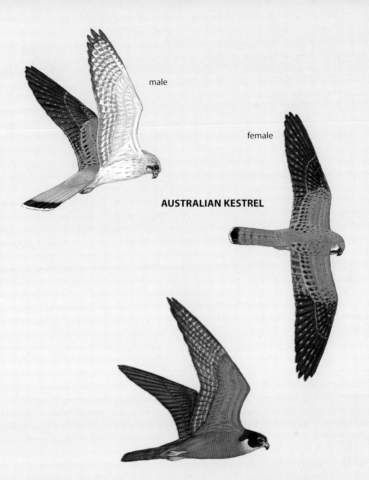

male

female

AUSTRALIAN KESTREL

ORIENTAL HOBBY

PEREGRINE FALCON

MELANESIAN SCRUBFOWL *Megapodius eremita* 34 cm

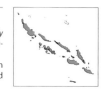

Unmistakable, dark fowl-like ground bird with a plump body, short tail and small, crested head. Geographically isolated from the New Hebrides Scrubfowl. Underparts and neck dark slate-grey; back and wings dark olive-brown, forehead and part of face bare and reddish, unfeathered legs and feet horn-coloured.
SEXES Alike. **IMM** Slightly duller. **HABITAT** Lowland rainforest and offshore islands. **STATUS** Fairly common breeding bird throughout the Solomons. **CALL** Loud chuckles, chortles and screams, uttered both day and night.

NEW HEBRIDES SCRUBFOWL *Megapodius layardi* 30–34 cm

Similar shape to geographically isolated Melanesian Scrubfowl. All dark blackish-brown, extensive red bare skin on forehead and face, unfeathered legs and feet yellow.
SEXES Alike. **IMM** Duller, with brown legs. **HABITAT** Lowland rainforest and vine thickets. **STATUS** Fairly common endemic bird throughout Vanuatu. **CALL** Loud hoarse clucking, uttered both day and night.

RED JUNGLEFOWL *Gallus gallus* 42–75 cm

Both male and female are unmistakable, a slightly smaller version of the familiar domestic fowl.
ADULT MALE Large red fleshy comb on head, long orange-red neck hackles and long drooping dark bronze-green tail. **ADULT FEMALE** Much less conspicuous, neck feathers blackish-brown with golden-yellow margins, remainder of plumage brown with some white streaks, tail short and black. **HABITAT** Rainforest and scrub. **STATUS** Introduced from South-East Asia, fairly common breeding bird in Vanuatu, and the Isle of Pines in New Caledonia. **CALL** Very similar to 'cock a doodle-do' of domestic fowl.

RED-BACKED BUTTONQUAIL *Turnix maculosa* 12–16 cm

Small terrestrial bird, similar to true quails. Geographically isolated from Painted Buttonquail.
ADULT FEMALE Greyish above, mottled with black, chestnut and buff. Chestnut-red collar on hindneck. Eyestripe, face, throat and breast orange-rufous, abdomen ochre. **ADULT MALE** Smaller and duller, with whitish underparts, sides of breast and flanks barred with black. **IMM** Darker, more mottled and scalloped. **HABITAT** Grasslands. **STATUS** In the Pacific found only in grasslands of the coastal plain of Guadalcanal Island in the Solomons. This habitat is disappearing quickly due to coastal development, and this subspecies is now endangered. **CALL** Loud 'oom', rapidly repeated.

PAINTED BUTTONQUAIL *Turnix varia* 17–23 cm

Small terrestrial bird, similar to true quails. Geographically isolated from Red-backed Buttonquail.
ADULT FEMALE Blackish above, mottled with chestnut, white and grey, brownish-grey line along the centre of the crown, with broad black stripe each side and a buffy-white eyestripe. White throat, breast pale grey with dense overlay of prominent rufous-buff scalloping. **ADULT MALE** Smaller and duller, with less rufous in plumage. **IMM** No rufous; greyer and heavily mottled. **HABITAT** Forest and woodland. **STATUS** In the Pacific found only in New Caledonia, where it is now extremely rare and endangered. **CALL** Low pitched 'oom', repeated eight times.

KAGU *Rhynochetos jubatus* 50–60 cm

Unmistakable, night-heron-sized flightless bird, with shaggy erectile crest. Head, entire underparts and crest pale ash-grey, back, wings and tail pale grey washed with brown. Longish orange-red bill and short orange-red legs. When the broad, rounded wings are spread in display there is conspicuous black, white and brown banding across the primaries.
SEXES Alike. **IMM** Similar to adult, but browner and finely banded. **HABITAT** Rainforest. **STATUS** Endemic to mainland New Caledonia; drastic decline since European settlement, now endangered and extremely vulnerable to predation by dogs outside the few protected areas. **CALL** 'Gou-gou-gou' likened to the barking of a small dog. Loud hissing sound when alarmed.

MELANESIAN
SCRUBFOWL

NEW HEBRIDES SCRUBFOWL

RED JUNGLEFOWL

female

male

displaying

RED-BACKED
BUTTONQUAIL

male

female

KAGU

male

female

PAINTED
BUTTONQUAIL

WOODFORD'S RAIL *Nesoclopeus woodfordi* 30 cm

Medium-sized secretive, flightless rail, plainly marked and dark plumaged, with stout body, short legs and short stout bill. Head, neck and underparts blackish-grey; some races have faint buff barring on flanks and undertail-coverts. The upperparts are black with a slight rufous wash. Bill colour varies according to race, being black, grey or yellow. Legs and feet also vary, being either grey or greenish-yellow.
SEXES Alike. **IMM** White chin, the underparts are browner, with pale edges to breast feathers. **HABITAT** Lowland rainforest, with preference for forested river valleys, secondary growth, swamp forest and abandoned gardens. **STATUS** Endemic to the Solomons, it is local and uncommon on Santa Isabel and possibly extinct on Bougainville and Guadalcanal. **CALL** An unmusical series of three metallic shrieks unvarying in pitch.

NEW CALEDONIAN RAIL *Gallirallus lafresnayanus* 45–48 cm

Large thickset flightless rail with long slender slightly decurved yellowish bill and short stout horn-coloured legs. Uniform dark brown upperparts and dark grey underparts, with a pale brownish wash on the breast.
SEXES Alike. **IMM** Largely black with chocolate-brown wash on upperparts, sides of neck and breast. **HABITAT** Dense rainforest and forested river valleys. **STATUS** This diurnal and crepuscular rail is endemic to mainland New Caledonia and thought to be extinct, but may still survive in inaccessible areas of forest relatively free from introduced animals such as dogs, cats, rats and pigs. **CALL** Unknown.

BUFF-BANDED RAIL *Gallirallus philippensis* 30–33 cm

Medium-sized rail with stout body, small rounded head, short grey legs and short wedge-shaped reddish bill. Chestnut head with prominent pale grey supercilium, remainder of upperparts brownish-olive, with black centre and large white tip to feathers. Underparts pale grey, heavily barred black and white, with a pale buff wash to the centre of the lower belly and thighs. Some races have a conspicuous rufous-buff band across the upper breast.
SEXES Alike. **HABITAT** Rank grasslands, roadside edge, swampy areas and along watercourses. **STATUS** Common resident. **CALL** Harsh creaky 'preep,' usually repeated four or five times.

ROVIANA RAIL *Gallirallus rovianae* 30 cm

Similar to Buff-banded Rail in size and shape, but upperparts uniform dark chestnut-brown. Broad reddish-chestnut stripe from the bill, through the eye to the sides of neck contrasts with pale grey supercilium. Underparts dark grey, very finely barred black and white on sides of neck, flanks and undertail-coverts. Birds from New Georgia have heavy black and white barring on the entire underparts and a conspicuous rufous-buff band across the upper breast.
SEXES Alike. **HABITAT** Forest, especially second growth, rank grasslands, roadside edge, abandoned gardens, open ground and airstrips. **STATUS** This recently described species, first described in 1991, is restricted to the islands of New Georgia, Kulambangra, Wana Wana, Kohinggo and Rendova, in the Central Solomons. There are two races involved, the Kulambangra race, is common on Kulambangra and the New Georgia race, appears to be rare throughout its limited range. **CALL** Rapidly repeated, high-pitched 'kitikete'.

RUFOUS-TAILED BUSH-HEN *Amaurornis moluccanus* 24–31 cm

Medium-sized, secretive, plainly marked rail, closely resembles a moorhen in shape, but is smaller. Upperparts dark olive-brown, throat pale grey, foreneck, breast and upper belly slate-grey, lower belly, thighs and undertail-coverts buffy-rufous. Short stout green bill; legs and feet olive-yellow.
SEXES Alike. **HABITAT** Dense stands of grass and reeds, usually near still or running fresh water, swampy grasslands and roadside ditches. **STATUS** Largely nocturnal, common and widespread resident throughout the Solomons, often heard but rarely seen. **CALL** Loud shrieks and yodelling 'woodle-woodle-woodle', particularly at night, often given by two birds in duet.

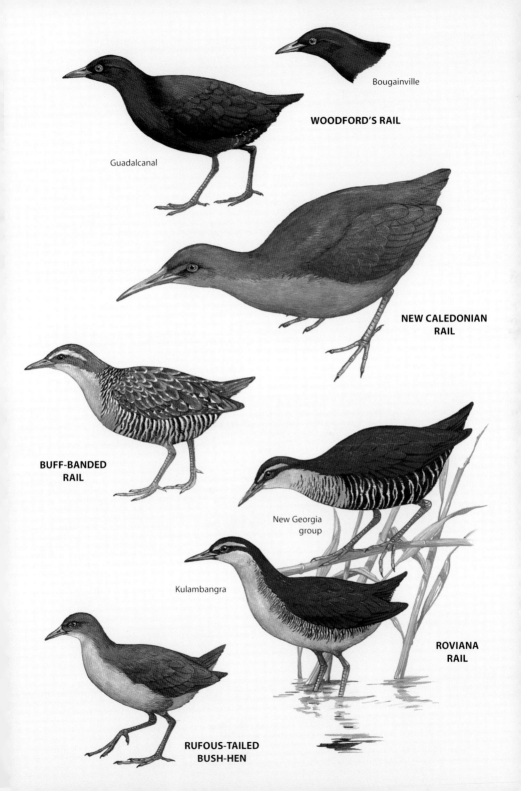

Bougainville

WOODFORD'S RAIL

Guadalcanal

**NEW CALEDONIAN
RAIL**

**BUFF-BANDED
RAIL**

New Georgia
group

Kulambangra

**ROVIANA
RAIL**

**RUFOUS-TAILED
BUSH-HEN**

SPOTLESS CRAKE *Porzana tabuensis* 17–20 cm

A small, secretive, plainly marked crake, with conspicuous deep red eye and red legs. Upperparts uniform dark chocolate-brown, head, neck and abdomen greyish-black, undertail-coverts narrowly barred with white. Black bill.
SEXES Alike. **HABITAT** Dense vegetation in freshwater swamps. **STATUS** Uncommon and localised resident. often heard but seldom seen. **CALL** A rapid trilling purr, somewhat similar to the sound of a motor-bike engine.

WHITE-BROWED CRAKE *Porzana cinerea* 17–20 cm

Small slim-bodied crake, with striking and diagnostic facial pattern. Greyish-black cap, broad black stripe from the base of the bill, through the eye to the crown, with contrasting bold white stripes above and below, remaining upperparts brownish with broad dark centres to feathers. Underparts mainly white, with greyish wash over neck, breast and flanks. Bill olive-brown at base, grading to olive-yellow at the tip. Legs and feet light green.
SEXES Alike. **IMM** As adult but underparts buffish-brown, with white throat and belly and indistinct facial pattern. **HABITAT** Vegetated swamps and wetlands. **STATUS** Uncommon resident. **CALL** Rapidly repeated 'chika-chika-chika'.

PURPLE SWAMPHEN *Porphyrio porphyrio* 44–48 cm

Unmistakable large powerful rail, with conspicuous massive red bill and frontal shield, long red legs and toes and conspicuous white undertail. Upperparts blackish olive-brown. Throat and shoulder are glossy light blue, underparts glossy purplish-blue.
SEXES Alike. **IMM** Duller than adult, brownish above, pale blue below, feathers edged with buff. **HABITAT** Freshwater swamps, wet meadows, lakes and rainforest, often far from water. **STATUS** Common resident. **CALL** Harsh screeching 'ke-owww'.

.

SAN CRISTOBAL MOORHEN *Gallinula silvestris* 27 cm

A distinctive medium-sized moorhen, extremely short tailed; flightless and forest-dwelling. Conspicuous bright red bill, legs and feet. Head, neck and breast dark blackish, chin and face blackish, mantle and wings brownish-black, with a slight olive wash to the wings. Frontal shield dark grey-blue.
SEXES Alike. **HABITAT** Dense undergrowth on steep slopes in mountain rainforest. **STATUS** Endemic to Makira Island, known from only one specimen collected in 1929 and one confirmed sighting in 1953. Older local people remember the bird, before the widespread introduction of cats and dogs. There were reported sightings by local people in a largely inaccessible area in 1974. **CALL** Unknown.

DUSKY MOORHEN *Gallinula tenebrosa* 35–40 cm

Medium-sized, dark moorhen, easily distinguished from Purple Swamphen by smaller size, much darker colour and prominent yellow tip to the bill. Plumage entirely blackish, with brownish wash on wings and white sides to undertail-coverts.
SEXES Alike. **IMM** Duller and browner above, paler below, bill and legs dull coloured. **HABITAT** Freshwater wetlands, rivers and artificial wetlands surrounded by reeds. **STATUS** Recently colonised New Caledonia, presumably from Australia, and is now an uncommon breeding bird. **CALL** A raucous, loud 'kurk'.

SPOTLESS CRAKE

WHITE-BROWED
CRAKE

imm

imm

PURPLE
SWAMPHEN

SAN CRISTOBAL
MOORHEN

imm

DUSKY MOORHEN

BLACK-TAILED GODWIT *Limosa limosa* 40–44 cm

Large, graceful, long-necked wader. At rest, similar to Bar-tailed Godwit, but differs in having longer legs, a slimmer body and longer neck, a flatter forehead, straighter bill and greyer, unmottled upperparts. In all plumages flight pattern diagnostic, owing to combination of prominent white wingbar, white band across lower rump and uppertail, and black tail band.
BREEDING PLUMAGE: Head, neck, mantle and upper breast, chestnut, belly and flanks white with irregular bold black barring. **SEXES** Alike. **IMM** Similar to non-breeding adult. **HABITAT** Mainly coastal, sheltered bays, estuaries, lagoons and tidal flats. Occasionally inland lakes and wetlands. **STATUS** Rare summer visitor. **CALL** A strident 'reeta-reeta-reeta', especially in flight.

BAR-TAILED GODWIT *Limosa lapponica* 37–39 cm

Large, graceful, long-necked wader. At rest similar to Black-tailed Godwit, but differs in having shorter legs, a larger and stockier body and shorter neck. Has a steeper forehead, more upturned bill and browner, more mottled upperparts. Lacks distinctive flight pattern of Black-tailed Godwit, with no wingbar, but has white rump, with white extending in a wedge up the back; tail is white with thin brown barring.
BREEDING PLUMAGE: Head, neck and underparts deep rufous. **SEXES** Alike. **IMM** Similar to non-breeding adult. **HABITAT** Mainly coastal, sheltered bays, estuaries, lagoons and tidal flats. **STATUS** Common summer visitor. **CALL** Sharp 'kerk-kerk'.

LITTLE CURLEW *Numenius minutus* 28–31 cm

The smallest curlew, similar in size to Pacific Golden Plover. Has a distinctive dark stripe behind the eye, prominent broad pale-buff supercilium and a short, only slightly decurved bill. Buffish-brown rump and back.
SEXES Alike. **HABITAT** Short, dry grasslands. **STATUS** Rare summer visitor to Bougainville Island in the Solomons. **CALL** A series of two or three whistled notes 'tchew-tchew-tchew'.

WHIMBREL *Numenius phaeopus* 40–45 cm

Medium-sized curlew with long decurved bill and striped head pattern: the only curlew in the region with a white rump and back. Larger, bulkier and longer-billed than Little Curlew and smaller and shorter billed than Far Eastern Curlew. Similar in size and shape to the far less common Bristle-thighed Curlew, but overall plumage much greyer-brown and different rump colour. The American race N. P. hudsonicus, has an all dark rump and back and could occur in the region.
SEXES Alike. **HABITAT** Mainly coastal, tidal flats, estuaries, grassy airstrips and offshore islands. **STATUS** Common summer visitor. **CALL** Distinctive, rapid trill, 'tee-tee-tee-tee-tee'.

BRISTLE-THIGHED CURLEW *Numenius tahitiensis* 40–44 cm

A stripe-headed curlew which resembles Whimbrel in size and shape, but plumage much more cinnamon above and below. In flight, shows distinctive bright cinnamon rump and uppertail and deep cinnamon underwing-coverts.
SEXES Alike. **HABITAT** Mainly coastal, tidal-flats, sand bars, offshore islands and grasslands. **STATUS** Rare summer visitor to the Santa Cruz Islands, plus a recent record from the Solomons. Probably a rare vagrant throughout the region. **CALL** A quick 'weoo-weet', very different call to that of Whimbrel.

FAR EASTERN CURLEW *Numenius madagascariensis* 60–66 cm

A very large curlew, without head stripes, with very long, decurved bill. Much larger and bulkier than Whimbrel, with dark back, rump and underwing. Plumage rather uniform grey-brown.
SEXES Alike. **HABITAT** Mainly coastal, tidal flats, estuaries, harbours and coastal lagoons. **STATUS** Uncommon summer visitor. **CALL** High-pitched, distinctive 'cur-loo'.

non-br

non-br

BLACK-TAILED
GODWIT

br

br

BAR-TAILED
GODWIT

LITTLE CURLEW

WHIMBREL

BRISTLE-THIGHED
CURLEW

FAR EASTERN
CURLEW

MARSH SANDPIPER *Tringa stagnatilis* 22–26 cm

Medium-sized wader, pale grey, delicate and long-legged. General shape and plumage similar to Greenshank but smaller and slimmer, with proportionally longer legs and much finer and straighter needle-like bill. In flight, conspicuous triangular white rump and wedge up the back.
SEXES Alike. **HABITAT** Prefers freshwater swamps but also frequents brackish lagoons, saltpans and rarely tidal flats. **STATUS** Rare summer visitor to Bougainville Island in the Solomons. **CALL** Loud and clear 'teoo'.

COMMON GREENSHANK *Tringa nebularia* 30–35 cm

Large, heavily built, long-legged wader. Similar to Marsh Sandpiper but larger with stouter build and noticeably longer, more robust, slightly upturned bill. Head and neck white with fine grey streaking, rest of upperparts grey; whole of underparts white.
SEXES Alike. **HABITAT** Tidal flats, saltmarsh, mangroves and inland swamps and lakes. **STATUS** Rare summer visitor to the Solomons. **CALL** Loud, ringing, evenly spaced 'tchu-tchu-tchu'.

WOOD SANDPIPER *Tringa glareola* 19–23 cm

A medium-sized sandpiper with short straight bill and long legs. In all plumages shows prominent white supercilium, extending well behind the eye, and white eyering. Dark grey-brown above, strongly spotted with white; underparts white, breast washed with grey and slightly streaked; legs and feet dull yellowish. In flight, shows conspicuous white rump and pale underwing.
SEXES Alike. **IMM** As adult, but upperparts browner, distinctly spotted with buff. **HABITAT** Freshwater wetlands and lakes. **STATUS** Rare summer visitor to Bougainville Island in the Solomons. **CALL** High-pitched, slightly descending 'chiff-iff-iff', especially when alarmed.

COMMON SANDPIPER *Tringa hypoleucos* 19–21 cm

A small sandpiper, with straight medium length bill, easily recognised by distinctive, frequent 'teetering' - wagging body and tail up and down, and very distinctive flight of rapid shallow wingbeats, alternating with glides on down-curved wings. The only wader that regularly occurs inland, along rivers and streams. Dark brown above and white below, with sharply demarcated brown breast and diagnostic white shoulder patch, in front of closed wing. Short, olive-yellow legs. In flight shows prominent, narrow white wingbar.
SEXES Alike. **HABITAT** Estuaries, muddy streams and banks of larger rivers. **STATUS** Common summer visitor. **CALL** A penetrating 'swee-wee-wee'.

TEREK SANDPIPER *Tringa cinerea* 22–24 cm

A medium-sized sandpiper, easily recognised by distinctive long, slightly upcurved, orange-based bill; short orange-yellow legs and very active method of feeding. Pale, brownish-grey upperparts and sides of breast, and white underparts. In flight, shows distinctive, broad white trailing-edge to wing and grey rump and tail.
SEXES Alike. **HABITAT** Coastal. Mainly tidal flats, estuaries, harbours and mangroves. **STATUS** Uncommon summer visitor to Bougainville Island in the Solomons. **CALL** Fluty, twittering 'weet-weet-weet'.

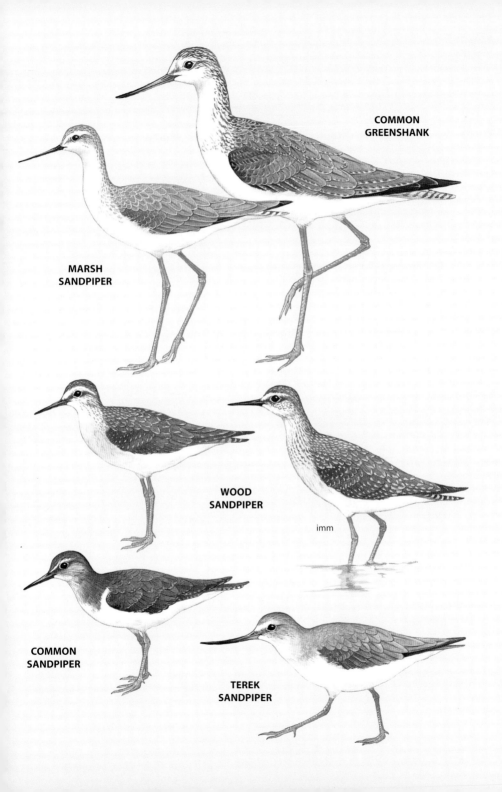

COMMON
GREENSHANK

MARSH
SANDPIPER

WOOD
SANDPIPER

imm

COMMON
SANDPIPER

TEREK
SANDPIPER

SWINHOE'S SNIPE *Gallinago megala* 27–29 cm

Medium-sized, cryptically-plumaged wader, easily distinguished from all other waders in the region by the long, straight bill, short rounded wings and distinctive striped head markings. Distinctive secretive behaviour, often hides amongst swamp vegetation. When flushed from cover has distinctive 'zig-zagging' flight.
SEXES Alike. **HABITAT** Freshwater marshes and flooded pasture. **STATUS** Uncommon summer visitor to Bougainville Island in the Solomons. **CALL** Short, rasping 'shrek'.

GREY-TAILED TATTLER *Tringa brevipes* 25 cm

Tattlers in all plumages are distinct from all other waders in having uniform grey upperparts, including entire wings and tail. A medium-sized wader with straight medium-length bill and rather short yellow legs. Has well-defined white supercilium and dark loral stripe. In all plumages very similar to slightly larger Wandering Tattler, but differs in always being paler and having a slightly broader and longer supercilium. The uppertail-coverts show faint whitish barring. Most reliably separated by call and habitat preference.
BREEDING PLUMAGE: Neck, breast and flanks are lightly streaked and barred with grey, belly is always extensively white. Undertail-coverts plain white or with a few narrow grey bars. **SEXES** Alike. **IMM** Similar to non-breeding adult, but upperparts show small, neat whitish-buff spotting; edges of tail feathers are clearly notched whitish. **HABITAT** Coastal, estuaries, harbours, tidal flats, mangroves and occasionally rocky shores. **STATUS** Fairly common summer visitor. **CALL** Plover-like, up-slurred whistle, with two or three notes 'troo-eet' or 'troo-eet-eet'.

WANDERING TATTLER *Tringa incana* 27 cm

Very similar to slightly smaller Grey-tailed Tattler, but differs in always being slightly darker and having a slightly narrower and shorter supercilium, mainly in front of the eye. Uppertail and tail plain grey. Most reliably separated by call and habitat preference.
BREEDING PLUMAGE: Except for very small area on belly, all underparts are heavily barred with dark grey. Heavily barred undertail-coverts are diagnostic. **SEXES** Alike. **IMM** Similar to non-breeding adult. **HABITAT** Found almost exclusively on rocky coasts and reefs, very occasionally on tidal flats. **STATUS** Uncommon summer visitor. **CALL** Rippling trill of 6–10 accelerating notes 'whee-we-we-we...', at same pitch but decreasing in volume.

RUDDY TURNSTONE *Arenaria interpres* 22–24 cm

Distinctive stocky, medium-sized wader with short, slightly uptilted, wedge-shaped bill and short orange-red legs. Dark grey-brown upperparts with distinctive smudgy grey-brown pattern on head and breast, rest of underparts white. Striking dark-and-white pattern in flight. Habit of turning stones over in search of invertebrates is diagnostic.
BREEDING PLUMAGE: Sharply patterned black and white on head and breast and black and chestnut on wings, underparts pure white. **SEXES** Alike. **IMM** Similar to non-breeding adult, but upperparts browner with conspicuous buff edges to feathers. **HABITAT** Coastal, rocky coasts, tidal pools, tidal flats and sandy beaches. **STATUS** Fairly common summer visitor. **CALL** Clear rapid 'trik-tuk-tuk-tuk'.

RED-NECKED PHALAROPE *Phalaropus lobatus* 18–19 cm

Distinctive small marine wader, with small head, slender neck, short straight needle-like bill and short grey legs and feet, with lobed toes. Whitish head and neck with grey crown and hindneck and conspicuous oval-shaped black patch from in front of eye to ear-coverts. Remainder of upperparts ash-grey, feathers narrowly edged with white. Underparts white.
BREEDING PLUMAGE: Upperparts become dark grey, chin and throat white with a chestnut-red band on foreneck and sides of neck, broad buff lines on mantle and scapulars. **FEMALE** More brightly coloured than male. **HABITAT** Normally pelagic during the non-breeding season, occasionally occurs on inland lakes. **STATUS** Not officially recorded from the region, but should occur in the northern Solomons. **CALL** Sharp repeated 'chek'.

GREY-TAILED TATTLER

br

non-br

imm

SWINHOE'S SNIPE

br

WANDERING TATTLER

non-br

imm

non-br

imm

RUDDY TURNSTONE

br

RED-NECKED PHALAROPE

female br

non-br

RED-NECKED STINT *Calidris ruficollis* 14–16 cm

Very small grey and white sandpiper with short black bill and short black legs. The only very small wader in the region with a white breast. Upperparts pale brownish-grey, most feathers with dark shafts and narrowly edged with white, in fresh plumage. Shows noticeable white supercilium and dark loral stripe, from the lores through the eye to the ear-coverts. Underparts white with diffuse pale brownish-grey patches on sides of breast. **BREEDING PLUMAGE:** The upperparts are mottled black, brown and chestnut, the head, neck and upperbreast become light rufous, rest of underparts white. **SEXES** Alike. **IMM** Similar to non-breeding adult. **HABITAT** Mainly coastal, sheltered bays, estuaries, tidal flats and occasionally saltmarsh and inland lakes. **STATUS** Uncommon summer visitor. **CALL** Short 'chit'.

LONG-TOED STINT *Calidris subminuta* 14–16 cm

Very small, pale-legged sandpiper, of inland marshes. Like a miniature Sharp-tailed Sandpiper. Feathers of crown and back have black centres with orange-rufous edges; breast is a creamy colour with fine dark streaking; rest of underparts white. Legs and feet yellowish. **SEXES** Alike. **HABITAT** Prefers shallow freshwater wetlands with a covering of vegetation. **STATUS** Rare vagrant to the Solomons. **CALL** Trilling 'trrrrt'.

SANDERLING *Calidris alba* 19–21 cm

A small, thickset wader, with short straight, fairly heavy bill. In non-breeding plumage, the palest sandpiper of the region. Pale grey above and white below, with distinctive black shoulder-patch. Typically seen in small highly active flocks on sandy beaches. **BREEDING PLUMAGE:** Upperparts blackish, feathers edged with varying amount of chestnut and white. Head, neck and upperbreast rufous spotted with black; remaining underparts white. **SEXES** Alike. **IMM** Bold black and white chequered upperparts, with bold black shoulder-patch and white underparts. **HABITAT** Mostly open sandy beaches. **STATUS** Uncommon summer visitor. **CALL** Liquid 'twick-twick'.

BROAD-BILLED SANDPIPER *Limicola falcinellus* 16–18 cm

Small, short-necked, stint-like wader, with short legs and diagnostic heavy based, long straight black bill, which is noticeably down-curved at the tip. In all plumages shows conspicuous dark crown stripe and dark eyeline, separated by a whitish split supercilium. Upperparts uniform dull grey, feathers edged with white with darker shaft streaks, blackish shoulder-patch sometimes evident. Breast lightly streaked grey-brown, remainder of underparts white. **BREEDING PLUMAGE:** Upperparts are blackish-brown, feathers edged with white and chestnut; white edges to mantle and scapulars form conspicuous snipe-like pale lines on upperparts. Upperbreast and flanks with heavy black streaking; remainder of underparts white. **SEXES** Alike. **IMM** Resembles adult in breeding plumage. **HABITAT** Coastal, estuaries, harbours, tidal flats and lagoons. **STATUS** Rare vagrant to the Solomons **CALL** A trilled 'chrrect'.

RED-NECKED
STINT

br

LONG-TOED STINT

non-br

br

br

imm

SANDERLING

non-br

non-br

br

BROAD-BILLED SANDPIPER

CURLEW SANDPIPER *Calidris ferruginea* 18–23 cm

Small, slim, long-necked sandpiper with longish black legs and diagnostic long, decurved black bill with fine tip. Upperparts plain brownish-grey, most feathers narrowly edged with white. Underparts white, with varying brownish-grey wash on sides of breast. In flight, has bold white wingbar and distinctive squarish white patch across lower rump and uppertail-coverts.
BREEDING PLUMAGE: Upperparts richly marked black and chestnut, feathers tipped greyish-white, head, neck and underparts rich chestnut-red. **SEXES** Alike. **IMM** Upperpart feathers brownish, with pale buff edges. Foreneck and breast washed pale buff, overlayed with fine dark streaking. **HABITAT** Estuaries, bays, tidal flats, coastal lagoons and inland lakes and wetlands. **STATUS** Rare summer visitor to the Solomons and New Caledonia. **CALL** Gentle, rippling. 'chirrup'.

SHARP-TAILED SANDPIPER *Calidris acuminata* 17–22 cm

A small sandpiper with a medium-length, slightly decurved dark bill. Has distinctive capped appearance and a noticeable white supercilium. Mainly dull grey-brown above, feathers with ill-defined blackish centres. Brownish-grey wash on breast which is finely streaked with black, rest of underparts white with dark streaking on flanks, vent and undertail-coverts. Similar to Pectoral Sandpiper but differs in lacking sharp demarcation between streaked breast and clear white belly; lacks large pale area at base of bill and legs olive-grey, not yellowish.
BREEDING PLUMAGE: Rufous cap, upperparts dark brown, feathers broadly edged with rufous and tipped with white, producing a very scaly effect. Neck and upper breast rufous-brown overlaid with black spots and streaks, lower breast, flanks and undertail, with diagnostic bold blackish chevrons. **SEXES** Alike. **IMM** A strikingly plumaged bird with very noticeable bright rufous crown, richly coloured upperparts appear blackish, the feathers edged with chestnut or orange-buff and tipped with white; foreneck and breast, bright orange-buff, with a narrow gorget of fine streaking across the upper neck. **HABITAT** Brackish or freshwater wetlands. **STATUS** Uncommon summer visitor. **CALL** A soft repeated 'pleep'.

PECTORAL SANDPIPER *Calidris melanotos* 19–24 cm

Very similar to Sharp-tailed Sandpiper, but differentiated by a more uniformly and coarsely streaked foreneck and breast, forming a more pronounced gorget, which is always much more sharply demarcated from the white belly than in Sharp-tailed Sandpiper. The centre of the gorget is often shaped into a downwards point. Vent and undertail-coverts normally unmarked, but occasionally can show a few fine dark streaks, not heavily streaked as in Sharp-tailed Sandpiper. Bill appears bi-coloured, with pale base to one third to half of both mandibles, in contrast to Sharp-tailed Sandpiper which normally only shows a small pale base to the lower mandible. The legs usually appear yellowish, not olive-grey to greenish-yellow, as in Sharp-tailed Sandpiper.
SEXES Alike. **HABITAT** Brackish or freshwater wetlands. **STATUS** Rare vagrant to the Solomons and Vanuatu. **CALL** A low 'krrip-krrip'.

RUFF *Philomachus pugnax* Male 26–32 cm, Female 20–25 cm

A distinctive, medium to large-sized wader, which varies greatly in size, plumage and leg colour. Despite variability, easily recognised by combination of small head, medium-length, slightly decurved bill, long neck, deep-bellied and hunched appearance and long legs. Upperparts scaly, similar to Sharp-tailed Sandpiper; underparts grey-white washed with grey on sides of breast. Bill black, sometimes with orange or reddish base. Colour of legs and feet highly variable, can be orange, yellow or green. In flight, broad oval-shaped white patches at both sides of tail are diagnostic.
SEXES Similar in non-breeding plumage, except in size, male much larger. **IMM** Upperparts dark brown, centre of feathers blackish-brown with narrow buff edges, producing a very scaly appearance. Breast buff coloured, remainder of underparts white. **HABITAT** Brackish or freshwater wetlands. **STATUS** Rare vagrant to the Solomons. **CALL** Typically silent in the region.

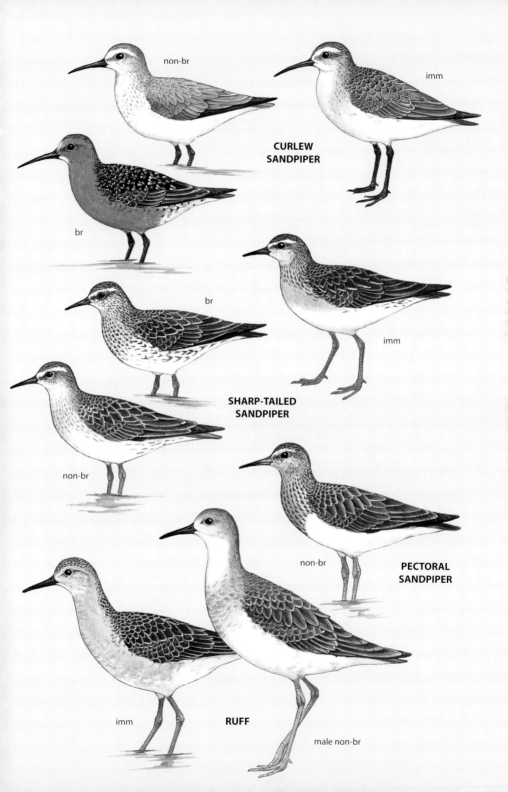

non-br

imm

CURLEW SANDPIPER

br

br

imm

SHARP-TAILED SANDPIPER

non-br

non-br

PECTORAL SANDPIPER

imm

RUFF

male non-br

BEACH THICK-KNEE *Burhinus giganteus* 54–56 cm

Very distinctive, large stocky wader, which inhabits sandy beaches. Upperparts uniform grey-brown. Conspicuous black and white head pattern and shoulder-patch, massive, slightly uptilted black bill with yellow base. Short, thick pale yellow legs with thick 'knees'. In flight, shows striking pattern of black, white and grey. **SEXES** Alike. **HABITAT** Sandy beaches, tidal flats, reefs and mangroves. **STATUS** Fairly common in the Solomons, now very rare in Vanuatu and New Caledonia. **CALL** A harsh 'weer-loo'.

SOUTH ISLAND OYSTERCATCHER *Haematopus finschi* 46 cm

Unmistakable large stocky black and white wader, with conspicuous red eye, long stout red bill and short stout pinkish legs. **SEXES** Alike. **HABITAT** Sandy and rocky beaches, tidal flats, estuaries, grasslands and farmland. **STATUS** Extremely rare vagrant to Vanuatu. **CALL** High-pitched 'kervee-kervee-kervee'.

ORIENTAL PRATINCOLE *Glareola maldivarum* 23–24 cm

Very distinctive, tern-like wader with long pointed wings, forked tail, short legs and short decurved bill. Upperparts, foreneck and breast uniform dark brownish-olive, chin and throat paler, bordered by indistinct short black streaks; rest of underparts whitish. Bill and legs black. In flight, shows chestnut underwing-coverts and white rump and tail, with black terminal tail band.
BREEDING PLUMAGE: Similar to non-breeding adult, but throat creamy-buff, with neat black border, gape and base of lower mandible bright red. **SEXES** Alike. **IMM** Similar to non-breeding adult but upperparts paler, the feathers edged with buff, giving a scaly appearance, and throat is paler, with an indistinct dark boarder. **HABITAT** Plains, flood plains and grasslands. **STATUS** Rare summer visitor to the Solomons. **CALL** Sharp 'chik-chik' or 'chet'.

PACIFIC GOLDEN-PLOVER *Pluvialis fulva* 23–26 cm

Medium-sized plover, with rounded head, slim neck, short bill, longish legs and upright stance. Noticeably smaller and slimmer than Grey Plover. Crown and upperparts brown, heavily mottled bright golden-buff and white; forehead, face and underparts pale yellow-buff to whitish, spotted and streaked greyish on the breast. In flight, distinguished from Grey Plover by dark, not white, rump, and grey underwings and axillaries.
BREEDING PLUMAGE: Upperparts black, boldly spotted and spangled golden, underparts, foreneck and sides of face black, with a narrow white frontal band and eyebrow stripe extending along the neck and flanks, overlaid with bold black barring on the flanks. **SEXES** Similar. **HABITAT** Tidal flats, estuaries, saltmarsh, grasslands and airstrips. **STATUS** Common summer visitor. **CALL** Melodious 'tee-tew'.

GREY PLOVER *Pluvialis squatarola* 27–31 cm

Medium-sized plover, noticeably larger and bulkier than Pacific Golden Plover. Crown and upperparts pale brownish-grey mottled whitish; underparts white, mottled and streaked brownish-grey. In flight, distinguished from Pacific Golden Plover by prominent white wingbar and white, not dark rump, and whitish underwings with contrasting black axillaries.
BREEDING PLUMAGE: Upperparts black, boldly spotted and spangled silvery-white; breast, foreneck and sides of face black, with a broad white frontal band and eyebrow stripe extending along the neck and upper breast. Vent and undertail white. **SEXES** similar. **HABITAT** Almost entirely coastal, mainly estuaries, lagoons and tidal flats. **STATUS** Rare summer visitor to the Solomons and New Caledonia. **CALL** Plaintive whistle 'pec-oo-wee'.

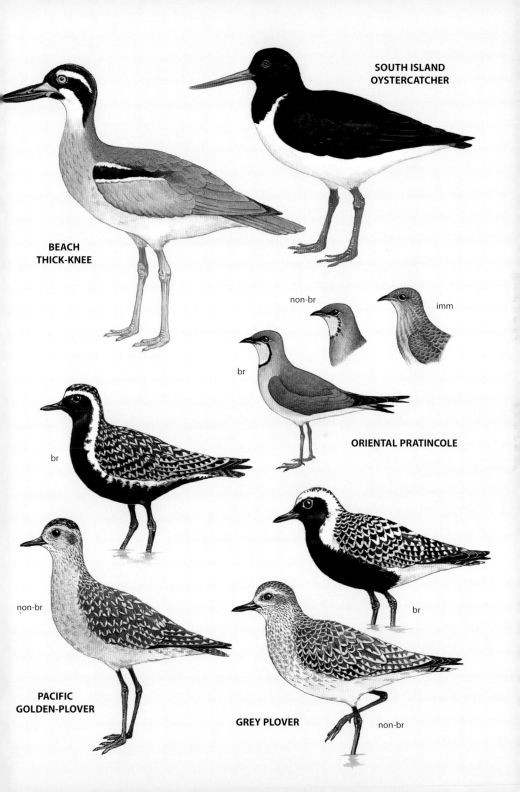

SOUTH ISLAND OYSTERCATCHER

BEACH THICK-KNEE

non-br

imm

br

ORIENTAL PRATINCOLE

br

br

non-br

PACIFIC GOLDEN-PLOVER

GREY PLOVER

non-br

LITTLE RINGED PLOVER *Charadrius dubius* 14–17 cm

A small, short-necked, slim plover, with a noticeable horizontal stance. Upperparts uniform dark brown, with conspicuous, narrow white collar which joins white foreneck and throat. White forehead and supercilium tinged with buff, breast-band normally restricted to brown patches at sides of breast; remaining underparts white.
BREEDING PLUMAGE: Distinctive black and white head pattern, bright yellow eyering and complete black breast-band. **SEXES** Alike. **IMM** Similar to non-breeding adult, but feathers of upperparts edged with warm buff. **HABITAT** Found mainly inland, along gravelly rivers, lakeshores and sand bars; particularly fond of bare ground including roads and tracks, airstrips and even industrial sites and rubbish tips. **STATUS** Extremely rare vagrant to the Solomons. **CALL** A clear descending 'pee-oo'.

DOUBLE-BANDED PLOVER *Charadrius bicinctus* 18–21 cm

A small, plump plover, with an upright stance, the only plover in the region with two breast-bands. Upperparts brownish, whitish forehead, lores and supercilium. Underparts white, with indistinct greyish-brown breast-bands.
BREEDING PLUMAGE: Shows black frontal band between crown and white forehead and a black loral stripe which extends down sides of neck to join narrow black upper breast-band, broader, dark chestnut lower breast-band. **SEXES** Similar. **IMM** Similar to non-breeding adult, but the feathers of the upperparts are edged with buff, producing a scaly appearance; has a buff hindneck collar and larger and more distinct buff supercilium. The breast-bands are greyish and very indistinct, often barely noticeable. **HABITAT** Prefers edges of inland lakes, especially brackish ones, also found in saltmarsh and grasslands and occasionally on sandy beaches and tidal flats. **STATUS** Rare vagrant to New Caledonia and Vanuatu. **CALL** Clear, incisive 'chip', often repeated three or four times.

MONGOLIAN PLOVER *Charadrius mongolus* 18–21 cm

A small, compact plover with slightly hunched-up posture, grey-brown upperparts, white underparts and dark grey legs. Similar to Greater Sandplover in all plumages, but is smaller, has shorter legs, a rounder head and a shorter, less robust bill. Differs from Double-banded Plover by paler upperparts and single breast-band. Much smaller and shorter-legged than Oriental Plover and has very different posture.
BREEDING PLUMAGE: Black frontal band and face mask, broad and irregular chestnut breast-band and chestnut hindneck collar. **SEXES** Alike. **HABITAT** Sheltered bays, harbours, estuaries and tidal flats. **STATUS** Fairly common summer visitor to the Solomons, scarce visitor to Vanuatu and New Caledonia. **CALL** Short, hard 'chitik'.

GREATER SANDPLOVER *Charadrius leschenaultii* 22–25 cm

A medium-sized, long-legged plover, with grey-brown upperparts, white underparts and pale greenish-grey legs. Similar to Mongolian Plover, but is larger, with more angular head, longer, heavier and more pointed bill and longer legs. Differs from Oriental Plover by larger head, shorter neck, more robust bill and shorter legs.
BREEDING PLUMAGE: Black frontal band and mask through the eye to ear-coverts, fairly narrow even chestnut breast-band, narrower than in Mongolian Plover, and a chestnut hindneck collar. **SEXES** Alike in non-breeding plumage, male much brighter in breeding plumage. **HABITAT** Almost entirely coastal: harbours, estuaries, tidal flats and beaches. **STATUS** Uncommon summer visitor to the Solomons, and scarce visitor to Vanuatu and New Caledonia. **CALL** Short, rippling trill, 'trrrt'.

ORIENTAL PLOVER *Charadrius veredus* 22–25 cm

A medium-sized, long-necked, long-legged plover, with characteristic upright stance, dark brown upperparts, white underparts and dull yellowish legs. Differs from Mongolian Plover and Greater Sandplover by slightly larger size, longer neck, more horizontal stance, longer yellowish legs, buff coloured breast and all-dark underwings.
BREEDING PLUMAGE Male: Head and neck whitish, broad chestnut breast-band with narrow black lower border, sharply demarcated from white belly. **Female:** As non-breeding adult, but with buffy breast. **IMM** Similar, but feathers of upperparts edged with buff. **HABITAT** Mainly stony flats and alongside rivers and lakes. **STATUS** Scarce summer visitor to the Solomons. **CALL** Sharp, whistled 'chip-chip-chip'.

LITTLE RINGED PLOVER

imm

br

non-br

DOUBLE-BANDED PLOVER

non-br

br

imm

MONGOLIAN PLOVER

br

non-br

br

GREATER SANDPLOVER

br

non-br

non-br

ORIENTAL PLOVER

SWINHOE'S
SNIPE

BLACK-TAILED
GODWIT

br

non-br

BAR-TAILED GODWIT

br

non-br

br

RUDDY
TURNSTONE

LITTLE CURLEW

BRISTLE-THIGHED
CURLEW

WHIMBREL

FAR-EASTERN
CURLEW

BEACH THICK-KNEE

MARSH SANDPIPER

non-br

GREENSHANK

non-br

TEREK SANDPIPER

non-br

WOOD SANDPIPER

COMMON SANDPIPER

WANDERING TATTLER

non-br

GREY-TAILED TATTLER

non-br

br

br

ORIENTAL PRATINCOLE

br

SOUTH ISLAND OYSTERCATCHER

SANDERLING

RED-NECKED STINT

LONG-TOED STINT

non-br

non-br

non-br

br

br

br

PECTORAL SANDPIPER

SHARP-TAILED
SANDPIPER

BROAD-BILL
SANDPIPE

non-br

non-br

non-br

CURLEW
SANDPIPER

RED-NECKED
PHALAROPE

non-br

non-br

br

br

br

RUFF

non-br

PACIFIC GOLDEN PLOVER

non-br

br

GREY PLOVER

non-br

br

LITTLE RINGED PLOVER

non-br

br

DOUBLE-BANDED PLOVER

non-br

br

MONGOLIAN PLOVER

non-br

br

GREATER SANDPLOVER

non-br

br

ORIENTAL PLOVER

non-br

br

SILVER GULL *Larus novaehollandiae* 36–44 cm

A medium-sized gull, with pale grey mantle and wings and white head, neck and underparts. Noticeable white wedge on upperwing, from carpal joint onto bases of outer primaries, wingtips black with prominent white mirrors. Bill, eyering, legs and feet bright red; iris white.
NON-BREEDING PLUMAGE: Similar to breeding plumage, but red bill, eyering, legs and feet duller. **SEXES** Alike. **IMM** Brown mottling on mantle and upperwing-coverts, narrow dark brown subterminal band or spots on the tail, soft parts pinkish-brown. **HABITAT** Open beaches, sheltered bays, estuaries and farmland. **STATUS** Common breeding bird in New Caledonia, rare vagrant to Vanuatu. **CALL** A loud screaming 'keey-ow'.

BLACK-HEADED GULL *Larus ridibundus* 38–44 cm

A medium-sized gull, with pale grey mantle and wings and white neck and underparts. Similar in size and shape to Silver Gull but slightly smaller and slimmer. In breeding plumage easily separated from Silver Gull by distinctive dark brown head. In all plumages easily identified in flight by broad white wedge on leading edge of primaries and narrow black border to trailing edge. Narrow white incomplete eyering; bill, legs and feet red; iris brown.
NON-BREEDING PLUMAGE: Head white, dusky patch in front of and below eye and prominent blackish ear-spot. **SEXES** Alike. **IMM** Conspicuous mottled brown bar on wing-coverts and narrow black subterminal band on tail. **HABITAT** Open beaches, sheltered bays, estuaries, farmland and rubbish tips. **STATUS** Rare vagrant to Bougainville Island in the Solomons. **CALL** Nasal, melodious 'kwarrrr'.

GREAT CRESTED-TERN *Sterna bergii* 40–50 cm

Large slender tern, grey above and white below, with black cap and shaggy crest, and narrow white forehead. Easily separated from all other terns by combination of large size, shaggy crest and greenish-yellow bill.
NON-BREEDING PLUMAGE: Similar to breeding plumage but with more white on forehead and crown. **IMM** Heavy grey-black mottling to upperparts and uniform grey-black primaries. **HABITAT** Open beaches, sheltered bays, estuaries, offshore islands and offshore waters. **STATUS** Common resident. **CALL** A loud 'wep-wep'.

LESSER CRESTED-TERN *Sterna bengalensis* 38–43 cm

Large slender tern, very similar to Great Crested-Tern, but smaller and more graceful. Separated in all plumages from all other terns by diagnostic, long bright orange bill.
NON-BREEDING PLUMAGE: Similar to breeding plumage, but with white forehead and crown. **IMM** Dark grey mottling to saddle, rump and uppertail-coverts, upperwing uniform grey-black with conspicuous broad white panel across central innerwing-coverts. **HABITAT** Open beaches, sandy cays, coral reefs and offshore waters. **STATUS** Rare vagrant to Bougainville Island in the Solomons. **CALL** Loud rasping 'kek-kereck'.

SILVER GULL

imm

br

BLACK-HEADED GULL

imm

non-br

GREAT CRESTED-TERN

imm

non-br

LESSER CRESTED-TERN

imm

non-br

br

WHISKERED TERN *Chlidonias hybridus* 23–25 cm

A medium-sized freshwater tern, with a slightly forked tail and red bill and legs. Pale grey above and white below, with white head finely streaked black on hindcrown and distinctive black band from eye to nape. Similar to White-winged Tern but has a pale grey, not white crown, streaked head, rather than a solid somewhat smudgy head pattern, and no ear-covert mark extending below the eye.
BREEDING PLUMAGE: Unmistakable; has neat black cap and blackish-grey abdomen. **IMM** Dusky cap and distinctive buff and black barring on saddle. **HABITAT** Lakes, swamps and estuaries. **STATUS** Uncommon transient to Bougainville Island in the Solomons. **CALL** A hoarse 'eeirk'.

WHITE-WINGED TERN *Chlidonias leucopterus* 20–23 cm

A medium-sized freshwater tern, with a slightly forked tail, black bill and red legs and feet. Slightly smaller and slimmer than Whiskered Tern. Pale grey above and white below, white head, crown and centre of nape mottled with black. Similar to Whiskered Tern but has white, not grey, rump and a rather solid somewhat smudgy, not streaked, head pattern. The ear-covert mark extends below the eye and there is a distinct white hindcollar.
BREEDING PLUMAGE: Unmistakable; strikingly black and white, black head and body, white rump and tail and diagnostic white forewing-coverts. **IMM** Similar to immature Whiskered Tern, but the saddle is a more solid brownish-black, with indistinct pale edges to the feathers. There is a distinct white hindcollar and the rump is white. **HABITAT** Lakes, swamps and estuaries. **STATUS** Uncommon transient to Bougainville Island and recently observed by the author at Lake Tengano, on Rennell Island in the Solomons. **CALL** High-pitched 'kreek-kreek'.

ROSEATE TERN *Sterna dougallii* 33 cm

Slender medium-sized sea tern, with long deeply forked tail. Only slightly larger than Black-naped Tern, much smaller and slimmer than Common Tern. Pale grey above and white below, forecrown white with black crown. Bill black, legs and feet red. Distinguished by long outer tail feathers which project well beyond the wings at rest, very pale upperparts and completely white underwing.
BREEDING PLUMAGE: Shows full black cap and bright red bill, legs and feet. **IMM** Blackish forehead and crown, bold black 'V'-shaped barring on saddle, producing a scaly appearance and dusky carpal bar. **HABITAT** Offshore waters, around coral cays and offshore islands. **STATUS** Uncommon breeding bird in the Solomons and New Caledonia; wanderers occur in the waters off Vanuatu. **CALL** A grating 'aaark-aaark'.

COMMON TERN *Sterna hirundo* 33–37 cm

Slender medium-sized sea tern, with long deeply forked tail. Much larger and bulkier than Black-naped and Roseate Terns. Grey above and white below, white forehead with black crown. Bill, legs and feet black. Distinguished by tips of tail feathers falling level with wingtips at rest, much greyer upperparts, noticeable blackish carpal bar and smudgy black trailing edge on outer underwing, none of these features being present in Black-naped or Roseate Terns.
BREEDING PLUMAGE: Shows full black cap and lacks carpal bars. **IMM** Resembles non-breeding adult but has broader more prominent black carpal bar. **HABITAT** Oceanic and coastal waters. **STATUS** Abundant summer visitor to the Solomons and very uncommon visitor to Vanuatu and New Caledonia. **CALL** A strident 'ker yah' and 'kik-kik-kik'.

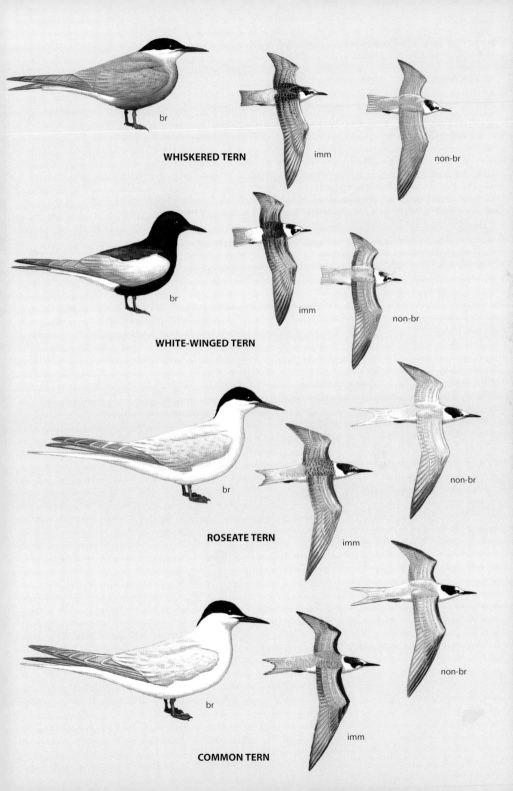

WHISKERED TERN

br

imm

non-br

WHITE-WINGED TERN

br

imm

non-br

ROSEATE TERN

br

imm

non-br

COMMON TERN

br

imm

non-br

BLACK-NAPED TERN *Sterna sumatrana* 30–32 cm

Small slender sea tern, with long deeply forked tail. Adult has diagnostic narrow black band from the eye to the nape. Mantle and wings very pale grey, can appear almost white at a distance. Underparts have strong pink wash in breeding season. Only black on the wing is confined to the edge of the outermost primary.
SEXES Alike. **IMM** Upperparts boldly patterned with black and white mottling and has noticeable dusky carpal bar. **HABITAT** Offshore islands and sandy or coral cays. **STATUS** Common resident. **CALL** Short 'krep-krep'.

LITTLE TERN *Sterna albifrons* 20–25 cm

Very small slender sea tern, with forked tail and rapid wingbeats, often hovers. White head and crown with fine black streaking on hindcrown and nape, upperparts pale grey, sharply contrasting with blackish outer three or four primaries and narrow black carpal bar; underparts white. Black bill, legs and feet.
BREEDING PLUMAGE: Crown, nape and line from eye to bill black, white triangular patch on forehead reaching to above eye, bill bright yellow with small black tip, legs and feet bright orange. **IMM** Slightly dusky above. **HABITAT** Coastal areas, lagoons, estuaries, rivers, lakes and tidal flats. **STATUS** Uncommon summer visitor to the Solomons. **CALL** A chattering 'crik-crik-crik'.

FAIRY TERN *Sterna nereis* 22–27 cm

Similar in size, shape and flight to Little Tern. In all plumages distinguished from Little Tern by white lores and different coloured bill. Non-breeding plumage shows fine black and white streaking on forecrown and blackish bill with orange centre. Lacks dark carpal bar.
BREEDING PLUMAGE: White forehead not extending above eye; crown and nape black. Bill, legs and feet orange. **IMM** Dusky mottling on head and upperparts. **HABITAT** Lagoons, estuaries, river mouths, open beaches and offshore islands. **STATUS** Fairly common resident around the coasts of New Caledonia. **CALL** Chattering 'kee-ick-kee-ick', similar to call of Little Tern.

COMMON WHITE-TERN *Gygis alba* 28–33 cm

Unmistakable small, delicate, snowy-white tern, with slightly forked tail, large black eyes and slightly uptilted black bill.
SEXES Alike. **IMM** Pale buffish mottling on back and wings and behind the eye. **HABITAT** Coastal lagoons, offshore islands and coral cays. **STATUS** Breeds in small numbers in New Caledonia. Regular visitor to the Solomons and Vanuatu, but breeding there has not been proved. **CALL** Guttural 'heech-heech'.

BLACK-NAPED TERN

imm

br

br

LITTLE TERN

imm

non-br

br

FAIRY TERN

imm

non-br

br

**COMMON
WHITE-TERN**

imm

GREY-BACKED TERN *Sterna lunata* 35–38 cm

A medium-sized sea tern, with long deeply forked tail. Similar to Bridled Tern, but differs in having much greyer upperparts, slightly whiter underparts and less white on outer tail feathers.
SEXES Alike. **IMM** White forehead and crown, crown streaked with black, merging with solid black nape. Feathers of mantle and wings are edged buff-brown and white, producing very scaly upperparts. **HABITAT** Coastal lagoons, offshore islands, coral cays and the open ocean. **STATUS** Uncommon resident in the northern Solomons, probably breeds in small numbers. **CALL** High-pitched 'ki-dee'.

BRIDLED TERN *Sterna anaethetus* 35–38 cm

A medium-sized sea tern, with long deeply forked tail. Similar to Grey-backed Tern, but differs in having much darker upperparts, slightly greyer underparts and more white on outer tail feathers.
SEXES Alike. **IMM** Duller, less well defined head pattern; upperparts grey-brown, feathers edged with buff, underparts white. **HABITAT** Coastal lagoons, offshore islands, coral cays and the open ocean. **STATUS** Uncommon breeding bird in the Solomons and New Caledonia, a vagrant in Vanuatu. **CALL** Barking 'wep wep'.

SOOTY TERN *Sterna fuscata* 36–42 cm

A medium-sized sea tern, with long deeply forked tail. Similar to Bridled Tern, but differs in having a much deeper white forehead which extends backwards only as far as the eye. In Bridled Tern the white forehead is much narrower and extends in a narrow supercilium to well behind the eye. The entire upperparts are much darker, almost black in Sooty Tern, compared to brown-grey in Bridled Tern.
SEXES Alike. **IMM** Dark sooty brown, mantle and wing feathers edged buff-white, underparts blackish-grey. **HABITAT** Coastal lagoons, offshore islands, coral cays and the open ocean. **STATUS** Common breeding bird throughout the region. **CALL** Raucous 'wideawake'.

BLUE-GREY NODDY *Procelsterna cerulea* 25–31 cm

A small, distinctive, polymorphic sea tern, with moderately forked tail. Dark morph, all-grey head, wings and body, with slightly paler underparts. Pale morph, whitish head merging into pale grey upperparts and greyish-white underparts. Both colour morphs have a partial white spectacle behind the eye and a small black spot in front of the eye, a short slender black bill, black eyes and black legs and feet. The feet have conspicuous yellow webbing.
SEXES Alike. **IMM** A brownish wash to the underparts. **HABITAT** Coastal lagoons, offshore islands and coral cays. **STATUS** Breeds in small numbers in New Caledonia. **CALL** Soft purring 'crorr'.

BROWN NODDY *Anous stolidus* 40–45 cm

A large chocolate-brown sea tern with a wedge-shaped tail, which is slightly notched when fanned. Dark brown all over except for prominent pale grey crown, almost white on forehead. Similar to Black Noddy, but plumage much browner. It is noticeably larger and bulkier, with larger stouter black bill and is much more laboured in flight.
SEXES Alike. **IMM** Lacks pale cap, faint grey-brown barring on mantle and wings. **HABITAT** Coastal lagoons, offshore islands, coral cays and the open ocean. **STATUS** Common breeding bird throughout the region. **CALL** Harsh croaking 'kra-kra'.

BLACK NODDY *Anous minutus* 35–40 cm

Medium-sized, slender sooty-black sea tern with a wedge-shaped tail, which is slightly notched when fanned. Uniform black all over except for conspicuous white forehead and crown. Similar to Brown Noddy, but plumage much blacker, it is much smaller and slimmer, with thinner black bill and more graceful flight.
SEXES Alike. **IMM** As adult, but whitish forehead and crown sharply demarcated from blackish nape and with pale edges to feathers on the mantle. **HABITAT** Coastal lagoons, offshore islands and coral cays. **STATUS** A common breeding species in the Solomons and New Caledonia, stragglers reaching Vanuatu. **CALL** Harsh rattling 'kik-krrrrr'.

GREY-BACKED TERN

imm

BRIDLED TERN

imm

SOOTY TERN

imm

BLUE-GREY NODDY

dark morph

pale morph

BROWN NODDY

imm

BLACK NODDY

imm

SOUTH POLAR SKUA *Catharacta maccormicki* 53 cm

The largest skua in the region; a large, powerfully built, heavy-bodied, broad-winged, gull-like seabird. Much broader winged and shorter tailed than the smaller, more delicate jaegers. Polymorphic, with two main colour morphs, pale and dark, and varying intermediate morphs. Pale morph: diagnostic contrast between blackish-brown upperparts and greyish-white head, neck and underbody. Dark morph: dark brown to blackish usually with slightly paler nape and sometimes pale band at base of bill. All colour morphs show prominent large white patches across base of primaries on both the upper and underwings.
SEXES Alike. **IMM** Pale morph similar to adult but head and underbody greyer. Dark morph, pale edges to feathers of upperparts. **HABITAT** During migration far offshore, in the open ocean. **STATUS** Not officially recorded in the region, but immature birds undertake regular migration into the northern Pacific and undoubtedly pass through the region in small numbers. **CALL** Silent at sea.

POMARINE JAEGER *Stercorarius pomarinus* 65–78 cm

A robust, small-headed, barrel-chested gull-like seabird with conspicuous white wing-flashes. Unmistakable in adult plumage with two elongated spoon-shaped central tail feathers, however these are often worn or absent. Polymophic, with two main colour morphs, pale and dark, and varying intermediate morphs. Adult breeding pale morph: sooty black cap, yellowish nape with white throat and belly, upperparts uniform blackish-brown. Adult non-breeding pale morph: dark brownish-grey cap, sometimes extending to chin and throat, forming dusky hood; upperparts uniform blackish-brown, black-and-white barring on rump and uppertail-coverts; underparts white with broad brownish-grey breast-band and barring along flanks, bold black and white barring on undertail-coverts. Adult breeding dark morph: uniform blackish-brown, with neck and throat washed yellowish-brown. Adult non-breeding dark morph: dark and whitish barring on rump.
SEXES Alike. **IMM** Differs from non-breeding adult in having axilliaries and underwing completely barred. **HABITAT** Prefers the open ocean. **STATUS** Transient and winter visitor, in small numbers. **CALL** Silent at sea.

PARASITIC JAEGER *Stercorarius parasiticus* 46–67 cm

A gracefully built rather falcon-like seabird with conspicuous white wing-flashes. Slimmer, less deep-chested and swifter in flight than Pomarine Jaeger. Unmistakable in adult plumage with elongated pointed tips to central tail feathers, however, these are often worn or absent. Polymorphic, with two main colour morphs, pale and dark, and varying intermediate morphs. Adult breeding pale morph: most birds have a sooty black cap, yellowish nape with white throat and belly, some individuals have a complete greyish-brown breast-band, while others have incomplete breast-bands, upperparts uniform blackish-brown. Adult non-breeding pale morph: pale brownish-grey cap, occasionally extending to chin and throat forming dusky hood with upperparts blackish-brown, with white or buff scaling on mantle and back, underparts white with broad brownish-grey breast-band, narrow dark barring along flanks and bold black and white barring on undertail-coverts. Adult breeding and non-breeding dark morphs are very similar, both uniform blackish-brown, with yellowish cheeks and hind-collar.
SEXES Alike. **IMM** Differs from non-breeding adult in having axillaries and underwing completely barred. **HABITAT** On wintering grounds prefers more inshore waters than Pomarine Jaeger. **STATUS** Transient and winter visitor in small numbers. **CALL** Silent at sea.

LONG-TAILED JAEGER *Stercorarius longicaudus* 33–40 cm plus 15–20 cm central tail feathers

Smallest, most buoyant and graceful jaeger, rather tern-like in flight. Unmistakable in adult plumage with extremely long elongated central tail feathers. In breeding plumage has distinctive pale blue-grey upperparts with black cap and primaries, white at base of primaries confined to innermost two primaries. Underparts, throat and breast white, with grey belly. In non-breeding plumage lacks elongated tail feathers, has dusky cheeks and nape and pale scaling to upperparts, shows black and white barring to upper and undertail-coverts and greyish barring on underparts.
SEXES Alike. **IMM** Whitish head and diagnostic barred undertail and underwing-coverts. **HABITAT** Oceanic. **STATUS** Very rare transient and winter visitor. **CALL** Silent at sea.

SOUTH POLAR SKUA

pale morph

dark morph

pale morph non-br

POMARINE JAEGER

dark morph br

imm

PARASITIC JAEGER

pale morph br

dark morph non-br

imm

br

non-br

imm

LONG-TAILED JAEGER

METALLIC PIGEON *Columba vitiensis* 38 cm

A large dark heavily built pigeon with diagnostic and conspicuous pure white chin, throat and cheek patch. Upperparts dark grey with a pronounced iridescent purplish-green sheen. Head and underparts pale pinkish-brown, with grey tail. Bill cherry red, with a yellow tip. Legs and feet bright red.
SEXES Alike. **IMM** Duller, with no iridescent sheen, and the throat is dull brownish-grey. **HABITAT** Primary forest of lowlands, highlands and small offshore islands. **STATUS** Uncommon resident throughout the region. **CALL** A loud booming 'whoo-whoo', at a constant pitch.

YELLOW-LEGGED PIGEON *Columba pallidiceps* 40 cm

A large dark heavily built pigeon, somewhat similar to Metallic Pigeon. Head and neck greyish-white, wings and tail black, underparts dark grey. All body feathers are broadly edged with pink, purple and green iridescence, the colour varying according to light conditions. The feather edging is particularly evident on the upperwing. Bare skin around the eye bright red. Bill is also bright cherry red, legs and feet yellow-orange.
SEXES Alike. **IMM** Brownish head with reduced iridescence throughout plumage. **HABITAT** A ground-feeding bird of primary forest from the lowlands to the mountains. **STATUS** An endangered and rare species, restricted in distribution to the Bismarck Archipelago (where there are only one or two sightings this century) and to the Solomons. Recently observed by the author in highland forest on Makira Island. Only one or two other sightings this century. **CALL** Unknown.

CLOVEN-FEATHERED DOVE *Drepanoptila holosericea* 28 cm

This extremely attractive dove is unmistakable. A medium-sized, compact dove with short squarish tail and broad rounded wings. The bird has a very rounded and steep, bulging forehead.
ADULT MALE Head and upperparts deep green, with indistinct whitish-grey bars across wings and tail. The bird has a pure white stripe down the centre of the throat, a deep green breast, and narrow white and black breast-band. Belly to undertail-coverts yellow. The legs are fully feathered, with conspicuous fluffy pure white feathers. Iris reddish-brown, bill greyish-brown and the feet are pinkish-brown. **ADULT FEMALE** Duller green, with much more subdued markings and most of abdomen green. **IMM** Similar to female, but markings barely discernible. Feathers of tertials, wing-coverts and flight feathers are edged with yellow. **HABITAT** Mainly dense montane forests. **STATUS** Endemic to New Caledonia, where it is locally common. **CALL** Loud, slow and regular 'oo-oo-oo-oo'.

NICOBAR PIGEON *Caloenas nicobarica* 34 cm

This extraordinary medium-sized, stocky pigeon is readily identified by its conspicuously short tail, deep-chested appearance, long broad wings and elongated neck, which has a distinctive ruff of lance-shaped feathers. Plumage predominantly blue-black, in good light showing brilliant iridescent green and bronze sheen and a conspicuous short pure white tail. Iris black, bill, legs and feet grey.
SEXES Alike. **IMM** Lacks elongated neck feathers and is entirely brownish-black, including the tail. **HABITAT** A ground- dwelling inhabitant of dense lowland rainforest; nests colonially on small offshore islands, but visits coastal lowlands of larger islands to forage for food. **STATUS** An uncommon breeding bird mainly in the northern islands of the Solomons where there has been a marked decline in numbers in recent years, caused by hunting and loss of habitat. **CALL** Usually silent, but occasionally utters harsh guttural croaks and soft 'cooing'.

METALLIC
PIGEON

YELLOW-LEGGED
PIGEON

CLOVEN-FEATHERED DOVE

NICOBAR
PIGEON

SPOTTED DOVE *Streptopelia chinensis* 30–33 cm

A large dove, with a long, strongly graduated tail. Head pale grey, with a slight pinkish wash. Nape and back of neck jet-black with conspicuous white spotting. Wings and back dark grey-brown, with prominent dark shaft-streaks and pale edging to feathers. Uppertail dark grey-brown, outer tail feathers have broad white tips, forming prominent white corners to tail in flight. Underbody pinkish-brown, grading to creamy-grey on belly and vent. Iris yellow, with black outer ring; bill grey-black, legs and feet pinkish-red.
SEXES Alike. **IMM** Overall dull brown, with no black and white markings on the neck. **HABITAT** A bird of towns, villages, gardens and occasionally cultivated land and forested areas. **STATUS** Introduced from Asia to New Caledonia where it is locally common. **CALL** Mellow 'coo-whoo-coo'.

EMERALD DOVE *Chalcophaps indica* 23–27 cm

A small plump short-tailed, ground-frequenting dove. Similar to Stephan's Dove but geographically separated in this region.
ADULT MALE Head, neck and underparts rufous-brown; mantle and wing-coverts bright iridescent green with a prominent white shoulder-patch, primaries brown; lower back and rump blackish-brown crossed by two broad, pale grey bars, tail blackish. Iris dark brown; bill orange-red, legs and feet bright red. **ADULT FEMALE** Similar to male but duller, with greyish shoulder-patch and indistinct barring on rump. **IMM** Head and body pale brown, scalloped with dark brown, wings green, scalloped with chestnut-bronze. **HABITAT** Dense forest. **STATUS** Common resident in Vanuatu and New Caledonia. **CALL** Low-pitched penetrating 'coo' repeated continuously.

STEPHAN'S DOVE *Chalcophaps stephani* 23–25 cm

A small plump short-tailed, ground-frequenting dove. Similar to Emerald Dove but geographically separated in this region.
ADULT MALE Head, neck, mantle, underparts and tail rich purplish-brown. Forehead brilliant white, wing-coverts iridescent green, two alternating blackish and ochreous bars across lower back and rump. Iris dark brown; bill orange-red, legs and feet purplish-red. **ADULT FEMALE** similar, but more brownish, less purplish and the forehead is grey. **IMM** Similar to female but lacks grey forehead and has a small area of pale rufous around the eye. **HABITAT** Dense lowland forest. **STATUS** A fairly common resident throughout the Solomons. **CALL** A low mournful 'woooah', followed by a long series of 'pu' notes, starting very softly and gradually increasing in volume.

CRESTED CUCKOO-DOVE *Reinwardtoena crassirostris* 40–42 cm

A large, distinctive rainforest pigeon, with a very long graduated tail. Mantle, wings and tail blackish with a very distinctive long thin brownish-grey erectile crest, formed by the stiff elongated feathers of crown and nape. Head, neck, upper back and complete underparts grey. Iris red, bare skin around the eye red; a stout reddish bill with yellow tip, legs and feet red.
SEXES Alike. **IMM** Lacks the crest, has a darker head and is more brownish, with rusty fringes to most feathers. **HABITAT** Hill and mountain forests, favouring mountain valleys above 500 m. **STATUS** Endemic to the Solomons, where it is rare and localised. **CALL** A far-carrying, mournful, two-note 'hoo-woooahha', the second long note rising in pitch before gradually descending.

MACKINLAY'S CUCKOO-DOVE *Macropygia mackinlayi* 27–32 cm

A large, slender, distinctive rainforest pigeon, with a very long graduated tail.
ADULT MALE Upperparts rufous-brown, slightly darker on wings and tail. Underparts pale cinnamon, black-based, bifurcate breast feathers form distinct black spots, the vent is bright cinnamon. Iris red; bill black, and legs and feet red. **ADULT FEMALE** similar to the male, but slightly duller and the breast is more strongly mottled with black. **IMM** Much duller than adult and is scalloped with dark brown and ochre. **HABITAT** Primary and secondary forest at all altitudes, prefers the understorey and more open areas, clearings and gardens. **STATUS** Common resident in the Solomons and Vanuatu. **CALL** Melodious, mellow 'vo-ku', slightly rising then dropping in pitch.

imm

SPOTTED DOVE

imm

imm

STEPHAN'S DOVE

EMERALD DOVE

MACKINLAY'S CUCKOO-DOVE

CRESTED CUCKOO-DOVE

WHITE-BIBBED GROUND-DOVE *Gallicolumba jobiensis* 24–25 cm

A small plump dove of the forest floor.
ADULT MALE Easily identified by black crown and line through the eye, conspicuous white supercilium, bright purple upperparts and white throat and breast; remainder of underparts blackish. **ADULT FEMALE** Duller greyish-brown with greenish wash to mantle, scapulars and some wing-coverts. **IMM** Dark brown with distinct rufous edges to most feathers, particularly on the wing-coverts. **HABITAT** Prefers dense coastal forest of the lowlands and small offshore islands. **STATUS** Rare resident of Vella Lavella, Gizo and Guadalcanal islands in the Solomons. **CALL** Variously described as a 'belch', a grunt, or a short frog-like note.

SANTA CRUZ GROUND-DOVE *Gallicolumba sanctaecrucis* 22–25 cm

A small, plump, short-tailed dove of the forest floor.
ADULT MALE Head pale grey, crown, nape and rest of upperparts chocolate-brown, with a glossy purple wash, strongly iridescent violet-purple shoulder-patch. Throat and breast shield whitish, washed pinkish-buff, belly chocolate-brown. **ADULT FEMALE** Paler, more brownish, with a greenish gloss to the upperparts. **IMM** Uniform brown. **HABITAT** The few recent records are from primary forest and patches of remnant forest, from 300 to 1000 m. **STATUS** A rare species which is restricted to the islands of Tinakula and Utupua, in the Santa Cruz Islands, and the island of Espiritú Santo in Vanuatu. **CALL** A low, moderately loud 'woot', repeated monotonously.

TANNA GROUND-DOVE *Gallicolumba ferruginea* 22–25 cm

A small ,plump, short-tailed dove of the forest floor.
ADULT FEMALE Head rusty-brown, back dark reddish-purple, wings dark green, primaries brownish-grey with very narrow pale edges. Throat and breast rusty-brown, belly grey. Iris yellow; bill black, and legs and feet red. **HABITAT** Dense forest. **STATUS** Extinct. No specimens, and known only from Forster's drawing of 1774. Confined to Tanna Island in southern Vanuatu. It is possible that the bird was seen elsewhere than Tanna Island, or that the bird may be an extinct race of Santa Cruz Ground-Dove.

BRONZE GROUND-DOVE *Gallicolumba beccarii* 18–20 cm

A very small, plump, short-tailed dove of the forest floor.
ADULT MALE Upperparts glossy green, with a bronzy iridescent wash and a prominent iridescent maroon shoulder-patch. Head, neck, throat and breast blueish-grey, sharply demarcated from the blackish-brown abdomen. **ADULT FEMALE** Duller and browner, lacks the maroon shoulder-patch. **IMM** Similar but browner, with rufous edges to wing and breast feathers. **HABITAT** Primary forest from lowlands to highlands. **STATUS** Rare and retiring, found on several islands in the Solomons. **CALL** A series of low 'cook-cook-cook-cook-coook' notes, all at the same pitch.

THICK-BILLED GROUND-DOVE *Gallicolumba salamonis* 26 cm

A small, plump dove of the forest floor, with a conspicuously heavy bill. Upperparts rich chestnut, with faint purplish iridescent sheen to scapulars and lesser wing-coverts. Throat and breast shield pale buff, contrasting with chocolate-brown abdomen. Bill brown, legs red.
HABITAT Primary forest. **STATUS** Endemic to Malaita, Makira and Ramos islands in the Solomons. Known from only two specimens. Presumed extinct. Has not been recorded since 1927. **CALL** Unknown.

CHOISEUL PIGEON *Microgoura meeki* 28–31 cm

A large, plump, short-tailed pigeon of the forest floor. Head, mantle, shoulder-patch and breast blue-grey; bare blue-grey frontal shield, surrounded by black face, a conspicuous long hairy-looking crest of blue-grey feathers; wings brown, abdomen bright rufous-cinnamon. Tail is purplish-black.
HABITAT Primary forest. **STATUS** Endemic to Choiseul and Ramos islands in the Solomons; probably extinct, no reliable sightings since 1904. Older local people remember the bird, before the widespread introduction of cats and dogs. **CALL** Local people have imitated the call as a low 'crooo-crooo-crooo'.

WHITE-BIBBED GROUND-DOVE

SANTA CRUZ GROUND-DOVE

female

male

TANNA GROUND-DOVE

female

female

male

BRONZE GROUND-DOVE

THICK-BILLED GROUND-DOVE

CHOISEUL PIGEON

TANNA FRUIT-DOVE *Ptilinopus tannensis* 28–30 cm

A medium-sized, plump fruit-dove.
ADULT MALE Predominantly grass-green all over, with yellowish wash to head, some greyish-white spots on the edge of the shoulder, conspicuous bright yellow spots at the tip of some tertial and secondary feathers, lemon-yellow undertail-coverts, with green centres, and a fairly obscure greyish terminal tail band. Iris ochre; bill greyish-brown, legs and feet very pale red. **ADULT FEMALE** Similar to male, but with reduced or sometimes no spotting on the wings and pale yellow on the lower abdomen. **IMM** Similar to female, but lacks the yellowish head and any spotting on the wings. Most feathers but particularly those on the mantle, wings and underparts are edged with yellow. **HABITAT** Found in a wide range of wooded habitats as long as there are tall fruit-bearing trees but prefers primary forest, also found in open woodland, plantations and gardens. It is predominantly a lowland species but ascends up into the hills to as high as 500 m. **STATUS** Endemic to Vanuatu and Banks Island, where it is fairly common. **CALL** A deep, fairly loud but not far-carrying 'woo'.

SUPERB FRUIT-DOVE *Ptilinopus superbus* 22–24 cm

Small compact fruit-dove, with short rounded wings and short tail.
ADULT MALE Rich purple cap, broad orange-rufous hindneck collar, yellowish-green upperparts, grey breast with purplish spotting and prominent thick black lower breast-band, whitish abdomen with green patches on flanks and thighs. Vent and undertail-coverts dull white, blotched green. Iris yellow; bill greenish-grey, legs and feet brownish-buff. **ADULT FEMALE** Mostly green with a bluish-purple patch on rear crown, lacks hindneck collar and breast-band. **IMM** Similar to female, but lacks the crown patch, most feathers but mainly those on the mantle, wings and breast are edged with yellow. **HABITAT** Prefers primary forest but also found in shrubby secondary growth and in mangroves close to rainforest. **STATUS** Found throughout the Solomons, where it is uncommon and unobtrusive, often difficult to observe owing to its preference for feeding amongst dense foliage in the upper canopy. **CALL** 5 or 6 deep guttural 'whoots'.

RED-BELLIED FRUIT-DOVE *Ptilinopus greyii* 21–24 cm

Small compact fruit-dove, with short rounded wings and short tail.
ADULT MALE Purplish-pink crown bordered with whitish-yellow at the sides and rear, mantle, wings and tail green, with yellow edging on wing-coverts, throat whitish-yellow, grey neck and underparts with prominent purplish-red patch on lower breast; undertail-coverts orangey-pink, greyish terminal tail band. Iris orange-red; bill olive, legs and feed pinkish-red. **ADULT FEMALE** Similar to the male but purplish-red patch on lower breast is less extensive. **IMM** Upperparts are almost entirely green, with most feathers edged yellow, the underparts are grey washed with green and the undertail-coverts are pale yellow. **HABITAT** A bird of lowland primary forest, usually occupying the denser parts of the canopy. **STATUS** Endemic to Vanuatu, the Santa Cruz Islands and New Caledonia. It is a common and conspicuous bird throughout Vanuatu and the Santa Cruz Islands, however, it is markedly more common in the Loyalty Islands than it is on mainland New Caledonia. **CALL** A loud resonant cooing, 'coo-coo-coo-coocoocoocoocoo', increasing in speed.

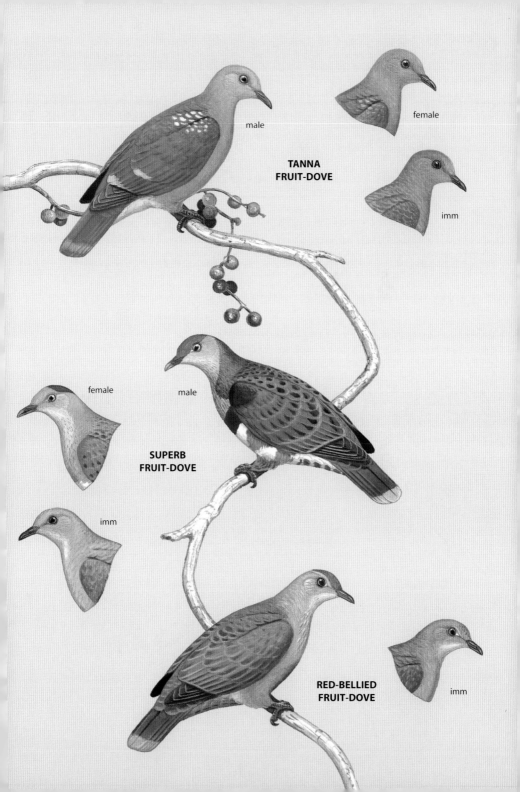

TANNA FRUIT-DOVE

male

female

imm

SUPERB FRUIT-DOVE

female

male

imm

RED-BELLIED FRUIT-DOVE

imm

YELLOW-BIBBED FRUIT-DOVE *Ptilinopus solomonensis* 18–21 cm

Small, compact fruit-dove, with short rounded wings and short tail.
ADULT MALE Head and upperparts dark green, forehead dark reddish-mauve (this may be reduced to a small mark on the lores, or extend back to the eye). Bright sulphur-yellow, crescent-shaped breast-band, dark green flanks, with a large mauve patch on the belly, undertail-coverts bright yellow. Iris yellow; bill greyish with a yellow tip, legs and feet bluish-purple. **ADULT FEMALE** Almost entirely dark green, with yellow fringes to belly feathers and bright yellow undertail-coverts. **IMM** Similar to female, but most feathers edged yellow, especially on the wing-coverts. **HABITAT** Primary and secondary growth from the lowlands up into the highest mountains. **STATUS** A common species throughout many islands of the Solomons. **CALL** A series of 'coos', which rise both in volume and speed towards the end.

SILVER-CAPPED FRUIT-DOVE *Ptilinopus richardsii* 21 cm

Small, compact fruit-dove, with short rounded wings and short tail. Head, hindneck, throat and breast pale greenish-grey, crown silver-grey, upper throat and chin yellowish. Upperparts green, with clear pink spots on the scapulars and tertials, obvious yellow terminal tail band. Belly and undertail-coverts bright orange. Iris reddish-orange; bill greenish with a purple cere and yellow-green tip, legs and feet deep reddish-purple.
SEXES Alike. **IMM** Dark green with bold yellow edges to the feathers of the upperparts, belly bright yellow with a few scattered orange feathers. **HABITAT** Lowland rainforest, often on small coral islands. **STATUS** Endemic to the islands of Ugi, Malaupaina, Malaulalo, Santa Ana, Bellona and Rennell in the Solomons, where the bird is abundant. **CALL** Low-pitched 'whoo-oom-whoo-oom-whoo-oom', progressively decreasing in volume.

CLARET-BREASTED FRUIT-DOVE *Ptilinopus viridis* 21 cm

A small, plump fruit-dove, with short rounded wings and short tail. Back, wings and tail dark green, with pale grey shoulder-patch and spots on the tertials. Entire throat and upper breast dark purplish-crimson, sharply demarcated from the dark green belly and undertail-coverts. Iris pale yellow; bill dull yellowish-grey, legs and feet greyish-pink.
SEXES Alike. **IMM** Lacks the dark purplish-crimson breast and has less distinct shoulder-patch and yellow edges to the wing-coverts. **HABITAT** Primary forest, secondary growth and gardens. **STATUS** A moderately common bird of lowland and mountain forests throughout the entire western Solomons, east to Guadalcanal and Malaita islands. **CALL** 'coo-coo', with the emphasis on the second note.

WHITE-HEADED FRUIT-DOVE *Ptilinopus eugeniae* 21 cm

A small, plump fruit-dove, with short rounded wings and short tail. Back, wings and tail dark green, with pale grey shoulder-patch and spots on the tertials. Conspicuous, bright snowy-white head; throat and upper breast dark purplish-crimson, sharply demarcated from the dark green belly and yellow undertail-coverts. Iris tawny-red; bill purplish-maroon with a golden-yellow tip, legs and feet dark purple.
SEXES Alike. **IMM** Green head with greyish forehead and throat, lacks the dark purplish-crimson breast and has less distinct shoulder-patch and yellow edges to wing-coverts. **HABITAT** Primary forest, secondary growth and gardens. **STATUS** Endemic to the islands of Makira, Ugi and Malaupaina in the Solomons, where it is moderately common. **CALL** A soft double cooing, with the emphasis on the second note.

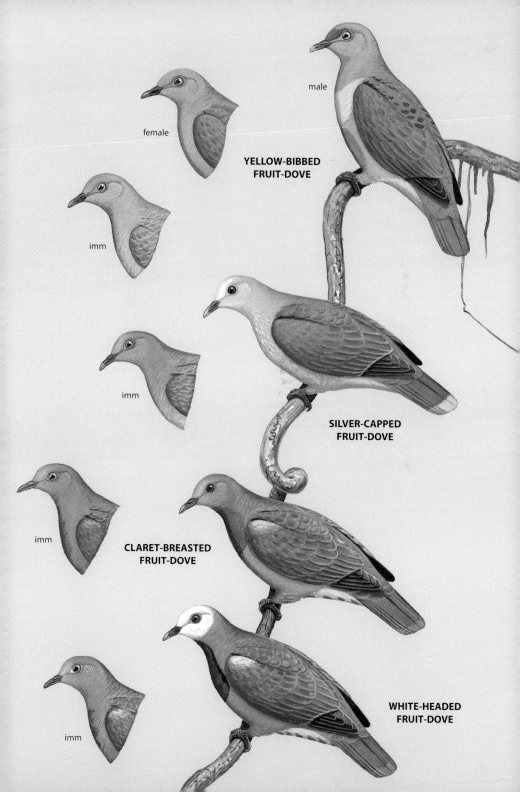

female

male

**YELLOW-BIBBED
FRUIT-DOVE**

imm

imm

**SILVER-CAPPED
FRUIT-DOVE**

imm

**CLARET-BREASTED
FRUIT-DOVE**

**WHITE-HEADED
FRUIT-DOVE**

imm

PACIFIC IMPERIAL-PIGEON *Ducula pacifica* 35–39 cm

A large grey pigeon with a conspicuous black knob at the base of the upper mandible and shiny green wings and tail.
ADULT MALE Head, neck and upper back pale grey; mantle, wings and tail dark green with a bluish iridescence. Underparts pale grey washed with pink, flanks and thighs grey, undertail-coverts chestnut. Iris red; bill and knob black, legs and feet bright cherry red. **ADULT FEMALE** Similar to male but slightly smaller, with a smaller knob and much paler in colour. **IMM** Similar to female but lacks the knob and iridescence on the mantle, wings and tail. **HABITAT** An island species, usually found only on small islands. Predominantly a bird of lowland forest but has been recorded as high as 1000 m. **STATUS** A common bird on Rennell Island and nearby much smaller islands. Does not occur elsewhere in the Solomons; fairly common throughout Vanuatu and the Santa Cruz Islands, rather uncommon in the Loyalty Islands of New Caledonia and only very occasionally visits mainland New Caledonia. **CALL** Deep, far-carrying 'roooo-prrroooooo', often followed after a short pause by a soft, low drawn-out 'hoooooooo'.

ISLAND IMPERIAL-PIGEON *Ducula pistrinaria* 38–44 cm

A large grey pigeon, similar to Pacific Imperial-Pigeon but lacks knob on bill and has conspicuous white ring around the base of the bill and around the eye. In flight, diagnostic underwing-coverts are conspicuously pale grey, showing marked contrast with the blackish flight feathers. Head, neck and upper back slaty-grey; mantle, wings and tail dark iridescent green. Throat pinkish-grey, rest of underparts slaty-grey, contrasting strongly with the chestnut undertail-coverts. Iris dark red; bill pale greyish-blue, legs and feet red.
SEXES Alike. **IMM** Similar but duller and paler, with narrow buff edges to the feathers of the wings and underparts. **HABITAT** An island species, usually found only on small islands and coastal forest of larger islands. Frequents primary and taller secondary forest, mangroves and occasionally gardens. **STATUS** Not particularly common, found on small islands and coastal forest throughout the Solomons. This is a highly mobile species, with birds frequently observed flying over the sea, sometimes in large flocks, in search of fruiting trees. **CALL** Fairly low 'wu-hoo-wu-hoo-wu-hoo-wu-hoo', gradually falling in pitch and volume.

RED-KNOBBED IMPERIAL-PIGEON *Ducula rubricera* 38–41 cm

A large grey pigeon with a conspicuous bright red knob at the base of the upper mandible, with shiny green wings and blue tail. Head, neck and upper back very pale grey; mantle and upperwings bright iridescent green, primaries, secondaries and tail iridescent blue-green. Upper throat pinkish-buff, lower throat and breast pale grey; belly to undertail-coverts dark rufous. Iris red; bill greyish, knob cherry red, legs and feet purplish-red.
SEXES Alike. **IMM** Like adult, but lacks red knob on bill. **HABITAT** A bird of lowland and hill forest, wherever there are fruiting trees. **STATUS** Widespread and very common throughout the Solomons. **CALL** A deep slow 'whoohoo', starting on a level pitch then rising and increasing in volume before dropping in pitch at the end.

imm

**PACIFIC
IMPERIAL-PIGEON**

**ISLAND
IMPERIAL-PIGEON**

**RED-KNOBBED
IMPERIAL-PIGEON**

CHESTNUT-BELLIED IMPERIAL-PIGEON *Ducula brenchleyi* 35–40 cm

A large dark pigeon, with a relatively slender build and long tail. Forehead and lores pale grey, crown and nape slaty-grey, washed with pink. Mantle, wings and tail dark sooty grey. Upper throat pinkish-buff, breast purplish-rufous with a faint grey wash. Belly to undertail-coverts rich purplish-chestnut. Iris red; bill greyish-black, legs and feet purplish-red.
SEXES Alike. **IMM** Similar to adults but lacks pink wash to nape; chin and throat yellowish-buff, underparts sooty grey washed with brown. **HABITAT** Occasionally observed in coastal secondary growth but prefers primary montane forest, especially ridge forest. **STATUS** This endangered species is endemic to the Solomons, where it is known from the islands of Guadalcanal, Malaita, Makira and a few smaller islands close to Makira. All recent reports are only from the island of Makira, where the bird is very uncommon and declining rapidly. **CALL** A deep prolonged 'coolooo', rising in pitch then descending.

BAKER'S IMPERIAL-PIGEON *Ducula bakeri* 40 cm

A large dark pigeon, with a fairly long tail. Head pale blue-grey; mantle, wings and tail slaty-grey; collar, back and breast purplish-maroon, merging into the dark chestnut belly and slightly paler dull rufous undertail-coverts. Iris bright yellow, with a bright red outer ring; bill black, legs and feet bright red.
SEXES Alike. **IMM** Similar to adult, but much duller. **HABITAT** Found in primary montane forests of the larger islands of northern Vanuatu, from 600 m to the highest elevations. **STATUS** Endemic to northern Vanuatu, where the species is considered uncommon and declining. **CALL** A powerful and far-carrying 'twoo-too-too-too-too', repeated frequently at short intervals.

NEW CALEDONIAN IMPERIAL-PIGEON *Ducula goliath* 50–52 cm

A very large dark pigeon, with a slender build, long tail and long bill which is noticeably hooked at the tip. Head, neck and breast bluish-grey, the feathers of the neck are elongated and bifurcated and appear silvery. Mantle and wings chestnut-grey, lesser wing-coverts chestnut-maroon, forming a band across the upperwing. The tail is blackish, with a broad dark chestnut median band. Belly dark chestnut shading into paler buffy-yellow undertail-coverts. Iris cherry red, bill pinkish-red; legs and feet pink.
SEXES Alike. **IMM** Similar to adult, but plumage duller and browner, lacks elongated neck feathers and median tail band. **HABITAT** Undisturbed primary forest from sea level to the mountains, with a preference for riverine forest. **STATUS** Endemic to New Caledonia where it is still quite common in the more inaccessible areas, but as these are opened up it is heavily hunted, becoming locally extinct, which now threatens the long-term survival of the species. **CALL** Low-pitched, booming 'oom', not varying in pitch or volume.

PALE MOUNTAIN-PIGEON *Gymnophaps solomonensis* 38 cm

A large pale grey pigeon, with slender build and long tail. Often in fast moving flocks, their wings make a loud 'wooshing' noise as they fly overhead. Head, neck, upperback, rump, tail and entire underparts very pale ash-grey; the lower breast and abdomen can sometimes have a pinkish wash. Mantle and wings smoky-grey, each feather edged with black, producing a scaly appearance. Bare skin around the eye reddish, iris orange-red. Bill yellow, legs and feet dark purplish-red.
SEXES Alike. **IMM** Crown cinnamon-buff, feathers of underparts have minute blackish speckling and the feathers of the tertials, innerwing-coverts and undertail-coverts are edged with cinnamon. **HABITAT** Breeds in montane forest from 500 to at least 1550 m but foraging birds can be found at any altitude down to sea level. **STATUS** Endemic to the Solomons, where it is known from Bougainville, Kulambangra, Vangunu, Guadalcanal and Malaita islands. Moderately common on Kulambangra, uncommon elsewhere. **CALL** Short pigeon-like 'coooorr', uttered when in feeding groups.

CHESTNUT-BELLIED
IMPERIAL-PIGEON

BAKER'S
IMPERIAL-PIGEON

NEW CALEDONIAN
IMPERIAL-PIGEON

PALE
MOUNTAIN-PIGEON

FINSCH'S PYGMY-PARROT *Micropsitta finschii* 8–10 cm

A tiny green parrot with a short spine-tipped tail, usually observed in flight or feeding on lichen on treetrunks and branches.
ADULT MALE Plumage mostly green, with slightly paler underparts, chin bluish, centre of abdomen orange-red and tail blue. Some races lack orange-red centre to abdomen and have a blue patch on hind-crown. **ADULT FEMALE** Similar, but the chin is pink and lacks orange-red on the abdomen. **HABITAT** Found in primary forest of the lowlands and hill country up to an altitude of 750 m. **STATUS** Found throughout the Solomons, where the species is fairly common. **CALL** High pitched 'zeet', often repeated two or three times in quick succession.

RED-BREASTED PYGMY-PARROT *Micropsitta bruijnii* 8–9 cm

A tiny parrot with a short spine-tipped tail, usually observed in flight or feeding on lichen on treetrunks and branches.
ADULT MALE Unmistakable, with bright red underparts, dark blue nape and tail and buffy-pink cheek patches. **ADULT FEMALE** Plumage mostly green with dark blue crown and tail, pinkish cheek patch and yellowish-green underparts. **HABITAT** Montane forest and forest edge, normally above 750 m. **STATUS** Occurs only in Bougainville, Guadalcanal and Kulambangra islands in the Solomons, where it is local and scarce. **CALL** Shrill, penetrating 'tseet-tseet'.

SINGING PARROT *Geoffroyus heteroclitus* 23–25 cm

A medium-sized green parrot with a fairly short rounded tail.
ADULT MALE Mostly green with dull yellow head and greyish-mauve collar encircling the neck; a reddish-brown patch on the median wing-coverts; upper mandible pale yellow. **ADULT FEMALE** Similar, but head bluish-grey and upper mandible dark grey. **HABITAT** Forest and forest edge, partially cleared areas and gardens in the lowlands and hills. Often perches in the exposed branches of tall trees. **STATUS** Found throughout the Solomons, where it is moderately common. **CALL** Musical 'kreel-kreel-kreel'.

DUCORP'S COCKATOO *Cacatua ducorpsii* 31–35 cm

Unmistakable, the only species of cockatoo in the region. A large white parrot with a short tail and small erectile crest. Feathers of head with pink base, undersurface of wings and tail washed with yellow, bare blue skin around the eye.
SEXES Alike. **HABITAT** Lowland forest, cleared areas and gardens. **STATUS** Endemic to the Solomons, found throughout the islands with the exception of Makira. The species is common and widespread. **CALL** A harsh 'errk-errk'.

ECLECTUS PARROT *Eclectus roratus* 32 cm

Large robust parrot with a short tail. Exhibits extreme sexual dimorphism.
ADULT MALE Mostly green with red flanks and underwing, blue bend in wing, blackish-grey undertail with yellowish tip; upper mandible orange. **ADULT FEMALE** Mostly red, brownish-red on back and wings, blue on upper mantle, bend of wing, lower breast and abdomen; black bill. **HABITAT** Primary lowland forest, forest edge, partially cleared areas and occasionally gardens. **STATUS** Locally common throughout the Solomons, usually found in pairs. **CALL** Harsh screeching 'krraach-kraak'.

FINSCH'S PYGMY-PARROT

finschii

nanina
male

male

female

**RED-BREASTED
PYGMY-PARROT**

female

male

female

male

**SINGING
PARROT**

male

**DUCORP'S
COCKATOO**

male

female

**ECLECTUS
PARROT**

RED-FRONTED PARAKEET *Cyanoramphus novaezelandiae* 26–28 cm

Slender, long-tailed, green parakeet. Green above, yellowish-green below. Forehead, crown, a small patch behind the eye plus one on each side of the rump bright red, outer webs of flight feathers blue.
SEXES Alike. **HABITAT** Inhabits areas of dense primary forest. **STATUS** Found throughout mainland New Caledonia in undisturbed forest, but most recent sightings are from the southern part of the island. This unobtrusive parakeet is uncommon, localised in distribution and declining in numbers. **CALL** In flight, or when alarmed, birds give a repetitive 'kek-kek-kek-kek-kek'; when feeding, they produce a constant musical chatter.

HORNED PARAKEET *Eunymphicus cornutus* 32–35 cm

Slender, long-tailed, green parakeet, easily identified by conspicuous long crest. Plumage mostly green, earcoverts and hindneck dull yellowish, forehead and forepart of crown red; face black. Has a crest of two long black feathers tipped with chestnut. The Uvea Island race differs in lacking the yellowish on the head, has a narrow row of red feathers on the centre of the forehead and forecrown and a crest of six green feathers.
SEXES Alike. **HABITAT** Inhabits dense primary forest from sea level to the mountains; particularly fond of Kauri Pines. **STATUS** Endemic to New Caledonia, where it is found throughout the mainland and on the island of Uvea in the Loyalty Islands. The bird is now uncommon, localised and declining in numbers. It is seriously threatened by the continued clearing of native forest, and widespread trapping of birds to be kept as pets. **CALL** A raucous 'ko-kot'; when feeding, a peculiar chuckling sound is uttered.

CARDINAL LORY *Chalcopsitta cardinalis* 30–31 cm

Unmistakable. Plumage mostly red, darker more brownish-red on back and wings, feathers of underparts edged with buffy-yellow, producing a slightly scalloped appearance.
SEXES Alike. **HABITAT** Primary lowland and hill forests, particularly fond of coastal coconut plantations. **STATUS** Abundant throughout most of the Solomons, but rare on Makira. **CALL** A harsh, rasping 'zheet-zheet', similar to the call of Rainbow Lorikeet, but louder and harsher.

RAINBOW LORIKEET *Trichoglossus haematodus* 25–27 cm

Slender, long-tailed, strikingly coloured lorikeet. Head dark violet-blue, yellowish-green hindneck collar, upperparts and tail bright green, breast orange-red, feathers narrowly edged with black, giving a scaly appearance. Lower abdomen and undertail-coverts green, variably marked with yellow.
SEXES Alike. **HABITAT** Found in most types of wooded habitat, mainly in the lowlands although also in mountain forest. Is particularly fond of coastal coconut plantations. **STATUS** Abundant throughout the region. **CALL** Loud harsh shrieks, also twitters softly when feeding.

YELLOW-BIBBED LORY *Lorius chlorocercus* 28 cm

A medium-sized, colourful, short-tailed parrot. Plumage mostly red, top of head and a small patch on each side of the neck black, wings and lower half of tail green, a narrow yellow band across the upper breast. Violet thighs, and lower half of undertail dusky yellow.
SEXES Alike. **HABITAT** Found in primary forest and secondary growth at all altitudes. **STATUS** Endemic to the eastern Solomon Islands of Savo, Guadalcanal, Malaita, Ugi, Makira and Rennell, where the bird is moderately common. **CALL** A shrieking 'chu-er-wee'.

RED-FRONTED PARAKEET

CARDINAL LORY

mainland

Loyalty Is

HORNED PARAKEET

RAINBOW LORIKEET

YELLOW-BIBBED LORY

PALM LORIKEET *Charmosyna palmarum* 15–17 cm

The only small, slender, narrow-tailed, mostly green parrot in Vanuatu, Santa Cruz and Banks islands.
ADULT MALE Almost entirely green, paler and more yellowish on the underparts. Chin and feathers around base of bill are red, the mantle has a slight olive-brown wash, feathers on the undertail are narrowly tipped with yellow. **ADULT FEMALE** Less red on the chin and around the base of the bill, sometimes absent altogether; lacks olive-brown on mantle. **HABITAT** Montane forest, mainly above 1000 m. **STATUS** Endemic to Vanuatu, Santa Cruz and Banks islands, the population fluctuates but the bird is normally fairly common above 1000 m. **CALL** During flight a short, high-pitched 'tswit-tswit'; when feeding, produces a constant twittering.

MEEK'S LORIKEET *Charmosyna meeki* 16 cm

The only small, slender, narrow-tailed, mostly green parrot in the Solomons. Almost entirely green, with yellowish wash to the underparts and underwing-coverts; crown dull greyish-blue, narrow band of olive-brown on the mantle; underside of tail bright yellow.
SEXES Alike. **HABITAT** Mainly a bird of the foothill and mountain forests between 300 m and 1500 m, but can be seen occasionally at lower elevations in large flowering trees. **STATUS** Endemic to the islands of Bougainville, Isabel, Kulambangra, Guadalcanal and Malaita in the Solomon Islands, where it is uncommon and localised. **CALL** A high-pitched, short squeak.

RED-FLANKED LORIKEET *Charmosyna placentis* 15–16 cm

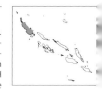

A small, slender, narrow-tailed lorikeet, with diagnostic facial streaking and conspicuous red flanks on the male.
ADULT MALE Mostly green; forecrown and underparts yellowish green, throat and sides of face red, ear-coverts streaked with violet-blue, underwing-coverts, flanks and sides of breast red, undertail yellow, patterned with red and black. **ADULT FEMALE** Similar to male but lacks yellowish forecrown and red on throat, sides of face, flanks and sides of breast. Ear-coverts boldly streaked with yellow. **HABITAT** Coastal coconut plantations and secondary growth of the lowlands. **STATUS** Found on Nissan and Bougainville islands in the Solomons, where the bird is plentiful. **CALL** A short, shrill 'seeet' screech.

NEW CALEDONIAN LORIKEET *Charmosyna diadema* 19 cm

The only small, slender, narrow-tailed, mostly green parrot in New Caledonia.
ADULT MALE Undescribed. **ADULT FEMALE** Mostly green, crown violet-blue, cheeks and throat yellowish, vent red, undertail yellow. **HABITAT** Montane forest. **STATUS** Presumed extinct. Endemic to mainland New Caledonia, where it is known from only two female specimens, collected before 1860. There are a few claimed sightings this century and persistent rumours that birds still occur in mountain forests in the north of the island. **CALL** Unknown.

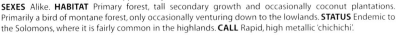

DUCHESS LORIKEET *Charmosyna margarethae* 20 cm

A small parrot with a long pointed tail. Mostly red except for dark green wings, back and undertail-coverts, the rump and uppertail-coverts golden-olive, hindcrown black; broad yellow band across breast bordered above and below with black. The yellow breast-band combines as a narrow band across the mantle, bordered above with a narrow black line; tail red, tipped with yellow.
SEXES Alike. **HABITAT** Primary forest, tall secondary growth and occasionally coconut plantations. Primarily a bird of montane forest, only occasionally venturing down to the lowlands. **STATUS** Endemic to the Solomons, where it is fairly common in the highlands. **CALL** Rapid, high metallic 'chichichi'.

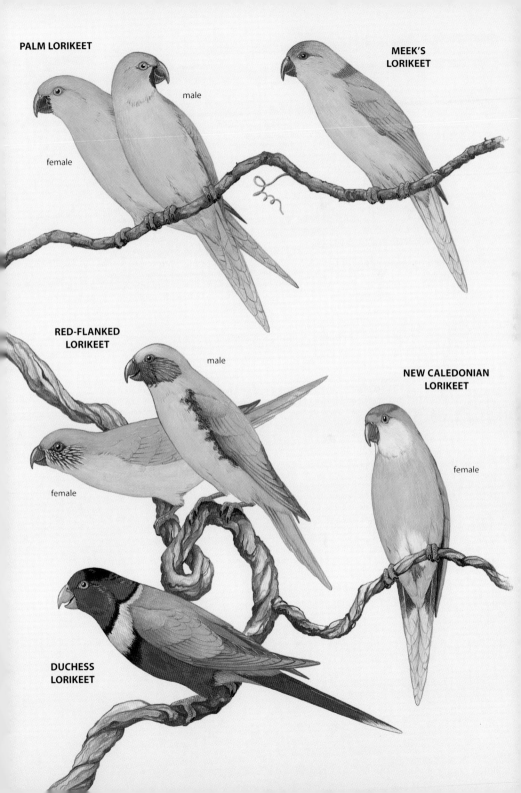

PALM LORIKEET

MEEK'S LORIKEET

male

female

RED-FLANKED LORIKEET

male

NEW CALEDONIAN LORIKEET

female

female

DUCHESS LORIKEET

ORIENTAL CUCKOO *Cuculus saturatus* 30–32 cm

A large falcon-like cuckoo; the female is polymorphic.
ADULT: Grey morph, upperparts, head and upper breast grey, lower breast and abdomen white, boldly barred with dark grey. Tail long and graduated, undertail dark grey with white partial barring. Rare female hepatic morph: the grey in the much commoner grey morph is replaced by rufous and the entire bird is barred with black. **IMM** Upperparts brownish with pale greyish-white edging to feathers and buffy spotting on the wings. Underparts white with buff wash, heavily barred dark brown. **HABITAT** Forest edge, partially cleared areas and gardens. **STATUS** Rare summer visitor to the Solomons. **CALL** Normally silent on wintering grounds.

BRUSH CUCKOO *Cacomantis variolosus* 21–24 cm

A medium-sized, rather plain coloured cuckoo, with a squarish tail, grey-white eyering and noticeably upright stance. More often heard than seen. Head and throat grey, upperparts brownish-olive, tail dark brown with indistinct white notches; breast greyish-buff shading to buffish on the lower abdomen, undertail grey with broad white tips to the feathers.
SEXES Alike. **IMM** Upperparts brown with bold buff spotting and barring, underparts white with a buffy wash and heavy brown barring. **HABITAT** Forest, forest edge and secondary growth, from sea level to 1200 m. **STATUS** Fairly common resident throughout the Solomons. **CALL** This highly vocal species has a very distinctive call, which it utters both day and night, comprising seven to eight shrill, mournful notes, on a descending scale and increasing in volume.

FAN-TAILED CUCKOO *Cacomantis flabelliformis* 24–25 cm

A medium-sized, slender cuckoo, with conspicuous white barring on the long, rounded tail. Somewhat similar to Brush Cuckoo, but can be separated by its slightly larger size, longer more rounded tail, bright orange-yellow eyering, cinnamon-buff rather than greyish-buff abdomen. Has considerably more white barring on the undertail and a very different call.
SEXES Alike. **IMM** Brown upperparts, with buff edging to most feathers, underparts creamy-white, finely barred grey, brown and buff. **HABITAT** Primary and secondary forest and gardens, both in the lowlands and highlands. **STATUS** An uncommon breeding bird in New Caledonia and very uncommon breeding bird in Vanuatu; birds winter in small numbers throughout the Solomons. **CALL** Fast, mournful trill, descending the scale, and repeated several times.

SHINING BRONZE-CUCKOO *Chrysococcyx lucidus* 16–18 cm

By far the smallest cuckoo in the region, the size of a honeyeater. Unmistakable. Crown to mantle coppery-bronze, remainder of upperparts bronze-green with marked greenish iridescence. Outer tail feathers banded black and white. Underparts white, with fine bronze-brown barring on the face and throat and much broader barring on the abdomen. The race C. l. lucidus, lacks the coppery-bronze head, has small white flecks on the forehead and the barring is bronze-green.
SEXES Alike. **IMM** Upperparts shiny bronze-green, underparts whitish with faint barring on the flanks. **HABITAT** Primary and secondary forest, forest edge, scrub and gardens. **STATUS** The race *C. l. plagosus*, is a fairly common resident in New Caledonia, Vanuatu, Santa Cruz, Banks Islands and the islands of Rennell and Bellona in the Solomons. The race *C. l. lucidus* breeds in New Zealand and winters in good numbers throughout the Solomons. **CALL** A series of double notes 'fee-ee-fee-ee...', with an upward inflection on the second note.

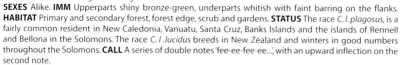

female
hepatic morph

imm

**ORIENTAL
CUCKOO**

imm

**BRUSH
CUCKOO**

imm

imm

**FAN-TAILED
CUCKOO**

plagosus

lucidus

imm

SHINING BRONZE-CUCKOO

AUSTRALIAN KOEL *Eudynamys cyanocephala* 40–46 cm

This shy bird is often difficult to see in the dense leafy trees and shrubs it frequents. The female is particularly shy, and the bird is usually located by its call.
ADULT MALE Glossy black with blue-grey bill, dark red eye and long, rounded tail. **ADULT FEMALE** Head and neck glossy black, remainder of upperparts brown with a bronze-green wash, feathers indistinctly barred and tipped white, flight feathers and tail heavily barred brown and white. Buffy-white malar streak above black throat stripe, rest of underparts whitish with a slight buff wash and fine brown barring. Bill horn coloured, eye dark red. **IMM** Similar to female but head rufous. **HABITAT** Rainforest; particularly fond of dense vegetation along river courses, occasionally in mangrove. **STATUS** Widespread but uncommon resident throughout the Solomons. **CALL** A shrill repeated 'coo-ee', the second note shorter and rising. It begins softly and gradually becomes louder until it is given at full volume, rising to a frantic climax and abruptly breaking off.

LONG-TAILED KOEL *Eudynamys taitensis* 38–41 cm

A large, long-tailed cuckoo which is shy and skulking, preferring to keep well concealed amongst the larger branches of the forest canopy. Upperparts dark brown, completely barred and spotted with russet, combined with white spotting on head, mantle and wings, barring particularly evident on the tail. Underparts buffy-white, with heavy dark brown streaks.
SEXES Alike. **IMM** Similar to adult but the white spots on the mantle and wings are larger and much more conspicuous; underparts rufous. **HABITAT** Found in any habitat on small islands, but prefers dense scrub and low trees. **STATUS** Widespread but uncommon winter visitor throughout the Solomons, from breeding grounds in New Zealand; mainly found on smaller, outer islands. **CALL** Usually silent on wintering grounds, but occasionally produces a harsh chatter.

BUFF-HEADED COUCAL *Centropus milo* 63–68 cm

A very large cuckoo with a heavy bill, short rounded wings and very long, broad tail. Clumsy and noisy as it walks, hops and bounds awkwardly up sloping branches to the forest canopy. Head, mantle and entire underparts pale buff, lower back, wings and tail black with a purplish-blue gloss. Dark red eye, blackish-grey bill and bluish-grey legs and feet. In the race C. m. milo, the belly and lower abdomen are black.
SEXES Alike. **IMM** Head, mantle and throat sooty black; wings, back and tail dark brown, heavily barred with black. Underparts dirty buff, mottled with black. **HABITAT** Primary forest and taller secondary growth, from the lowlands to the mountains. **STATUS** Endemic to the central Solomons, where it varies from being fairly common to uncommon. **CALL** A loud, raucous 'na-ow'.

AUSTRALIAN KOEL

female

imm

male

LONG-TAILED KOEL

imm

imm

albidiventris

BUFF-HEADED COUCAL

AUSTRALASIAN GRASS OWL *Tyto longimembris* 33–36 cm

A richly coloured owl with distinctive heart-shaped facial disc and very long, slender legs. Upperparts and wings are mottled chocolate-brown and orange-rufous, finely speckled with black and white. Facial disc buff coloured. The underparts are buffy-white with scattered small dark spots. Similar to Barn Owl, but upperparts much darker, lacks pale grey and yellowish-buff tones. Underparts buffy-white, rather than snowy-white; buff, not white, facial disk; has smaller eyes and noticeably longer legs. In flight, the legs protrude well beyond the tail.
SEXES Alike. **HABITAT** Tall grasslands and swampy areas. **STATUS** Occurs in New Caledonia where it is rare and very localised. **CALL** Loud hissing scream.

BARN OWL *Tyto alba* 31–34 cm

A very pale coloured owl with distinctive heart-shaped facial disc, long, slender legs and upright stance. Upperparts and wings are mottled pale grey and yellowish-buff, finely speckled with black and white. Facial disc white. The underparts are snowy-white, with scattered small dark spots. Somewhat similar to Australasian Grass Owl, but upperparts much paler, lacks chocolate-brown and orangey tones; underparts paler, snowy-white, rather than buffy. Has much paler facial disc, larger eyes and noticeably shorter legs; in flight, legs protrude only a little beyond the tail.
SEXES Alike. **HABITAT** Forest edge, plantations and farmland. **STATUS** A common bird in New Caledonia and Vanuatu. In the Solomons the bird is very localised and rare, may be increasing in numbers as areas of deforestation increase. **CALL** Main call a loud, drawn-out rasping 'shreeee'.

FEARFUL OWL *Nesasio solomonensis* 38–41 cm

A large owl with a powerful bill and large powerful talons. Crown and upperparts densely mottled rufous and dark brown. Underparts deep brownish-yellow, with narrow blackish shaft streaks, which are most pronounced on the breast.
SEXES Alike. **HABITAT** Primary and taller secondary forest, from the lowlands to the hills. **STATUS** Endemic to the islands of Bougainville, Choiseul and Isabel in the northern Solomons, where the bird is little known and rare. Local people say it feeds mainly on possums. **CALL** A long drawn-out 'hoo', rising in pitch at the end.

SOLOMON HAWK-OWL *Ninox jacquinoti* 25–30 cm

A medium-sized, extremely variable, short-tailed owl, which looks different on each island of the Solomons. Upperparts vary from chocolate-brown to rusty-brown. In some races the head is heavily spotted with small buffy-white spots and the mantle, wings and tail are profusely barred with rufous-buff. Other races have scattered white spots on the head and narrow, well-spaced, white bars on the tail. Those races with barred upperparts have creamy-buff underparts, with fine brown barring on the breast. Those with plain coloured upperparts have either white underparts, heavily barred with broad dark brown bars, or rufous-brown underparts, narrowly barred with dark brown.
SEXES Alike. **HABITAT** Primary and tall secondary forest. **STATUS** Endemic to the Solomons, found throughout all the islands with the exception of the New Georgia Group and Rennell Island. Widespread and common from sea level to the mountains. **CALL** A long low tremulous note, often repeated.

AUSTRALASIAN
GRASS OWL

BARN OWL

Isabel

FEARFUL
OWL

SOLOMON
HAWK-OWL

Guadalcanal

Makira

MARBLED FROGMOUTH *Podargus ocellatus* 33–38 cm

The large size, large flattened head, broad heavy bill, long tail and cryptic coloration make this nocturnal species unmistakable. Has bright orange iris, a buffy-white eyebrow and long, banded erect bristles above the bill; rest of plumage brown to rufous-brown with varying amounts of white markings on the scapulars and wing-coverts. The underparts are paler, delicately marbled with white, grey and buff.
SEXES Alike. **HABITAT** Primary forest, forest edge and tall secondary growth. **STATUS** Occurs on the islands of Bougainville, Choiseul and Isabel in the northern Solomons. The species is rare and little known. **CALL** Soft, repeated 'koo-loo'.

NEW CALEDONIAN OWLET-NIGHTJAR *Aegotheles savesi* 28 cm

The small size, large dark eyes, broad bill, long tail and cryptic coloration make this nocturnal species unmistakable. Has broad blackish head markings, which start above the eye, circle around the side of the face and return under the eye. Also has a pale hindcollar, bordered above and below with blackish. Upperparts and tail dark grey, freckled and barred light brown and buff. Paler, greyer underparts, are finely barred darker.
SEXES Alike. **HABITAT** Forest and forest edge. **STATUS** Endemic to New Caledonia, where it is presumed extinct; known from only one specimen, collected in 1880. **CALL** Unknown.

WHITE-THROATED NIGHTJAR *Eurostopodus mystacalis* 28–33 cm

The only nightjar in the region, a ground-frequenting, cryptically coloured, nocturnal bird, with long narrow wings and tail. Can sometimes be flushed from the forest floor in daylight hours, the flight is silent and has a peculiar stiff, jerky wingbeat. Upperparts blackish, irregularly mottled with grey and brown; dark grey tail, with well-spaced indistinct black barring. Wings blackish, heavily spotted with brown, grey and buff. Centre of throat blackish, with conspicuous white crescent on each side of throat; remaining underparts blackish, profusely barred dark brown.
SEXES Alike. **HABITAT** Forest edge, scrub and sandy beaches. **STATUS** Occurs in the northern Solomon Islands of Bougainville, Shortland Group, New Georgia Group and Isabel, where it is usually found on or near the beach. A 1939 sighting from New Caledonia was probably a vagrant from Australia. **CALL** An accelerating series of 'kook-kook-kook' notes.

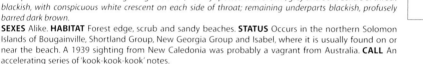

MARBLED FROGMOUTH

NEW CALEDONIAN OWLET-NIGHTJAR

WHITE-THROATED NIGHTJAR

MOUSTACHED TREESWIFT *Hemiprocne mystacea* 28–30 cm

The most slender and streamlined swift in the region. A beautifully plumaged bird with long, thin wings, slender body and very long, deeply forked tail. Head, wings and tail glossy blue-black; rest of plumage grey, with a whitish lower abdomen. Small chestnut patch on ear-coverts, bordered by conspicuous long white eyebrow stripe and long white moustachial plume. In flight, shows an indistinct pale band on underside of inner flight feathers.
SEXES Alike. **IMM** Mottled and barred with brown. **HABITAT** Mainly a bird of the lowlands, where it frequents the forest edge and is particularly fond of partially cleared areas where some trees remain. Often seen perched on the top of dead snags. **STATUS** Widespread and fairly common in suitable habitat throughout the Solomons. **CALL** The usual call, mainly given in flight, is a high-pitched, down-slurred 'kiiee', which has been likened to the sound produced by a plastic toy animal when squeezed.

FORK-TAILED SWIFT *Apus pacificus* 17–19 cm

A very typical swift with slender, cigar-shaped body and long, tapering, scythe-shaped wings and mostly blackish plumage. However, the combination of a pale throat, a long, deeply forked tail and broad white rump are diagnostic of this species. In flight, the tail is often held closed, appearing long and pointed.
SEXES Alike. **HABITAT** Aerial; over open country, forests and towns. **STATUS** This species, a long-distance migrant, breeding in Eastern Asia, Japan and Taiwan, has not officially been recorded in the region, but it is highly likely that strays do occur. Winters in New Guinea, Australia and occasionally New Zealand. Movements of this species are strongly influenced by weather patterns, with flocks often preceding thunderstorms. A slight shift to the east during migration would bring them into this region. **CALL** Shrill, excited twittering and a long, subdued buzzing note.

WHITE-THROATED NEEDLETAIL *Hirundapus caudacutus* 19–21 cm

A large, powerfully built swift, with a rather robust body and diagnostic short, square tail, tipped with short spines which are difficult to see in the field. Has distinctive combination of white throat and undertail-coverts; remaining underparts dark brown. The upperparts are darker, with a glossy green wash, a noticeably paler back and rump and a small white patch on the scapulars.
SEXES Alike. **HABITAT** Aerial; over forests, cleared areas, farmland, lakes and towns. **STATUS** Like the preceding species, this species has not officially been recorded in the region, but it is highly likely that strays do occur. This species is a long-distance migrant, breeding in the Himalayas, Eastern Asia, Japan and Taiwan. Winters mainly in New Guinea and Australia, regularly occurs in New Zealand and stragglers have occurred in Fiji. Movements of this species are strongly influenced by weather patterns, and flocks often precede thunderstorms. A slight shift to the east during migration would bring them into this region. **CALL** Rapid, high-pitched chattering.

**MOUSTACHED
TREESWIFT**

FORK-TAILED SWIFT

**WHITE-THROATED
NEEDLETAIL**

GLOSSY SWIFTLET *Collocalia esculenta* 9–10 cm

This is the smallest and by far the commonest swiftlet throughout the region. Differs from all other swiftlets by having glossy blue-black upperparts and contrasting white lower breast and belly. The colour of the rump is variable; some races have a pure white rump, others have only a small amount of white, and in others the entire upperparts are glossy blue-black, with no white on the rump.
SEXES Alike. **IMM** Duller, less glossy. **HABITAT** Aerial feeder over grasslands and forest, forest clearings and streams, mainly at lower elevations. Nests in caves. **STATUS** Abundant breeding bird throughout the region. **CALL** Tight, grating cheeps.

WHITE-RUMPED SWIFTLET *Collocalia spodiopygius* 11–12 cm

A dull-coloured swiftlet, with a whitish rump. Uniformly dull black-brown above with a pale off-white band on the rump, greyish below. Differs from Glossy Swiftlet by the dull colour and the absence of white on the underparts and from Uniform and Mayr's Swiftlets by the whitish bar on the rump.
SEXES Alike. **HABITAT** Aerial feeder over forest, cleared areas, beaches and gorges, from sea level to 1600 m. Nests in caves. **STATUS** An uncommon resident in the Solomons and New Caledonia. In Vanuatu the species was widespread and common up until the turn of the century, since when a steady decline has occurred and there have been no observations in Vanuatu for the last 20 years. **CALL** High-pitched squealing and short twittering notes.

UNIFORM SWIFTLET *Collocalia vanikorensis* 12–13 cm

A nondescript dark grey swiftlet, slightly darker above than below. Upperparts uniformly blackish-grey. Throat silvery-grey, rest of underparts dark grey. Differs from Glossy and White-rumped Swiftlets by its uniformly dark plumage. Very similar to slightly larger Mayr's Swiftlet, but differs in smaller-headed appearance, slightly paler plumage, uniformly coloured upperparts without rump band and the silvery-grey on the throat which does not extend onto the breast.
SEXES Alike. **HABITAT** Aerial feeder over forest, cleared areas, rivers and villages, from the lowlands up to 1000 m. Nests in caves. **STATUS** Common throughout the Solomons and fairly common in Vanuatu. **CALL** A soft twittering sound.

MAYR'S SWIFTLET *Collocalia orientalis* 14 cm

A large, large-headed, dusky swiftlet of forested mountains. Upperparts uniformly dull black, with a slight dark bluish gloss and contrasting grey band across the rump. Chin and upper throat greyish-brown, lower throat and breast silvery-grey, rest of underparts uniformly sooty-brown. Very similar to slightly smaller Uniform Swiftlet, but differing in larger-headed appearance, slightly darker plumage, grey rump band and the silvery-grey throat coloration extending onto the breast.
SEXES Alike. **HABITAT** Aerial feeder over forested mountains mainly above 1300 m. **STATUS** Found on the islands of Bougainville and Guadalcanal in the Solomons, where it is virtually unknown. Only one specimen and one or two sight records. **CALL** Unknown.

GLOSSY
SWIFTLET

WHITE-RUMPED
SWIFTLET

MAYR'S SWIFTLET

UNIFORM SWIFTLET

COMMON KINGFISHER *Alcedo atthis* 16 cm

A small, river-frequenting kingfisher, short-tailed and easily identified by orange-buff underparts. Entire upperparts and sides of head dark blue, with pale bluish-purple tips to feathers of crown and wing-coverts, indistinct orange-buff streak on ear-coverts, merging with buffy-white stripe on the side of the neck. Throat buffy-white, remainder of underparts orange-buff.
SEXES Alike. **HABITAT** Slow-flowing lowland streams and rivers. **STATUS** A fairly common resident, throughout the Solomons. **CALL** A high-pitched, whistled 'chee', repeated two or three times, usually given in flight.

LITTLE KINGFISHER *Alcedo pusilla* 11 cm

A tiny, short-tailed, unobtrusive, seldom seen kingfisher. Confined to waterside vegetation; spends long periods perched motionless on low branches overhanging water. Uniform blue upperparts and white underparts, with a white spot above the beak in front of the eye and on sides of neck. Race A. p. richardsi has a complete blue breast-band, and race A. p. bouganvillei has an incomplete, blue-speckled breast-band.
SEXES Alike. **HABITAT** A bird of coasts and coastal lowlands, inhabiting wooded pools, forest streams and mangroves. **STATUS** Uncommon resident occurring on most Solomon islands. **CALL** A high-pitched, repeated 'tsee', given in flight.

VARIABLE KINGFISHER *Ceyx lepidus* 13–14 cm

A tiny, short-tailed, unobtrusive and shy, forest-inhabiting kingfisher. A very variable kingfisher, no fewer than five races occur in the Solomons alone. Upperparts vary from bluish-green to bluish-purple, with head and wing-coverts spangled pale blue, middle of the back, rump and uppertail-coverts are paler blue. The loral spot, neck blaze and underparts are always the same colour and vary from yellowish-orange to white. Easily separated from somewhat similar Little Kingfisher by yellowish-orange underparts, when present, and the complete lack of any breast-band.
SEXES Alike. **HABITAT** A bird of the forest interior, sometimes close to forest pools or small forest streams, but often found far from water. **STATUS** A fairly common resident throughout the Solomons. **CALL** A shrill, wheezy 'tzeeip', usually given in flight.

FOREST KINGFISHER *Todirhamphus macleayii* 20 cm

A medium-sized, forest-inhabiting kingfisher; in flight shows diagnostic white patch in centre of wing.
ADULT MALE Top of head and nape deep blue, very conspicuous white loral spot in front of eye, broad black stripe from bill to ear-coverts, bordered below by complete white collar, upperparts deep blue. Australian birds have a greenish tinge on the back, underparts uniformly white. **ADULT FEMALE** Has only partial collar, not extending as far as the nape. **IMM** White areas scalloped with buff. **HABITAT** Forest, woodland and farmland. **STATUS** One recent observation on Kulambangra Island in the Solomons. It is resident in New Ireland and large numbers of migrants from Australia winter in New Guinea and New Britain. **CALL** Harsh 'krree-krree-kree'.

ULTRAMARINE KINGFISHER *Todirhamphus leucopygius* 18 cm

A medium-sized, forest-inhabiting kingfisher, with diagnostic pale purple rump and undertail-coverts.
ADULT MALE Top of head and nape deep ultramarine blue, broad black stripe from bill to ear-coverts extending as a narrow line onto the nape, bordered below by complete white collar. Upperparts deep ultramarine blue, back white and rump pale purple. Underparts pure white, with pale purple undertail-coverts. **ADULT FEMALE** Similar to male but lacks white back. **IMM** White areas scalloped with buff. **HABITAT** Primary forest, tall secondary growth and partially cleared areas. **STATUS** Endemic to the Solomons, where it is uncommon to fairly common, from sea level to 700 m. **CALL** A rattling, repeated 'kakatakakata-ta'.

COMMON KINGFISHER

LITTLE KINGFISHER

richardsi

bougainvillei

gentiana

VARIABLE KINGFISHER

meeki

FOREST KINGFISHER

imm

male

female

ULTRAMARINE KINGFISHER

imm

CHESTNUT-BELLIED KINGFISHER *Todirhamphus farquhari* 20 cm

This medium-sized, forest-inhabiting kingfisher is unmistakable, the only blue-backed kingfisher in its range.
ADULT MALE Top of head and nape dark blue, washed with black, conspicuous white loral spot in front of eye, broad black stripe from bill to nape, bordered below by complete white collar. Upperparts dark blue, throat and underparts white, breast yellowish-orange shading to rich chestnut on belly and undertail-coverts. **ADULT FEMALE** Similar to male but has a white patch on the lower abdomen. **HABITAT** Strictly a bird of the forest interior, above 200 m. **STATUS** Endemic to the islands of Espiritú Santo, Malo and Melekula in central Vanuatu, where it is fairly common. **CALL** Shrill, high-pitched, 'teck', repeated as much as 20 or more times, starting slowly, before simultaneously speeding up and rising in pitch.

COLLARED KINGFISHER *Todirhamphus chloris* 24–27 cm

This medium-sized kingfisher is extremely variable, with no fewer than 12 races found throughout the region, some of which closely resemble Sacred Kingfisher. Can be separated by combination of larger size, larger, heavier bill, rufous superciliary stripe, when present, and white underparts in most races. Upperparts bluish-green or olive-green, with conspicuous buff loral spot in front of eye or long buffy to rufous superciliary stripe and complete white, buff or pale orange collar and underparts.
SEXES Alike. **IMM** Duller, with dark scalloping. **HABITAT** Found in a wide variety of habitats including mangroves, creeks, coconut groves, coastal scrub, cultivated uplands, secondary growth and rainforest. **STATUS** Common resident throughout the Solomons and Vanuatu, from sea level to the highest mountains. **CALL** A harsh 'chack-chack-chack', descending the scale.

BEACH KINGFISHER *Todirhamphus saurophaga* 28–30 cm

This large coastal kingfisher is unmistakable, with its long, heavy bill, bluish-green back, bright blue rump, wings and tail and very conspicuous white head and underparts.
SEXES Alike. **HABITAT** Mangroves, beaches, rocky coasts and headlands, tidal reefs and small offshore islands. **STATUS** Found throughout the Solomons, where it is rather uncommon, always within 100 metres of the shoreline. **CALL** Similar to Collared Kingfisher but a louder and deeper 'kee-kee-kee'.

SACRED KINGFISHER *Todirhamphus sanctus* 20–22 cm

This medium-sized, forest-inhabiting kingfisher, closely resembles Collared Kingfisher, but differs in combination of smaller size, small, less heavy bill and usually has much buffier underparts. Top of head and nape dark green, conspicuous buff loral spot in front of eye, broad black stripe from bill to nape, bordered below by complete buffy-white collar. Upperparts dark green to bluish-green, underparts white, variably washed with buff, deepening in colour on the flanks, belly and undertail-coverts.
SEXES Alike. **IMM** White areas scalloped with buff. **HABITAT** Forest clearings, farmland, swamps and tidal mudflats. Found from sea level to 1700 m. **STATUS** Uncommon resident in Guadalcanal and Makira islands in the eastern Solomons and abundant resident in New Caledonia. Large numbers of birds from Australia winter throughout the Solomons during the months of April to October. **CALL** A nasal 'keenk-keenk-keenk-keenk'.

MOUSTACHED KINGFISHER *Actenoides bougainvillei* 32 cm

Unmistakable. Large, orange kingfisher, with a bright red bill.
ADULT MALE Bluish-purple moustachial streak and narrow line from behind the eye to nape, dark ultramarine wings and tail and pale azure-blue rump. Head, mantle and entire underparts orange-rufous. **ADULT FEMALE** Similar to male, but the back is olive-green. **HABITAT** Primary forest, from the lowlands to the mountains, at least to 1350 m. **STATUS** Endemic to the islands of Bougainville and Guadalcanal in the Solomons. Almost unknown; a dozen specimens were collected in southern Bougainville in the late 1930s, but has not been recorded there since. Three specimens were collected from Guadalcanal during the 1940s and 1950s and it was not seen again until observed by David Gibbs in 1994 at 1325 m, in the central highlands. **CALL** A loud, ringing laugh, 'ko-ko-ko'.

CHESTNUT-BELLIED KINGFISHER

male

female

COLLARED KINGFISHER

alberti

BEACH KINGFISHER

juliae

SACRED KINGFISHER

imm

COLLARED KINGFISHER

MOUSTACHED KINGFISHER

female

male

BLUE-TAILED BEE-EATER *Merops philippinus* 23–26 cm excluding tail streamers

Similar to Rainbow Bee-eater, but differs in larger size, bronzy-green not rufous-chestnut crown and nape, chestnut, not yellowish-buff throat, lacks black throat band and rufous on upperwing. Has blue not blackish tail and the tail streamers taper to a point.
SEXES Alike. **IMM** Duller and the tail streamers are shorter. **HABITAT** Open country, lowland grassland, air strips and cultivated areas. **STATUS** A breeding and locally nomadic species in New Guinea and the Bismarck Archipelago, so strays could easily occur in the northern Solomons. **CALL** A pleasant, rolling 'diririp', much lower-pitched than the call of the Rainbow Bee-eater.

RAINBOW BEE-EATER *Merops ornatus* 19–21 cm excluding tail streamers

Similar to Blue-tailed Bee-eater, but differs in smaller size, conspicuous rufous-chestnut not bronzy-green crown and nape, yellowish-buff not chestnut throat. Has black throat band and rufous patch on the upperwing, a blackish not blue tail and the tail streamers are very narrow with a spatulate tip.
SEXES Alike. **IMM** Duller and lacks tail-streamers. **HABITAT** Lowland forest clearings. **STATUS** Breeds in Australia, the main wintering grounds are in New Guinea, but small numbers winter on Nissan Island and in the northern Solomons. **CALL** Rolling 'pirr-pirr', much higher-pitched than the call of the Blue-tailed Bee-eater.

DOLLARBIRD *Eurystomus orientalis* 28–30 cm

A medium-sized, stocky bird, with a large dark brown head, a short, broad red bill, short neck, greenish-blue body and very short legs. In flight, shows diagnostic pale crescent-shaped 'dollar' marks at the base of the primaries. Dollarbirds spend much of their time perched conspicuously on the top of tall dead trees.
SEXES Alike. **IMM** Duller, more brownish-grey, with grey bill and legs. **HABITAT** Forest edge, secondary growth, partially cleared areas and cultivated land. **STATUS** Widespread and common resident throughout the Solomons. **CALL** Loud, harsh, rasping 'chak', repeated after a few seconds.

BLYTH'S HORNBILL *Aceros plicatus* 75–90 cm

Unmistakable. A huge black bird, with a white tail, an immensely large bill and remarkably loud flight.
ADULT MALE Bill horn coloured, with reddish-brown base; bare skin around the eye and throat is bluish-white. Iris is reddish-brown, head, neck and upper breast buffy-orange, back, wings and abdomen black, with a slight greenish gloss, the tail is white. **ADULT FEMALE** Smaller than the male and the entire plumage is black, except for the white tail. **IMM** Surprisingly, resemble adult males. **HABITAT** Primary forest, from sea level to 1500 m. **STATUS** Uncommon resident throughout the Solomons, with the exception of Makira Island, where it does not occur. **CALL** Deep grunts and honking noises.

BLACK-FACED PITTA *Pitta anerythra* 15 cm

The only pitta in the region. A plump ground-frequenting bird, with a large head, short rounded wings, very short tail and long legs. Head, chin, cheeks and nape black, remainder of upperparts rich green, with an iridescent turquoise-blue shoulder-patch; the race on Isabel Island has a chestnut crown. Underparts vary from buff to pale brown.
SEXES Alike. **IMM** Duller. **HABITAT** Primary forest, forest edge and overgrown gardens. **STATUS** Endemic to the islands of Bougainville, Choiseul and Isabel in the Solomons. Occurs from sea level to 600 m. Generally uncommon, but at times can be locally common, it is always shy and retiring. **CALL** High-pitched, two-syllabled 'kree-kree-o', given mainly in the early morning, late evening and during periods of rain.

BLUE-TAILED BEE-EATER

RAINBOW BEE-EATER

imm

imm

BLUE-TAILED BEE-EATER

imm

DOLLARBIRD

BLYTH'S HORNBILL

female

male

BLACK-FACED PITTA

BOUGAINVILLE HONEYEATER *Stresemannia bougainvillei* 17–18 cm

This medium-sized nondescript honeyeater is easily identified in its limited range, by its lack of distinguishing features, drab olive plumage and long, slightly down-curved bill.
ADULT MALE Upperparts uniform brownish-olive, underparts lighter and greyer. **ADULT FEMALE** Smaller and duller, with indistinct streaking on crown. **IMM** Similar to adult female. **HABITAT** Montane forest, from 700 m, to at least 1950 m. **STATUS** Endemic to the mountains of Bougainville Island in the Solomons, where it is scarce and little known. **CALL** A short series of mellow whistled notes, the first note rising and falling, the following notes also alternately rising and falling. There is also a harsh, raspy 'chht-chht'.

DARK-BROWN HONEYEATER *Lichmera incana* 13–17 cm

Another medium-sized, nondescript honeyeater, easily identified in its limited range by its drab olive plumage, diagnostic silvery-grey ear-coverts and long, slightly down-curved bill. Crown dark brownish-grey, ear-coverts silvery-grey, back, wings and tail, olive-brown. Throat ashy grey, remainder of underparts dirty-grey washed with olive.
SEXES Similar, except in size, the male noticeably larger. **IMM** Paler and lacks silver-grey on ear-coverts. **HABITAT** Almost all habitats from sea level to the lower hills in primary forest, forest edge, secondary growth, mangroves, scrub, gardens, villages and towns. **STATUS** Endemic to Vanuatu and New Caledonia, where it is common and widespread. **CALL** A loud, harsh 'tchoo-tchoo-tchoo'.

GUADALCANAL HONEYEATER *Guadalcanaria inexpectata* 18–20 cm

This medium-sized honeyeater is easily identified in its limited range by the diagnostic bright yellow throat plumes and conspicuous dark streaking on the throat and breast. Upperparts slate-grey, wings and tail yellowish-olive. Throat whitish, remainder of underparts pale grey, with dark grey streaking on throat and upper breast. Ear-coverts silvery-grey, bordered below by conspicuous bright yellow throat plumes.
SEXES Similar, except in size, the male noticeably larger. **HABITAT** Montane forest, particularly moss forest between 1450 and 1560 m. **STATUS** A little-known endemic, which is confined to the mountains of Guadalcanal Island in the Solomons. **CALL** Loud, musical 'per-twee, per-twee'.

NEW CALEDONIAN FRIARBIRD *Philemon diemenensis* 27–30 cm

The only large, brownish honeyeater, occurring in New Caledonia. Upperparts brown; top of head, wings and tail washed with slate-grey, with a noticeable dark moustachial streak. Underparts buffy-brown, with conspicuous long, pointed, silvery-white feathers on the throat and upper breast.
SEXES Similar, except in size, the male noticeably larger. **IMM** Paler, more washed-out and lacks silvery-white throat and breast feathers. **HABITAT** Primary forest, secondary growth and gardens. **STATUS** Endemic to New Caledonia, where the bird is fairly common. **CALL** Loud, varied squeaks and disjointed notes.

SAN CRISTOBAL MELIDECTES *Melidectes sclateri* 25–28 cm

The only large honeyeater occurring on the island of Makira. Upperparts greenish-brown, rump and tail rufous-brown. Head brownish, with conspicuous buffy-white streaking, very distinct, blackish moustachial streak which runs from the base of the bill, below the ear-coverts and onto the nape. Underparts pale yellowish-buff, overlaid with narrow, indistinct black streaking on the throat and breast.
SEXES Alike. **HABITAT** Primary forest and forest edge. Although found from the lowlands to the highlands, it is much commoner in the mountains. **STATUS** Endemic to the Island of Makira in the Solomons, where the bird is fairly common. **CALL** Loud, raucous, repeated series of nasal slurs.

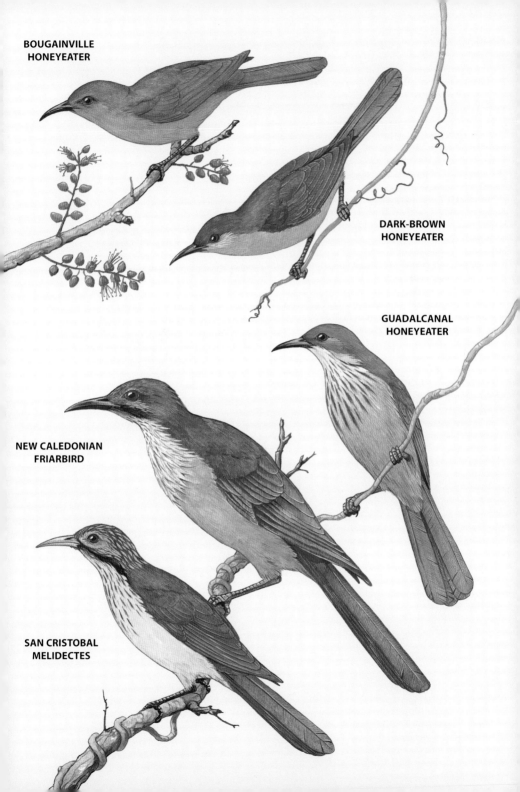

BOUGAINVILLE
HONEYEATER

DARK-BROWN
HONEYEATER

GUADALCANAL
HONEYEATER

NEW CALEDONIAN
FRIARBIRD

SAN CRISTOBAL
MELIDECTES

NEW CALEDONIAN MYZOMELA *Myzomela caledonica* 11–12 cm

The only myzomela occurring on mainland New Caledonia and nearby Isle of Pines.
ADULT MALE Head, back, rump and breast scarlet, lores, wings and tail black. Flanks and belly off-white. **ADULT FEMALE** Greyish-brown above, with a slight olive wash, greyish-buff below, whiter on the belly. **IMM** Similar to female. **HABITAT** Found in flowering trees and shrubs along forest edge, plantations and gardens. **STATUS** Endemic to mainland New Caledonia and the Isle of Pines, where it is common and widespread. **CALL** A loud, clear, tinkling song.

CARDINAL MYZOMELA *Myzomela cardinalis* 11–12 cm

The only scarlet and black myzomela occurring throughout its range.
ADULT MALE Head, back, rump and breast scarlet, lores, wings, belly and tail black. The belly is scarlet in the Solomons race. **ADULT FEMALE** Mostly greyish-olive, with dull, ill-defined patches of scarlet on head, back and rump. **IMM** Similar to female. **HABITAT** Primary forest, forest edge, secondary growth, plantations, gardens and mangroves. **STATUS** Occurs on Makira and Rennell islands in the Solomons, Santa Cruz Islands, Vanuatu and the Loyalty Islands. Common throughout its range. **CALL** A high-pitched 'tzwee' and a melodious, jingling song.

SCARLET-NAPED MYZOMELA *Myzomela lafargei* 12–13 cm

The only myzomela that occurs throughout its range.
ADULT MALE Head, throat and upperparts black, with a conspicuous large red patch on the hindneck. Underparts uniformly mustard. **ADULT FEMALE** Upperparts greyish-olive, underparts yellowish-olive, with greyish wash to the throat. **IMM** Similar to female, but males have small patch of red on the crown. **HABITAT** Primary forest, forest edge, secondary growth and mangroves. **STATUS** Endemic to the northern Solomon islands of Buka, Bougainville, the Shortland group, Choiseul and Isabel, where the bird is common. **CALL** Loud 'chtt'.

YELLOW-VENTED MYZOMELA *Myzomela eichhorni* 12–13 cm

The only myzomela that occurs throughout its range. Entire upperparts olive-grey, wing feathers edged with yellowish-olive, rump and throat scarlet. Entire underparts olive-yellow.
SEXES Alike. **HABITAT** Primary forest and tall secondary growth. **STATUS** Endemic to the central Solomon islands of Gizo, Kulambangra, New Georgia, Vangunu, Rendova, Tetipari, Ganonga, Vella Lavella and Bagga, where the species ranges from common to fairly common. **CALL** A sharp 'zeeeet-zeeeet', uttered in flight when chasing other birds.

BLACK-HEADED MYZOMELA *Myzomela melanocephala* 12–13 cm

The only myzomela that occurs throughout its range. Mostly pale olive-brown all over, with darker wings and tail and a conspicuous black face mask.
SEXES Alike. **HABITAT** Primary forest, tall secondary growth and gardens. **STATUS** Endemic to the central Solomon Islands of Florida, Savo and Guadalcanal, where the bird is common. **CALL** Short, sharp, high-pitched 'chiip-chiip', uttered when excited.

RED-BELLIED MYZOMELA *Myzomela malaitae* 12–13 cm

The only myzomela occurring on the island of Malaita.
ADULT MALE Head, upperparts and vent greyish-black, rump and underparts scarlet. **ADULT FEMALE** Upperparts pale olive-brown, underparts pale yellowish-olive, scarlet rump, throat and forecrown. **IMM** Similar to female. **HABITAT** Primary forest of the foothills and mountains. **STATUS** Endemic to the island of Malaita in the Solomons, where it is uncommon. **CALL** High-pitched 'see-see', usually given in flight.

SOOTY MYZOMELA *Myzomela tristrami* 11–12 cm

Unmistakable. The entire plumage is glossy sooty black.
SEXES Alike. **IMM** Dull black above; grey, mottled with black below. **HABITAT** Primary forest, secondary growth, plantations and gardens. **STATUS** An abundant endemic in the easternmost Solomon islands of Makira, Ugi and Santa Anna. **CALL** Wheezy, upslurred 'tweeest', uttered when excited.

NEW CALEDONIAN MYZOMELA

male

female

CARDINAL MYZOMELA

male

female

SCARLET-NAPED MYZOMELA

male

female

YELLOW-VENTED MYZOMELA

BLACK-HEADED MYZOMELA

RED-BELLIED MYZOMELA

male

female

SOOTY MYZOMELA

CROW HONEYEATER *Gymnomyza aubryana* 36–41 cm

A very large, distinctive, all black honeyeater, with a long graduated tail. Conspicuous area of bare facial skin below the eye varies from reddish-orange to bright yellow. Has long down-curved bill, the upper mandible greyish and the lower mandible yellow. Legs and feet are also yellow.
SEXES Similar, except in size, the male noticeably larger. **HABITAT** Dense, primary forest. **STATUS** Endemic to mainland New Caledonia; this shy, retiring species is now confined almost exclusively to the southern part of the island in the River Blue National Park and the Dzumac Mountains. **CALL** A loud prolonged, ringing note.

BARRED HONEYEATER *Phylidonyris undulata* 17–20 cm

A medium-sized, distinctivly marked honeyeater. Brown above; crown, sides of head, nape and mantle scalloped with white. Underparts greyish-white, with a small area of dense blackish barring from chin to upper throat; breast and flanks heavily scalloped brownish.
SEXES Similar, except in size, the male noticeably larger. **IMM** Similar to the adult, but scalloping on the underparts is very indistinct, barely visible. **HABITAT** Primary forest, tall secondary growth and gardens. **STATUS** Endemic to New Caledonia, where it is most common in the lower hills and mountain forests. **CALL** A flute-like whistle.

NEW HEBRIDES HONEYEATER *Phylidonyris notabilis* 18–21 cm

A distinctive, medium-sized honeyeater, with a longish, down-curved black bill. Forehead, crown and face black, narrowly streaked with white, more heavily streaked above the eye, forming a distinct eyestripe; rest of upperparts rufous-brown. Underparts whitish, sides of breast and flanks have numerous long, thin brownish streaks.
SEXES Similar, except in size, the male noticeably larger. **IMM** Duller and lacks streaking on the abdomen. **HABITAT** Primary forest and tall secondary growth. **STATUS** Endemic to Vanuatu and Banks Island, occurring from the lowlands to the mountains, but it is much commoner in the mountain forests. **CALL** A prolonged 'toowyt'; the rich and varied song is a pleasant series of flute-like notes and whistles, rendered as 'teewee-twytwyttee'.

NOISY MINER *Manorina melanocephala* 24–27 cm

A large, pugnacious and distinctive honeyeater. Forehead and lores white, black crown extends in an arc through and behind the eye and onto the cheeks, with a patch of bright yellow bare skin behind the eye; rest of upperparts greyish, finely barred with white, slightly darker on back and wings, wing feathers edged with olive-yellow. Underparts pale grey, with indistinct greyish-black barring, progressively becoming whiter on belly and undertail-coverts.
SEXES Similar, except in size, males noticeably larger. **IMM** Similar to adults, but have brownish wash on back, rump and wings. **HABITAT** Open woodland, plantations and gardens. **STATUS** In the 1950s this species was introduced from Australia to the Three Sisters Islands, off the coast of Makira. No recent sightings, but isolated birds may still occur. **CALL** Harsh, piping 'pwee-pwee-pwee'.

CROW HONEYEATER

BARRED
HONEYEATER

NEW HEBRIDES
HONEYEATER

NOISY MINER

FAN-TAILED GERYGONE *Gerygone flavolateralis* 10 cm

A rather tame small, drab warbler, dark above and lighter below.
ADULT MALE Head olive-grey with a narrow, incomplete white eyering, wings and tail olive-brown, with subterminal white spots on the lateral tail feathers. Throat whitish-grey, flanks and abdomen lemon-yellow, rest of underparts pale grey. **ADULT FEMALE** Similar to male but paler. **IMM** The entire underparts are yellowish. **HABITAT** Primary forest, secondary growth, scrub and gardens. **STATUS** Endemic to Rennell Island in the southern Solomons, Vanuatu, mainland New Caledonia and the island of Mare in the Loyalty Islands. It is a common and confiding bird throughout its range. **CALL** A three-syllable soft twitter 'twee-wee-heet', repeated rapidly and incessantly throughout the day.

SCARLET ROBIN *Petroica multicolor* 11–13 cm

A small, rounded robin, with diagnostic scarlet breast and white wing patch.
ADULT MALE Jet-black above, with conspicuous white forehead patch, bold white wing-stripe and white edges to tail. Has a black throat and very striking scarlet breast; remainder of underparts greyish-white. **ADULT FEMALE** Pale brownish above, whitish forehead spot and wing-stripe, with reddish wash on breast; remainder of underparts off white **IMM** Similar to female, but lacks reddish wash on breast. **HABITAT** Primary forest, partially cleared areas, plantations and gardens. **STATUS** Occurs on the islands of Bougainville, Kulambangra and Makira in the Solomons and Vanuatu, where it is an uncommon bird, primarily of montane forest. **CALL** A faint, yet far carrying twitter 'teet-teet', frequently repeated. The song is a pleasant whistling trill 'twee-weeweeweet'.

YELLOW-BELLIED ROBIN *Eopsaltria flaviventris* 14–15 cm

A distinctive yellow-bellied robin of the forest floor. Dark brownish-grey above, washed with olive on back, wings and tail. Throat and centre of breast whitish, with indistinct greyish streaking on the sides and lower breast; remainder of underparts bright lemon-yellow.
SEXES Alike. **IMM** Brownish, with indistinct paler streaking, particularly on the crown. **HABITAT** Primary forest, from the lowlands to the mountains. **STATUS** Endemic to New Caledonia, where it is fairly common. **CALL** Monotonous, high-pitched 'chip-chip-chaa'.

**FAN-TAILED
GERYGONE**

male

imm

female

**SCARLET
ROBIN**

female

male

imm

**YELLOW-BELLIED
ROBIN**

imm

GOLDEN WHISTLER *Pachycephala pectoralis* 17–18 cm

An extremely variable whistler, as 12 races occur throughout the Solomon Islands alone, however, no other whistler occurs in the forested lowlands and lower mountains of the Solomons.
ADULT MALE All male Golden Whistlers have a black head; most races have a bright yellow nape band, upperparts vary from olive-green to sooty black with a greyish-black tail. All birds have either a pure white or golden-yellow throat, and in almost all races this is bordered below by a black breast-band. All have golden-yellow underparts. **ADULT FEMALE** Upperparts vary from grey-brown to olive-green, wings vary from grey-brown to cinnamon, underparts vary from olive-grey to yellow. **IMM** Similar to female. **HABITAT** Primary forest, secondary growth, plantations and gardens. **STATUS** A common bird, found throughout the Solomons, Vanuatu and the Loyalty Islands of New Caledonia. **CALL** A loud, whistling 'chee-chee-chee-tu-whit'.

BLACK-TAILED WHISTLER *Pachycephala melanura* 15–16 cm

The white throat of this species easily separates it from the Golden Whistler, in areas where the two species overlap, the Golden Whistler has a yellow throat.
ADULT MALE Black head, with a bright yellow nape band, a yellowish-olive mantle, back and rump. Wing feathers are edged with grey and the tail is jet-black. Has a prominent white throat, bordered below by a broad black breast-band; remainder of underparts bright orangey-yellow. **ADULT FEMALE** Greyish head, mantle, throat and upper breast; remaining upperparts uniform olive, abdomen bright golden-yellow. **IMM** Similar to female. **HABITAT** Mangrove swamps and adjacent vegetation, particularly fond of small offshore islands. **STATUS** A resident breeding species on Nissan, Buka and other small islands off the coast of Bougainville, and one or two coastal locations on Bougainville Island in the Solomons. **CALL** A loud, whistling 'whit-weet-woat-woat-weet'.

NEW CALEDONIAN WHISTLER *Pachycephala caledonica* 15 cm

A distinctively plumaged whistler which inhabits primary forests of New Caledonia.
ADULT MALE Greyish head merging into brownish-olive back, wings and tail. Pure white throat, bordered below by a narrow black breast-band, remainder of underparts ochraceous-orange. **ADULT FEMALE** Uniform olive-brown above, pale greyish-brown below, with a whitish throat. **IMM** Similar to female, but has prominent rufous markings on wing feathers. **HABITAT** Found only in undisturbed primary forest, from sea level to the mountains. **STATUS** A fairly common endemic of mainland New Caledonia and the nearby Isle of Pines. **CALL** Loud, rising 'whit-whit-whit'.

MOUNTAIN WHISTLER *Pachycephala implicata* 16 cm

A shy and unobtrusive inhabitant of montane forests on the islands of Bougainville and Guadalcanal in the Solomons. The two island subspecies are very distinct.
Guadalcanal form **ADULT MALE** Black head, olive back and wings, black tail, throat ash-grey, breast and abdomen yellowish-olive. **ADULT FEMALE** Grey head, brownish-olive back, whitish throat and yellow breast and abdomen. **IMM** Similar to female. Bougainville form **ADULT MALE** Black head, throat, upper breast and tail; back golden-olive, abdomen dull yellow, with a slight olive wash. **ADULT FEMALE** Grey head, greenish-olive back, whitish throat with a greyish wash, abdomen yellow. **IMM** Similar to female. **HABITAT** Montane forest from 1200 m to at least 1750 m. Often frequents the understorey, where difficult to observe. **STATUS** Uncommon endemic in the mountains of Bougainville and Guadalcanal islands in the Solomons. **CALL** A loud whistling 'whee-whee-whee-whee-whip'.

RUFOUS WHISTLER *Pachycephala rufiventris* 15–16 cm

A distinctively plumaged whistler of open, disturbed forest and grasslands.
ADULT MALE Head and upperparts grey; black facial mask extends as broad breast-band, encircling the white throat; remainder of underparts pale rufous. **ADULT FEMALE** Brownish-grey upperparts, whitish throat; remainder of underparts pale buff, with dark streaking on the throat and breast. **IMM** Similar to female. **HABITAT** Open forest, disturbed areas and savanna grasslands with scattered trees. **STATUS** Fairly common on mainland New Caledonia. **CALL** Loud, ringing 'joey-joey-joey', ending with a whipcrack-like 'ee-chong'.

New Caledonia
Vanuatu

Malaita

female
Nth Solomons

Nth Solomons

**GOLDEN
WHISTLER**

Ranongga
Vella Lavella

male

female

BLACK-TAILED WHISTLER

female

male

**NEW
CALEDONIAN
WHISTLER**

Guadalcanal

female

male

**RUFOUS
WHISTLER**

male

male

female

**MOUNTAIN
WHISTLER**

female

Bougainville

WILLIE-WAGTAIL *Rhipidura leucophrys* 20 cm

A large, confiding, black and white flycatcher of open country, with diagnostic white eyebrow. Head, throat, sides of breast and entire upperparts glossy black, with a prominent white eyebrow and narrow indistinct white whisker line; remainder of underparts white. Unlike other fantails, the tail is cocked and waved but not fanned. **SEXES** Alike. **IMM** Duller, with buffy eyebrows and buffy edges to feathers, particularly on the wing-coverts. **HABITAT** Any type of open country, grasslands, clearings, parkland and gardens. **STATUS** A common bird throughout the Solomons. **CALL** A compilation of squeaky whistled notes, characterised as 'sweet-pretty-creature'; often sings during the night.

WHITE-WINGED FANTAIL *Rhipidura cockerelli* 16–17 cm

This extremely variable species is the only black and white fantail in the Solomons and is often found in mixed-species foraging flocks. In all races the entire upperparts are black or greyish-black, with either a conspicuous white wing patch or white edging on the secondaries. All birds show varying amounts of black on the throat and upper breast and most races have elongated white spotting on the breast. Could possibly be confused with Black-and-white and Kulambangra Monarchs, but these species differ in having prominent white cheek patches, white wing patches on the wing-coverts, not the secondaries, and the outer tail feathers are broadly tipped white. **SEXES** Alike. **HABITAT** Primary forest, from sea level to 1300 m; prefers open areas within the forest. **STATUS** A fairly common Solomon Islands endemic found on most major island groups, with the exception of Makira and Rennell islands. **CALL** A series of high-pitched twittering notes.

DUSKY FANTAIL *Rhipidura tenebrosa* 16–17 cm

This shy and inconspicuous species, is the only fantail in the region with the combination of a dark abdomen and a tail which is broadly edged with white at the tip. The plumage is predominantly brownish-grey, with the abdomen slightly paler and the head blackish. Has a narrow indistinct white line under the eye, the chin and upper throat are mottled white. There are two prominent rufous wingbars, formed by the tips of the wing-coverts, and the tail feathers are broadly edged with white. Found amongst mixed-species foraging flocks; stays inside the forest, not venturing into clearings and remains close to the forest floor, wings drooped and tail spread, occasionally performing acrobatic flutters and loops in pursuit of flying insects. **SEXES** Alike. **HABITAT** Undisturbed montane forest. **STATUS** An uncommon and little-known endemic of the mountains of Makira Island in the Solomons. **CALL** A continuous, melodious, upward-spiralling trill.

WILLIE-WAGTAIL

imm

Choiseul
Isabel

**WHITE-WINGED
FANTAIL**

New Georgia
group

Vella Lavella
Ranongga

DUSKY FANTAIL

GREY FANTAIL *Rhipidura fuliginosa* 15–16 cm

A very tame and confiding fantail, always active and restless, with a permanently fanned tail. Upperparts slate-grey, slightly darker on the head; tail is blackish, narrowly tipped with white and the wings have two indistinct white wingbars. Has a short white eyestripe and a small indistinct white line behind the eye. The white throat is separated from the buff-coloured abdomen by a narrow black breast-band.
SEXES Alike. **HABITAT** Found in both primary and secondary forest; prefers clearings in the forest, forest edge, parks and gardens. **STATUS** A common and conspicuous bird of both lowlands and mountains throughout New Caledonia and Vanuatu. In the Solomons it is confined to the mountains of Makira Island, where it is also common. **CALL** A high-pitched and melodious song, made up of short twittering notes, and constantly repeated.

BROWN FANTAIL *Rhipidura drownei* 14 cm

Tame and inquisitive within its restricted range, there are two rather distinct races. Head greyish-brown with a narrow white line above the eye, the Guadalcanal race also has a narrow white line behind the eye. Back, wings and tail dusky greyish-brown. Throat white; breast and abdomen greyish-buff with indistinct white streaking. The Bougainville race has a rufous wash to the wings, tail and abdomen.
SEXES Alike. **HABITAT** Montane forest above 800 m. **STATUS** A little-known endemic, of mountain forests on the islands of Bougainville and Guadalcanal in the Solomons. **CALL** Has a rather soft, high-pitched song, which has a tinkling quality to it.

RENNELL FANTAIL *Rhipidura rennelliana* 14–15 cm

This very tame species is the only fantail occuring on Rennell Island. The entire upperparts are drab brownish-grey, with a short broad eyestripe. Tail is slightly darker, almost blackish, with white edges to the outer tail feathers. Underparts are smoky-grey, the throat and centre of the breast mottled off-white.
SEXES Alike. **HABITAT** Primary forest, forest edge, reluctant to enter open areas, preferring the shade of the forest. **STATUS** A very common bird, endemic to Rennell Island in the Solomons. **CALL** High-pitched, up-slurred rasp, uttered when excited.

STREAKED FANTAIL *Rhipidura spilodera* 17 cm

A very active and restless fantail, easily recognised by the distinctive triangular-shaped black spotting on the breast. Entire upperparts dark grey with a broad white eyestripe and a narrower white line behind the eye. The throat and breast are white with conspicuous and diagnostic triangular-shaped black spotting on the breast; remainder of the underparts brownish-grey.
SEXES Alike. **HABITAT** Frequents true forest and forest edge, avoiding open areas. **STATUS** A common endemic of the forests of Vanuatu and New Caledonia. **CALL** A melodious, short twittering song, consisting of four or more distinct syllables.

MALAITA FANTAIL *Rhipidura malaitae* 16 cm

A uniformly coloured, virtually unknown fantail, endemic to the higher mountains of Malaita Island. The upperparts are uniformly pale rust in colour, with slightly paler, more ochraceous underparts.
SEXES Alike. **HABITAT** Montane forest above 900 m. **STATUS** A virtually unknown fantail, endemic to the mountains of Malaita Island in the Solomons. **CALL** Unknown.

RUFOUS FANTAIL *Rhipidura rufifrons* 15 cm

A tame and confiding fantail, with conspicuous rufous forehead, rump and base of tail, with tail permanently fanned. Forehead bright rufous, crown, hindneck and upper back brown, with a slight rufous wash; becoming bright rufous-orange on the lower back, rump and base of the tail; remainder of tail black, edged with greyish-white. Upper throat white, lower throat and upper breast black dappled with white; remainder of the underparts fawn.
SEXES Alike. **HABITAT** Primary forest, forest edge, secondary growth and occasionally mangroves. **STATUS** A fairly common bird throughout the Solomons, from sea level to the mountains. **CALL** A series of high-pitched notes 'zeee-zeee-ze-ze-ze-ze-ze'.

GREY
FANTAIL

BROWN
FANTAIL

RENNELL
FANTAIL

STREAKED
FANTAIL

MALAITA
FANTAIL

RUFOUS
FANTAIL

VANIKORO MONARCH *Mayrornis schistaceus* 15 cm

A small, slender, mainly grey flycatcher, restricted in distribution to one small island in the Santa Cruz group of islands. Upper and underparts wholly slate-grey, the underparts slightly paler. The black tail has small but quite obvious white tips to several of the outer tail feathers.
SEXES Alike. **HABITAT** Primary forest and taller secondary forest. **STATUS** This little-known flycatcher is endemic to the island of Vanikoro, in the Santa Cruz Islands, where it is common from sea level to at least 270 m. **CALL** Typical monarch flycatcher musical rasp.

ISLAND MONARCH *Monarcha cinerascens* 17 cm

A large, grey flycatcher with a pale rufous belly, mainly confined to small offshore islands. Closely resembles the immature plumage of Black-faced and White-capped Monarchs. Differs from immature Black-faced Monarch by lacking the pale area around the eye and has slightly paler underparts; differs from immature White-capped Monarch by paler underparts which extend only to the upper breast, not reaching the lower throat.
SEXES Alike. **IMM** Similar to adults but with brownish edges to wing feathers. **HABITAT** Largely confined to forest and scrub on small offshore islands. Very occasionally it can be found in lowland rainforest on larger islands, as is the case on the islands of Kulambangra and New Georgia. **STATUS** Fairly common in the right habitat throughout the northern Solomons. **CALL** A harsh scolding chatter and a compilation of squeaky, twittering notes like a cuckoo-shrike.

BLACK-FACED MONARCH *Monarcha melanopsis* 16–19 cm

A distinctive, robust flycatcher, with prominent black forehead, lores and throat patch; remainder of the upperparts uniform blue-grey, with a paler grey to off-white area around the eye. Breast blue-grey, sharply demarcated from the rich rufous abdomen. In immature plumage separated from Island Monarch by pale area around the eye and slightly darker underparts.
SEXES Alike. **IMM** Lacks black markings on face and throat; wings and tail are brownish and the bill is blackish with a horn-coloured base to the lower mandible. **HABITAT** Primary forest, secondary growth and gardens. **STATUS** Breeds along the east coast of Australia and winters in northeastern Australia and southeastern New Guinea and its offshore islands. Although not officially recorded from the region, strays could easily occur anywhere in the northern Solomons. **CALL** Loud, whistling, nasal call, of two short notes, also a pleasant, rising then falling 'whee-chu', repeated several times.

VANIKORO MONARCH

ISLAND MONARCH

imm

BLACK-FACED MONARCH

BOUGAINVILLE MONARCH *Monarcha erythrostictus* 17 cm

A glossy blue-black flycatcher, with chestnut underparts and diagnostic face markings.
ADULT MALE Head, neck, upper breast, back, wings and tail glossy blue-black, with a prominent white crescent in front of the eye; lower breast and abdomen chestnut. **ADULT FEMALE** Similar to male but the face marking in front of the eye is more rounded and is rufous in colour. **HABITAT** Mainly primary forest, occasionally straying into nearby secondary growth. Found from sea level to the mountains. **STATUS** Endemic to the island of Bougainville in the northern Solomons, where it is common. **CALL** Rapidly repeated, scolding rasps.

CHESTNUT-BELLIED MONARCH *Monarcha castaneiventris* 17 cm

A glossy blue-black flycatcher, with chestnut underparts, lacking any facial or head markings. Excluding the Ugi Island race, all races have head, neck, upper breast, back, wings and tail glossy blue-black, lower breast and abdomen chestnut. The Ugi Island race is entirely glossy blue-black.
SEXES Alike. **HABITAT** Primary forest and taller secondary forest, found from sea level to the highest mountains. **STATUS** A common endemic of the islands of Choiseul, Isabel, Florida, Guadalcanal, Malaita, Makira, and Ugi in the Solomons. **CALL** Similar to closely related Bougainville and White-capped Monarchs, a series of harsh, buzzing, rasps.

WHITE-CAPPED MONARCH *Monarcha richardsii* 17 cm

A stunningly plumaged flycatcher, with diagnostic pure white crown and hindneck. Forehead, lores, sides of face, upper breast, back, wings and tail glossy blue-black; conspicuous snow white crown and hindneck, lower breast and abdomen chestnut.
SEXES Alike. **IMM** Closely resembles Island Monarch, but differs in having darker underparts, which extend to the lower throat, pale rufous extending only to the upper breast in the Island Monarch. **HABITAT** Primary forest from sea level to at least 800 m. **STATUS** A fairly common bird, endemic to the New Georgia group of islands in the central Solomons. **CALL** Flycatcher-like chatter and a two-note whistle, firstly ascending then descending.

BOUGAINVILLE MONARCH

female

male

CHESTNUT-BELLIED MONARCH

Ugi

imm

WHITE-CAPPED MONARCH

BUFF-BELLIED MONARCH *Neolalage banksiana* 15 cm

A small, striking, glossy black, white and yellow flycatcher which often holds its tail in a cocked position.
ADULT MALE Crown, back and tail black, wings black with a broad golden-yellow wing patch and golden-yellow edging to some of the primaries. Upper throat, face and sides of head white, with a narrow black breast-band; remainder of the abdomen, rump and tip of the tail golden-yellow. **ADULT FEMALE** Similar to the male, but slightly duller. **IMM** Similar pattern to adult, but duller; the black is browner, the white is greyish and the golden-yellow is whitish. **HABITAT** Interior of primary forest, very rarely venturing out into the open. Occurs from sea level to 1200 m. **STATUS** Fairly common endemic throughout Vanuatu. **CALL** A low, mournful, drawn-out trill 'treereeeeee'.

BLACK-AND-WHITE MONARCH *Monarcha barbatus* 15 cm

A small, distinctive, black and white flycatcher, with a conspicuous white wing patch, geographically separated from the closely related Kulambangra and White-collared Monarchs. Upperparts and throat bluish-black, with prominent white wing patch and white tips to several of the outer tail-feathers. White on cheek patch, sides of throat and abdomen.
SEXES Alike. **IMM** Upperparts and sides of head brown, throat greyish, remainder of underparts rufous, underside of tail is broadly tipped with white. **HABITAT** Primary forest and taller secondary forest, from sea level to 1300 m. **STATUS** Endemic to the islands of Bougainville, Choiseul, Isabel, Florida and Guadalcanal in the Solomons, where it is fairly common. **CALL** Harsh churring notes, often repeated.

KULAMBANGRA MONARCH *Monarcha browni* 15 cm

A small, variable, black and white flycatcher, with a conspicuous white wing patch, geographically separated from the closely related Black-and-white and White-collared Monarchs. Upperparts and throat bluish-black, with prominent white wing patch and extensive white tips to several of the outer tail-feathers, white cheek patch and abdomen. Birds on Vella Lavella Island lack the white wing patch.
SEXES Alike. **IMM** Upperparts and sides of head brown, throat greyish, remainder of underparts rufous, underside of tail is broadly tipped with white. **HABITAT** Primary forest and taller secondary forest, occurring from sea level to the mountains. **STATUS** Endemic to the New Georgia group of islands in the central Solomons, where it is fairly common. **CALL** Harsh, repeated chatter.

WHITE-COLLARED MONARCH *Monarcha viduus* 15 cm

A small, distinctive, black and white flycatcher, with conspicuous white hindcollar, geographically separated from the closely related Black-and-white and Kulambangra Monarchs. Upperparts and throat bluish-black, with prominent white hindcollar, broken white wing patch, white rump, broad white edge to all tail feathers, and white abdomen. The Ugi Island form has pear-shaped white mottling on the lower throat and upper breast.
SEXES Alike. **IMM** Upperparts and sides of head brown, throat greyish, remainder of underparts rufous, underside of tail is broadly tipped with white. Females and immatures of Ochre-headed Flycatcher are similar but differ in having paler underparts, greyish rather than brownish head, pale brownish, not blackish, undertail, lacking white tail tip. **HABITAT** Primary forest and taller secondary forest, occurring from sea level to the mountains. **STATUS** Endemic to the islands of Makira and Ugi in the Solomons, where it is fairly common in the lowlands becoming commoner in the mountains. **CALL** A harsh buzzing call, similar to Kulambangra Monarch.

BUFF-BELLIED MONARCH

imm

BLACK-AND-WHITE MONARCH

imm

New Georgia group

KULAMBANGRA MONARCH

Ranongga

Vella Lavella

Makira

WHITE-COLLARED MONARCH

Ugi

STEEL-BLUE FLYCATCHER *Myiagra ferrocyanea* 13–14 cm

A very active, small flycatcher, with an upright posture and characteristic habit of rapidly quivering its tail. Geographically separated from similar Ochre-headed and New Caledonian Flycatchers.
ADULT MALE Head, upper breast and entire upperparts black, with a purplish gloss; remainder of underparts white. **ADULT FEMALE** Crown, sides of head and mantle grey; back, rump, wings and tail rufous-brown, with distinct rufous edges to the primaries. Underparts whitish, some races with a pale rufous wash on the lower abdomen. **IMM** Similar to female. **HABITAT** Mainly forest, forest edge, secondary growth and partially cleared areas, occurring from sea level to at least 1500 m. **STATUS** Endemic to the Solomons, where it is a common bird on most island groups, but not found on Makira and Rennell Islands. **CALL** A drawn-out whistle 'tuuu-iii', rising at the end.

OCHRE-HEADED FLYCATCHER *Myiagra cervinicauda* 13–14 cm

A very active, small flycatcher, with a slight erectile crest and characteristic habit of rapidly quivering its tail. Geographically separated from similar Steel-blue and New Caledonian Flycatchers.
ADULT MALE Head, upper breast and entire upperparts black with a greenish-blue gloss; remainder of underparts white. **ADULT FEMALE** Crown, sides of head and hindneck grey; back, wings and tail brownish, rump and undertail fawn. **IMM** Similar to female. **HABITAT** Mainly primary forest, occasionally in taller secondary growth. An uncommon bird of lowland forests, becoming common in the mountains to at least 1600 m. **STATUS** Endemic to the island of Makira in the Solomons. **CALL** Repeated rasping 'zhay-zhay-zhay'.

NEW CALEDONIAN FLYCATCHER *Myiagra caledonica* 15–16 cm

A small, restless flycatcher, with a slight erectile crest, a very broad, flat bill and characteristic habit of rapidly quivering its tail. Geographically separated from similar Steel-blue and Ochre-headed Flycatchers.
ADULT MALE Head, upper breast and entire upperparts black with a greenish gloss, remainder of underparts white. **ADULT FEMALE** Crown, sides of head and mantle dark grey, back, wings and tail brownish. Throat and upper breast rufous-orange, remainder of underparts white. **IMM** Similar to female. **HABITAT** Prefers open woodland, plantations, secondary growth and mangroves, from sea level to the mountains. **STATUS** Occurs on Rennell Island in the Solomons and throughout Vanuatu and New Caledonia. **CALL** A short, harsh rasping 'zweat', rapidly repeated.

VANIKORO FLYCATCHER *Myiagra vanikorensis* 13–14 cm

A small, active flycatcher, with a slight erectile crest, upright stance and characteristic habit of rapidly quivering its tail. Geographically separated from similar Chestnut-bellied Monarch.
ADULT MALE Head, upper breast and entire upperparts glossy blue-black; remainder of underparts rufous-chestnut. **ADULT FEMALE** Entire upperparts dark grey, underparts rufous-orange with a whitish throat. **IMM** Similar to female. **HABITAT** Forest, forest edge, secondary scrub and open woodland. **STATUS** In this region known only from the island of Vanikoro, in the Santa Cruz group of islands. **CALL** A buzzy 'bzzuip-bzzuip'.

STEEL-BLUE FLYCATCHER

male

female

OCHRE-HEADED FLYCATCHER

male

female

NEW CALEDONIAN FLYCATCHER

female

male

VANIKORO FLYCATCHER

male

female

SOUTHERN SHRIKEBILL *Clytorhynchus pachycephaloides* 19 cm

A large drab-coloured flycatcher, with a conspicuously long, vertically compressed bill slightly hooked at the tip. Entire bird olive-brown, slightly paler below, with very obvious broad white tips on the lateral tail feathers. Birds from Vanuatu have buff-coloured underparts.
SEXES Alike. **IMM** Slightly duller. **HABITAT** Thick tangled growth, in the poorly lit interior of undisturbed primary forest, throughout both the lowlands and the highlands. **STATUS** A fairly common endemic of Vanuatu and New Caledonia. **CALL** A long drawn-out whistle.

BLACK-THROATED SHRIKEBILL *Clytorhynchus nigrogularis* 17–18 cm

A large grey and brown flycatcher, with a conspicuously long, vertically compressed bill slightly hooked at the tip.
ADULT MALE Forehead, face and throat, glossy black, surrounding a bold whitish ear-patch; crown and hindneck grey, back, wings and tail brown. Underparts whitish, washed with buff. **ADULT FEMALE** Entirely brown, slightly paler below. **IMM MALE** similar to female but has a black face and throat, an indistinct whitish ear patch and conspicuous white spotting on the black throat. **HABITAT** Prefers dense, tangled vines within mature forest. **STATUS** An uncommon bird, occurring on the Santa Cruz group of islands. **CALL** A descending, whinnying whistle and a human-like up-slurred whistle.

RENNELL SHRIKEBILL *Clytorhynchus hamlini* 19 cm

A large rufous-brown flycatcher, with a conspicuously long, vertically compressed bill slightly hooked at the tip. Uniformly rufous-brown above and cinnamon below, with a very conspicuous black mask covering the fore-head, face and throat.
SEXES Alike. **IMM** Duller, with less distinct facial mask. **HABITAT** Dense underbrush in undisturbed primary forest. **STATUS** A fairly common endemic to Rennell Island in the Solomons. **CALL** A descending mournful whistle.

SOUTHERN
SHRIKEBILL

Vanuatu

New Caledonia

imm male

BLACK-THROATED
SHRIKEBILL

female

male

RENNELL
SHRIKEBILL

SOLOMON ISLANDS DRONGO *Dicrurus solomenensis* 28–32 cm

The only all-black perching bird with a notched tail in the region. A pugnacious, forest-inhabiting bird, which is all black with a bluish iridescence, a conspicuous bright red eye, a long, curved bill and a long, slightly splayed tail.
SEXES Similar, except in size as males are a little larger. **IMM** Duller, lacks the iridescence. **HABITAT** The interior of montane forest, not venturing into open areas. Often found amongst mixed-species foraging flocks of warblers, fantails and flycatchers. **STATUS** This drongo is thought to be the same race of the Spangled Drongo *Dicrurus bracteatus*, which is widespread along the north and east coasts of Australia. The author is very familiar with this species and is of the opinion that the Solomon Islands bird should be given full species status, justified because of differences in wing length, tail shape, bill length and shape, habitat preference, behaviour and vocalisations. It is endemic to the mountainous interior of Guadalcanal and Makira islands in the Solomons. The type specimen at the British Museum (Natural History) is an adult female (no. 1884.1.19.8., collected at Wano, on Makira Island in the Solomon Islands in April 1882, by J. Stephens). **CALL** Subdued chattering and grating sounds, much softer and less varied than calls of the Spangled Drongo.

NEW CALEDONIAN CROW *Corvus moneduloides* 40–43 cm

A medium-sized black crow with an unusually shaped bill, endemic to New Caledonia, where it is the only crow. Entire plumage black with a purple and green gloss. Has a relatively short, stout bill, the culmen almost straight and the lower mandible angled upwards at the tip.
SEXES Alike. **HABITAT** Forest and open country with scattered trees. **STATUS** A fairly common bird, endemic to mainland New Caledonia, introduced to Mare Island in the Loyalty Islands Group. **CALL** A soft, rather high-pitched 'waaaw' and a high-pitched 'wa-wa'.

WHITE-BILLED CROW *Corvus woodfordi* 40–41 cm

A heavily built, short-tailed crow, with a massive white bill tipped with black. Endemic to the central Solomons, where it is the only crow. Entire plumage black with a slight greenish gloss to the upperparts; has a massive ivory-coloured bill, with a strongly arched culmen tapering to a sharp, black tip.
SEXES Alike. **HABITAT** Primary foothill forest. **STATUS** Uncommon, endemic to the central Solomon islands of Choiseul, Isabel and Guadalcanal. **CALL** High-pitched cawing 'aaw-aaw-aaw'.

BOUGAINVILLE CROW *Corvus meeki* 41 cm

A heavily-built, short-tailed crow, with a massive black bill. Endemic to the northern Solomons, where it is the only crow. Entire plumage black with a purplish gloss on the upperparts and a bluish-green gloss on the head and underparts. Has a massive black bill, with a strongly arched culmen, tapering to a sharp tip.
SEXES Alike. **HABITAT** Mainly lowland forest, but has been recorded as high as 1600 m. **STATUS** A fairly common endemic on the northern Solomon island of Bougainville and nearby small islands in the Shortland group. **CALL** Loud, raucous 'car-car-car'.

SOLOMON ISLANDS
DRONGO

NEW CALEDONIAN
CROW

WHITE-BILLED
CROW

BOUGAINVILLE
CROW

POLYNESIAN TRILLER *Lalage maculosa* 15–16 cm

The male of this species is distinguished from the similar Long-tailed Triller by having upperparts dull, not glossy black, a prominent white eyeline and a much shorter tail.
ADULT FEMALE Differs from female Long-tailed Triller in greyer upperparts, prominent brownish eyeline and much shorter tail. **IMM** Differs from Long-tailed Triller in having pale brownish upperparts with white tipped feathers and dull greyish underparts. **HABITAT** Forest, secondary growth and gardens, mainly in the lowlands. **STATUS** A common bird throughout Vanuatu and the Santa Cruz islands. **CALL** A loud 'pee-chew' and a ringing trill.

LONG-TAILED TRILLER *Lalage leucopyga* 17–18 cm

The male of this species is distinguished from the similar Polynesian Triller by having brighter, more glossy upperparts, no eyeline and a much longer tail.
ADULT FEMALE Differs from female Polynesian Triller in having much browner upperparts, no eyeline and a much longer tail. **IMM** Differs from Polynesian Triller in having underparts whitish, not dull grey. **HABITAT** Both lowland and mountain forest; commoner along the edge of the forest and in open areas. **STATUS** A common bird throughout New Caledonia, Vanuatu and the islands of Ugi and Makira in the Solomons. **CALL** A short rasping call-note and a loud melodious song 'tee-zeeia-tee-zeeia-tee-zeeia'.

WHITE-BREASTED WOODSWALLOW *Artamus leucorynchus* 15–17 cm

When perched, an unmistakable plump-bodied, black and white bird with an upright posture; diagnostic soaring flight, with rapid, stiff wing beats. Upperparts and throat dark bluish-grey, white breast and underparts sharply demarcated from bluish-grey throat, conspicuous white rump, short, thick, blue-grey bill with a slight black tip.
SEXES Alike **IMM** Brown upperparts, feathers edged with buff; creamy-buff underparts. **HABITAT** Forest clearings, forest edge, open wooded country and wetlands, mainly in the lowlands. **STATUS** Common and widespread throughout Vanuatu and New Caledonia. **CALL** A soft twittering chatter.

AUSTRALASIAN MAGPIE *Gymnorhina tibicen* 44 cm

A large conspicuous black and white ground-frequenting bird; pointed greyish-white bill with black tip.
ADULT MALE Black head, wings, underparts and terminal tail band, white nape, back, shoulder of wing, undertail-coverts and tail. **ADULT FEMALE** Nape and back greyish. **IMM** The black parts of adult plumage are greyish-black, mottled and barred with grey. **HABITAT** Any open area with scattered trees. **STATUS** Introduced to the island of Guadalcanal in the Solomons, but has not done well, and may no longer survive there. **CALL** Diagnostic, rich, mellow, organ-like carolling.

POLYNESIAN TRILLER

female

male

imm

LONG-TAILED TRILLER

male

female

imm

WHITE-BREASTED WOODSWALLOW

imm

AUSTRALASIAN MAGPIE

BLACK-FACED CUCKOO-SHRIKE *Coracina novaehollandiae* 33–36 cm

A large, grey cuckoo-shrike with characteristic undulating flight; easily identified by light grey upperparts, black forehead, face and throat and greyish-white underparts. Flight feathers black edged with pale grey, tail black with white tip.
SEXES Alike. **IMM** Lacks black throat, but has small black mask from the bill through the eye and onto the ear-coverts; young birds have fine grey barring on head and breast. **HABITAT** Forest, forest edge, grasslands with scattered trees and parks and gardens. **STATUS** Very uncommon winter visitor to the Solomons from breeding grounds in Australia. Exceptionally rare vagrant to New Caledonia. Two birds recently observed by the author on Amadee Islet, off Nouméa, followed by a more recent sighting near Nouméa by Yves Letocart. **CALL** A cheerful, rolling, 'shri-lunk-shri-lunk-shri-lunk', usually given in flight.

YELLOW-EYED CUCKOO-SHRIKE *Coracina lineata* 25–28 cm

An extremely variable, medium-sized cuckoo-shrike, with a diagnostic bright yellow eye.
ADULT MALE Variable, in most races uniformly dark blue-grey, with indistinct blackish lores. Birds from Makira Island have inconspicuous white and grey barring on breast and abdomen, while birds from Rennell Island have bold black and white barring on breast and abdomen, as in females. Differs from Oriental Cuckoo by smaller size, darker face and more closely barred underparts; differs from Melanesian Cuckoo-shrike by smaller size, much paler plumage and grey not black tail; differs from male Common Cicadabird by uniformly coloured wings lacking pale edging, and has a bright yellow eye. **ADULT FEMALE** Not variable, in all races uniformly dark blue-grey upperparts and throat, with indistinct blackish lores; breast and abdomen boldly barred black and white. **IMM** Similar to female, but paler below. **HABITAT** Foothills and lower montane forest, forest edge and isolated fig trees. **STATUS** Widespread and common throughout the Solomons. **CALL** Plaintive, down-slurred whistle 'tieeuw', repeated at intervals.

WHITE-BELLIED CUCKOO-SHRIKE *Coracina papuensis* 25–27 cm

A medium-sized, grey cuckoo-shrike, with narrow black face mask and contrasting white underparts. Pale grey upperparts and white underparts; narrow black facial mask from the bill to the eye, not extending onto ear-coverts as in immature Black-faced Cuckoo-shrike.
SEXES Alike. **IMM** Similar to adult, but has dusky mottling on the breast. **HABITAT** Occurs mainly in the lowlands, along the forest edge, in secondary growth, coconut plantations and grasslands with scattered trees. **STATUS** Common and widespread throughout most of the Solomons but absent from Makira Island. **CALL** High-pitched 'kitch-eek', often given in flight.

**BLACK-FACED
CUCKOO-SHRIKE**

imm

**YELLOW-EYED
CUCKOO-SHRIKE**

male

female

**WHITE-BELLIED
CUCKOO-SHRIKE**

imm

MELANESIAN CUCKOO-SHRIKE *Coracina caledonica* 32–37 cm

A large, dark cuckoo-shrike with a powerful bill and long tail. Mainly dark greyish, northern races more slaty-black; lores, sides of head, throat, wings and tail glossy black. Differs from somewhat similar Common Cicadabird by much larger size and darker face, throat, wings and tail.
SEXES Alike. **IMM** Mainly greyish with black wings, the wing-coverts and secondaries are edged with light grey. **HABITAT** Primary forest, from the lowlands to the highlands, usually more common in the foothills and mountain forests. **STATUS** An uncommon endemic bird which occurs throughout the entire region. **CALL** A piercing, often repeated 'zweeee'.

NEW CALEDONIAN CUCKOO-SHRIKE *Coracina analis* 28 cm

A medium-sized, grey cuckoo-shrike with diagnostic chestnut-brown undertail-coverts. Mainly slaty-grey with chestnut-brown shoulder-patch, wing-linings and undertail-coverts.
SEXES Alike. **IMM** Brownish wings and paler underparts which are uniformly streaked with black. **HABITAT** Thick primary forest, both in the lowlands and the mountains. **STATUS** A fairly common bird which is endemic to mainland New Caledonia. **CALL** Shrill resonant whistles and a 'tu-whit tu-whee' double call note.

SOLOMON CUCKOO-SHRIKE *Coracina holopolia* 20–23 cm

A medium-sized cuckoo-shrike with distinctive black underparts.
ADULT MALE Uniform grey upperparts, with black primaries and tail, secondaries edged grey; forehead, face, throat and entire underparts glossy black. The Malaita Island race has a narrow black collar across the hindneck. **ADULT FEMALE** Uniformly grey with blackish wingtips and tail, the undertail broadly tipped pale grey. Differs from similar male Common Cicadabird by much paler appearance. **IMM** Similar to female but complete underparts narrowly barred grey and white. **HABITAT** A bird of true forest, not venturing into open areas. Occurs from the lowlands, where it is decidedly uncommon, gradually becoming commoner in the mountains. **STATUS** Endemic to the Solomons. **CALL** Occasional short, rasping 'shweee', uttered when feeding in groups.

COMMON CICADABIRD *Coracina tenuirostris* 25 cm

A medium-sized cuckoo-shrike with marked sexual dimorphism.
ADULT MALE Blackish lores, becoming blackish grey on cheeks, ear-coverts and throat; remainder of plumage deep leaden grey, flight feathers black, broadly edged with pale grey, producing a marked contrasting pattern; tail leaden grey with a broad black tip narrowly edged with white. Differs from similar female Solomon Cuckoo-shrike by much darker appearance, particularly on the face. **ADULT FEMALE** Back is dark brown, wings and tail rufous; has a greyish cap, a conspicuous pale eyebrow and a narrow dark line running through the eye; sides of face narrowly streaked with black, entire underparts buffy to pale rufous. The Makira Island race has entire upperparts, wings and tail grey. **IMM** Similar to adult female, but the cap is brown. **HABITAT** Primary forest and secondary growth, from sea level to 1000 m. **STATUS** Uncommon, but widespread throughout the Solomons. **CALL** A cicada-like 'sheer-sheer-sheer'.

MELANESIAN CUCKOO-SHRIKE

imm

SOLOMON CUCKOO-SHRIKE

imm

male

female

NEW CALEDONIAN CUCKOO-SHRIKE

female
Makira

male

COMMON CICADABIRD

female
Russell, Florida
Guadalcanal, Malaita

OLIVE-TAILED THRUSH Zoothera lunulata 22–23 cm

Robust, well-camouflaged, ground-dwelling thrush, with conspicuous crescent-shaped black scaling above and below. Upperparts rufous-brown, more chestnut on the rump; face and underparts golden-buff. All feathers have a rounded black tip, giving the bird a scaly appearance; the lower abdomen and undertail-coverts are buffy-white and unmarked. Wings dark brown with blackish median and greater wing-coverts having a creamy spot at the tip, forming an indistinct double wingbar; in flight, prominent pale stripe shows on the underwing. **SEXES** Alike. **HABITAT** Primary hill forest. **STATUS** One specimen taken on Choiseul Island in the Solomons in 1924; no subsequent sightings. **CALL** Two clear notes, connected by a slurred upward slide 'tlee-oo-whee'.

NEW BRITAIN THRUSH Zoothera talaseae 20–23 cm

A little-known ground-dwelling thrush, shy and secretive, with dark upperparts and white underparts. Upperparts uniformly dull black, the median and greater wing-coverts with a white spot at the tip, forming an indistinct double wingbar. Underparts white, the flank feathers edged dark grey, forming a scaly pattern. In flight, prominent pale stripe shows on the underwing. **SEXES** Alike. **HABITAT** Montane mist forest. **STATUS** A rare inhabitant of Bougainville Island in the northern Solomons, four specimens were collected in 1980, there have been no subsequent observations. **CALL** Unknown.

SAN CRISTOBAL THRUSH Zoothera margaretae 20–23 cm

A little-known ground-dwelling thrush, shy and very secretive, with distinctive mottled underparts. The San Cristobal race has warm brown upperparts, the wing-coverts with a white spot at the tip forming an indistinct double wingbar. Underparts tawny, with the feathers broadly edged darker, producing bold dark scalloping on the breast and belly; the centre of the belly, lower abdomen and undertail-coverts are buffy-white and unmarked. The Guadalcanal race has darker, more uniform upperparts lacking any wingbars, and greyish underparts with heavier scalloping. **SEXES** Alike. **HABITAT** Montane forest from 200 m to at least 600 m. **STATUS** A little-known endemic of Guadalcanal and Makira islands in the Solomons. **CALL** A high-pitched, descending whistle.

SONG THRUSH Turdus philomelos 23 cm

Slender brown-backed bird, with a distinctive spotted breast. Uniform brown above with buff cheeks, slightly streaked with brown. Chin white, throat, breast and flanks buff, heavily spotted dark brown, lower abdomen and undertail-coverts creamy-white and lightly spotted; in flight, shows rusty-buff underwing-coverts. **SEXES** Alike. **HABITAT** Forest, woodland, parks and gardens, **STATUS** Introduced from Europe to Australia and New Zealand. A solitary bird observed in Vanuatu during the 1930s was probably a vagrant from New Zealand. **CALL** A thin 'sipp'; the song is a rich, clear, collection of repeated phrases.

ISLAND THRUSH Turdus poliocephalus 23 cm

An extremely variable, plump thrush, with distinctive bright yellow bill and legs. Very similar in appearance and behaviour to the familiar European Blackbird. The most usual colour morph is all black, but others are entirely blackish-brown, or blackish above and brown below, or all black with a rufous lower abdomen. Others have a white head, throat and upper breast, with the remaining plumage greyish-black, while others are slaty-grey with a black cap, wings and tail. **SEXES** Alike. **HABITAT** Occurs in primary forest, from the lowlands to the mountains, but is usually more common in montane forest. **STATUS** On the islands of Bougainville, Guadalcanal and Kulambangra, it is found only in the highest montane forests. On Rennell Island, also in the Solomons, there are no mountains and the bird occurs throughout lowland rainforest. In Vanuatu occurs from sea level to the highest mountains. In New Caledonia and the Loyalty Islands this species has seriously declined in numbers during the last 40 years and is now very rare, and may even be extinct in the Loyalty Islands. **CALL** A short 'tchooh', becoming a rapid high-pitched chatter when the bird is alarmed. Also has a varied musical song, made up of repeated phrases.

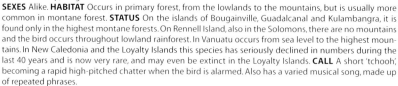

OLIVE-TAILED
THRUSH

NEW BRITAIN
THRUSH

SONG
THRUSH

SAN CRISTOBAL
THRUSH

ISLAND
THRUSH

RUSTY-WINGED STARLING *Aplonis zelandica* 18–20 cm

Arboreal, dull-coloured starling with a heavy bill and a short tail. The only dark-eyed brownish starling in the region. Upperparts dark grey-brown with blackish cap and lores, wings dark brown with a bright rufous-chestnut patch on the primaries; rump rufous-brown, tail brown. Underparts greyish-brown, with a buff wash.
SEXES Alike. **HABITAT** Primary forest. On small, low-lying islands it frequents lowland forest, but on larger islands it is mainly restricted to upland forest. **STATUS** An uncommon bird endemic to Vanuatu, Banks and the Santa Cruz islands. **CALL** A short, melodious 'zee-twee,' frequently repeated.

MOUNTAIN STARLING *Aplonis santovestris* 17–18 cm

An inconspicuous rufous-brown starling of cloud forest undergrowth. A stocky bird with a short tail and conspicuous white eyes. Crown blackish-brown, back brown, lower back and rump rufous-chestnut, wings and tail blackish-brown. Throat brownish; remaining underparts warm rufous-brown.
SEXES Alike. **HABITAT** A rare endemic which frequents the undergrowth of heavily mossed cloud forest above 1400 m. on the highest peaks of Espiritú Santo Island, Vanuatu. **STATUS** Thought to have been extinct, but rediscovered by a Vanuatu Natural Science Society Expedition in 1991. **CALL** A high, evenly-pitched, whistled 'cheep', frequently repeated.

BROWN-WINGED STARLING *Aplonis grandis* 21–23 cm

Large, blackish starling, with a greenish-blue gloss and diagnostic pale brown primaries. Head, hindneck, breast and throat black with a dull purplish gloss, remainder of plumage glossy greenish-black. Outerwing feathers pale brown.
SEXES Alike. **IMM** Similar to adult but duller, primaries dull brown. **HABITAT** Both primary and taller secondary forest and partly cleared areas with scattered trees, in the lowlands and hills, up to about 750 m.
STATUS A common endemic of the Solomons, found throughout the archipelago with the exception of Makira and Rennell islands. On Makira, it is replaced by San Cristobal Starling. **CALL** High-pitched whistles and squeaks.

SAN CRISTOBAL STARLING *Aplonis dichroa* 19 cm

A smaller version of the Brown-winged Starling, from which it is geographically separated. Has a far greater amount of brown in the wing. Overall plumage glossy greenish-black, with the tertials, secondaries and primaries brown.
SEXES Alike. **IMM** Similar to adult but duller, flight feathers dull brown. **HABITAT** Both primary and taller secondary forest and partly cleared areas with scattered trees. Found in the lowlands and hill country. **STATUS** A common endemic of Makira Island in the Solomons. **CALL** Loud clear whistles and clicking sounds.

**RUSTY-WINGED
STARLING**

**MOUNTAIN
STARLING**

**BROWN-WINGED
STARLING**

**SAN CRISTOBAL
STARLING**

STRIATED STARLING   *Aplonis striata*   17–18 cm

A stocky, short-tailed, blackish starling, with reddish-orange eye; the only native starling in New Caledonia.
ADULT MALE Black, with a slight bluish gloss. **ADULT FEMALE** Upperparts dull black, underparts pale greyish, with indistinct dark streaking on the throat. **IMM** Similar to female. **HABITAT** Forest edge, taller secondary growth, partially cleared areas and coconut plantations. **STATUS** Common and widespread, endemic to mainland New Caledonia and the nearby Loyalty Islands. **CALL** Flute-like whistle.

SINGING STARLING   *Aplonis cantoroides*   19–20 cm

A starling with a fairly thick bill and a short square tail. The only glossy-green starling with a short square tail.
Adults are all-black with a greenish gloss and conspicuous bright red eye.
SEXES Alike. **IMM** Whitish underparts, heavily streaked with black. **HABITAT** Occurs along the forest edge, in partially cleared areas with scattered trees, coconut plantations and villages. **STATUS** A common bird throughout the Solomons with the exception of Rennell Island, where it is replaced by the Rennell Starling. **CALL** A musical, down-slurred 'tey-eww'.

METALLIC STARLING   *Aplonis metallica*   23–24 cm

This starling is easily recognised by its long, pointed, graduated tail, elongated, lanceolate neck feathers, bright red eye and communal nesting habits. Differs from similar but much rarer White-eyed Starling by narrower bill, violet-purple, highly glossed, elongated neck feathers, lack of a crest, bright red eye and no tail-streamers.
SEXES Alike. **IMM** Whitish underparts, heavily streaked with black. **HABITAT** A highly gregarious bird of lowland and hill forests, staying mainly along the forest edge, visiting trees in clearings and occasionally mangroves. **STATUS** A common bird throughout the Solomons. **CALL** Harsh, nasal, down-slurred 'nraa-nraa'.

ATOLL STARLING   *Aplonis feadensis*   20 cm

Confined to small offshore islands, this starling is readily identified by the combination of short, stocky build, short, rounded wings, blackish plumage with a slight bluish-green gloss, short square tail and bright yellow eye.
SEXES Alike. **IMM** Pale edging to the feathers of the abdomen, producing a scaly effect. **HABITAT** Forest, forest edge and coconut plantations. **STATUS** Occurs on Nissan, Fead and Ongtong Java islands in the northern Solomons. **CALL** Loud rising 'wee-ee'.

RENNELL STARLING   *Aplonis insularis*   18 cm

A small, short-tailed starling, blackish with a slight bluish-green gloss and yellow-orange eye. Found only on Rennell Island in the Solomons.
SEXES Alike. **IMM** Uniform dark greyish, with a slight greenish gloss. **HABITAT** Forest, forest edge, secondary growth and coconut plantations. **STATUS** Endemic to Rennell Island in the southwest Solomons, where the bird is abundant. **CALL** Loud clear whistles and piercing harsh cries.

WHITE-EYED STARLING   *Aplonis brunneicapilla*   26–27 cm

Somewhat similar to the Metallic Starling but differs by being slightly more heavily built. The bill is much heavier, with a strongly curved culmen. Has white eye, head and neck feathers, oily-black not elongated, and violet-purple, and the elongated central tail-streamers make the tail much longer than that of the Metallic Starling. The tail-streamers are often broken off and the tail then becomes shorter than that of the Metallic Starling.
SEXES Alike. **IMM** Duller, with some indistinct white streaking on the breast and eye dark. **HABITAT** Forest, forest edge, gardens and cleared areas with scattered trees. **STATUS** An uncommon to rare bird which sometimes occurs within flocks of Metallic Starlings. Endemic to the Solomon Islands of Bougainville, Choiseul, Rendova and Guadalcanal. **CALL** A single harsh 'kwaitch', regularly repeated.

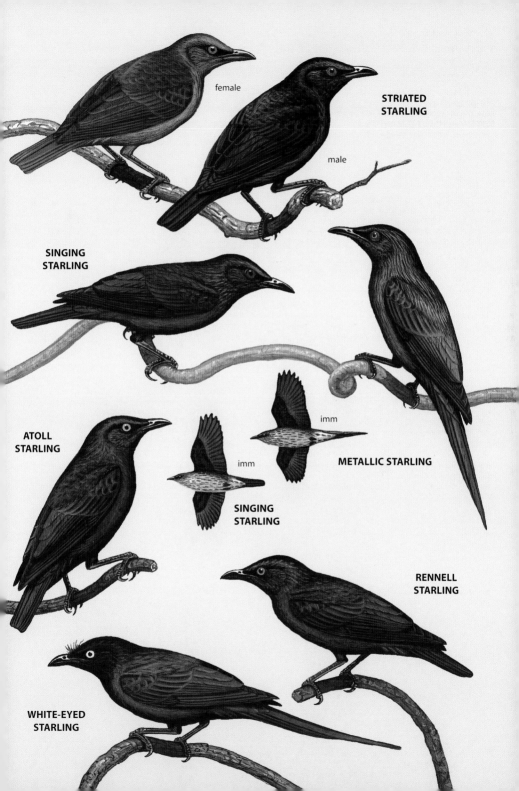

female

STRIATED
STARLING

male

SINGING
STARLING

ATOLL
STARLING

imm

imm

SINGING
STARLING

METALLIC STARLING

RENNELL
STARLING

WHITE-EYED
STARLING

POLYNESIAN STARLING *Aplonis tabuensis* 18 cm

A variable, stocky, short-tailed starling of the Santa Cruz Islands. Uniform earth-brown upperparts with a slight purplish gloss on the crown; secondaries are edged with white, producing a white wing patch on the folded wing. Throat yellowish-orange, breast and belly brown with whitish streaks, undertail-coverts white.
SEXES Alike. **HABITAT** Secondary growth, partly cleared areas, gardens and villages. **STATUS** A common bird in the Santa Cruz Islands. **CALL** A buzzing, 'tzeeip-breee'.

COMMON STARLING *Sturnus vulgaris* 20–22 cm

This familiar starling is easily recognised by its long, slender bill, flat forehead, short tail and triangular-shaped wings. Mainly blackish, with a green and purple gloss, with the exception of the wings, which are broadly edged with brown. In fresh plumage, speckled with buff above and white below; the speckles (the tips of the feathers) wear off, leaving an even glossy black plumage.
SEXES Alike. **IMM** Grey-brown above, slightly paler below, with whitish throat and indistinct streaking on the abdomen. **HABITAT** Towns, villages, farmland, parks and gardens. **STATUS** One sighting early this century, from Vanuatu. **CALL** Harsh, rasping 'tch-cheer', clear whistles and clicking sounds.

YELLOW-FACED MYNA *Mino dumontii* 25 cm

A large, robust, short-tailed myna, with broad rounded wings. Mainly black, with a large conspicuous area of bare orange-yellow skin surrounding the eye; short, broad, white wingbar and white rump and uppertail-coverts. Centre of lower abdomen bright yellow, becoming white on the undertail-coverts. Bill, legs and feet yellow. In flight shows prominent white wing patches.
SEXES Alike. **IMM** Similar, but duller. **HABITAT** Primary forest and particularly forest edge, partly cleared areas and gardens. **STATUS** One of the most conspicuous birds of lowland forest, throughout most of the Solomons. **CALL** A variety of high-pitched, clear, nasal whistles.

COMMON MYNA *Acridotheres tristis* 23–24 cm

A large, robust, short-tailed myna, with broad, rounded wings. Occurs only close to human habitation. Head and neck black, with a narrow patch of yellow skin below and behind the eye; remainder of body rich vinous-brown, slightly paler on the underparts; short, broad, white wingbar and white undertail-coverts. Bill, legs and feet yellow. In flight shows prominent white wing patch.
SEXES Alike. **IMM** Similar to adult but duller. **HABITAT** Towns, villages and farmland. **STATUS** Introduced from southern Asia, occurring widely in towns and villages throughout the region. **CALL** Loud, raucous, scolding and chattering.

POLYNESIAN
STARLING

imm

COMMON
STARLING

non-br

YELLOW-FACED
MYNA

COMMON
MYNA

BARN SWALLOW *Hirundo rustica* 17 cm

Chestnut-red forehead and throat, blue-black breast-band and deeply forked tail are diagnostic. Differs from Pacific Swallow by slightly larger size, presence of a breast-band, much whiter underparts and in breeding plumage, long, narrow tail-streamers.
SEXES Alike. **IMM** Similar to adults but duller, and tail streamers have not developed. **HABITAT** Occurs mainly in the lowlands, particularly over large freshwater swamps and nearby grasslands. **STATUS** Not officially recorded from the region. Small numbers regularly winter in New Guinea and northern Australia and stragglers are likely to occur in the northern Solomons. Breeds in the northern hemisphere **CALL** High-pitched 'tswee' and soft twittering.

PACIFIC SWALLOW *Hirundo tahitica* 13 cm

A small swallow, with a moderately long, forked tail. Upperparts glossy blue-black, flight feathers and tail blackish-brown, forehead face and throat chestnut, underparts greyish-white. Differs from Barn Swallow by lacking a breast-band, has greyer underparts and lacks tail streamers.
SEXES Alike. **IMM** Similar to adults but duller and has faint streaking on the underparts. **HABITAT** Open areas, rivers, lakes, swamps, villages, coastal areas and small offshore islands. **STATUS** A fairly common breeding bird throughout the region. **CALL** Weak twittering.

TREE MARTIN *Hirundo nigricans* 12–13 cm

A small swallow, easily separated from Barn and Pacific Swallows by combination of creamy-white rump, squarish, slightly notched tail, pale chestnut forehead and lightly streaked, buffy-white underparts.
SEXES Alike. **IMM** Underparts are far more buffy and streaking is heavier and more extensive, covering the entire underparts. **HABITAT** Open areas, grasslands, lakes, swamps, forest clearings and airstrips. **STATUS** An uncommon, non-breeding migrant from Australia. Winters in small numbers in the northern Solomons. **CALL** Sharp 'tweet' and pleasant twittering.

BARN SWALLOW

PACIFIC SWALLOW

TREE MARTIN

RED-VENTED BULBUL *Pycnonotus cafer* 20 cm

A crested bulbul, often found perched on power lines, fences and houses. A confiding, mainly earth-brown bird, with slightly crested black head, black throat and mottled brown body, conspicuous white rump, scarlet vent and white-tipped blackish tail.
SEXES Alike. **IMM** Slightly duller. **HABITAT** Gardens in towns and villages. **STATUS** Captive birds released in Nouméa in New Caledonia in 1982, small numbers can still be found in Nouméa township. **CALL** Low-pitched, whistled 'be-quick-quick'.

YELLOW WAGTAIL *Motacilla flava* 17–18 cm

Slender, long tailed, ground-dwelling bird, with the characteristic habit of wagging its tail up and down. Differs from Grey Wagtail by much shorter tail, and an olive, not grey back; lacks conspicuous olive-yellow rump and has much darker legs.
BREEDING PLUMAGE: Olive upperparts and bright yellow underparts. **NON-BREEDING PLUMAGE** and **IMM** Brownish-olive upperparts, with pale eyebrow, pale buff to whitish underparts. **HABITAT** Edges of swamps and wet grassland. **STATUS** Rare vagrant to Bougainville Island in the northern Solomons. **CALL** A shrill 'tsweep'.

GREY WAGTAIL *Motacilla cinerea* 19–20 cm

Slender, long tailed, ground-dwelling bird, with the characteristic habit of wagging its tail up and down. Differs from Yellow Wagtail by much longer tail, and a grey, not olive back; has a conspicuous olive-yellow rump and much paler, flesh-coloured legs.
ADULT MALE BREEDING PLUMAGE: Grey upperparts, with white eyebrow and mustachial stripe, diagnostic black throat patch and bright yellow underparts. **ADULT MALE NON-BREEDING PLUMAGE** and **ADULT FEMALE** Lack white mustachial stripe and black throat-patch. **IMM** Similar to female but differs in underparts being whitish, with yellow undertail-coverts. **HABITAT** Fast-flowing rocky streams, edges of lakes and gravel roads. **STATUS** Not yet recorded from the region, but likely to stray into the northern Solomons as it is a much more common winter visitor to New Guinea than is Yellow Wagtail. **CALL** Short, high-pitched metallic 'chittich'.

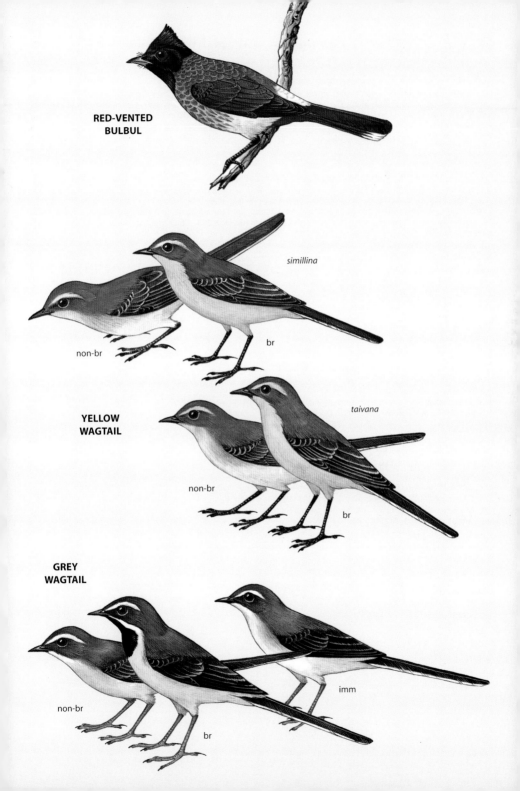

**RED-VENTED
BULBUL**

simillina

non-br

br

**YELLOW
WAGTAIL**

taivana

non-br

br

**GREY
WAGTAIL**

non-br

br

imm

LOUISIADE WHITE-EYE *Zosterops griseotinctus* 10–12 cm

Restricted in distribution to small islands. The bright yellow underparts, white eyering and lack of black on the forehead separates this species from all other white-eyes occurring in the Solomons.
SEXES Alike. **HABITAT** Primary forest, forest edge and secondary growth. **STATUS** In this region, occurs only on Nissan Island in the far northern Solomons, where it is abundant. **CALL** A 'chew' contact call and a loud 'chip-chip-chip', given in flight.

RENNELL WHITE-EYE *Zosterops rennellianus* 12 cm

Endemic to Rennell Island, where it is the only white-eye, without a white eyering. Upperparts uniform olive-green, slightly yellower below; no eyering; bright orange bill and pale orange legs.
SEXES Alike. **HABITAT** Restricted to primary forest, not venturing into disturbed areas. **STATUS** Endemic to Rennell Island in the Solomons, where it is common and widespread. **CALL** A quiet, high-pitched tinkling whistle.

BANDED WHITE-EYE *Zosterops vellalavella* 12 cm

Endemic to Vella Lavella and Mbava Islands, where it is the only white-eye. Upperparts uniform yellowish-olive, white eyering, yellow upper throat separated from white belly by a pale olive breast-band, yellow bill and legs.
SEXES Alike. **HABITAT** Primary forest and secondary growth. **STATUS** Endemic to the islands of Vella Lavella and Mbava in the northern New Georgia group of islands in the central Solomons. **CALL** A series of down-slurred notes, with unpredictable silent gaps.

GANONGGA WHITE-EYE *Zosterops splendidus* 12 cm

Endemic to the Island of Ranongga, where it is the only white-eye. Upperparts uniform olive, forehead and lores blackish, broad white eyering; underparts golden-yellow with olive flanks; bill black, legs yellowish-pink.
SEXES Alike. **HABITAT** Primary forest and secondary growth. **STATUS** Endemic to Ranongga Island, in the northern New Georgia group of islands in the central Solomons. **CALL** A series of staccato, down-slurred notes.

SPLENDID WHITE-EYE *Zosterops luteirostris* 12 cm

Endemic to Gizo Island, where it is the only white-eye. Upperparts uniform olive, forehead and lores black, white eyering, entire underparts bright golden-yellow, tail blackish. Bill and legs bright yellow.
SEXES Alike. **HABITAT** Taller secondary growth. **STATUS** A fairly common endemic of Gizo Island, in the northern New Georgia group of islands in the central Solomons. **CALL** A series of up-slurred notes, somewhat similar to the call notes of Collared Kingfisher.

SOLOMON ISLANDS WHITE-EYE *Zosterops kulambangrae* 12 cm

Upperparts uniform olive-green, forehead and lores blackish, narrow white eyering, entire underparts olive-yellow, bill all-black, legs and feet yellowish. Differs from Kulambangra White-eye by smaller size, brighter upperparts, much narrower eyering, all-black bill and yellowish, not grey legs.
SEXES Alike. **HABITAT** Primary forest and taller secondary forest. **STATUS** Endemic to the New Georgia group of islands, from Kulambangra southwards. **CALL** A short musical 'cheep-cheep'.

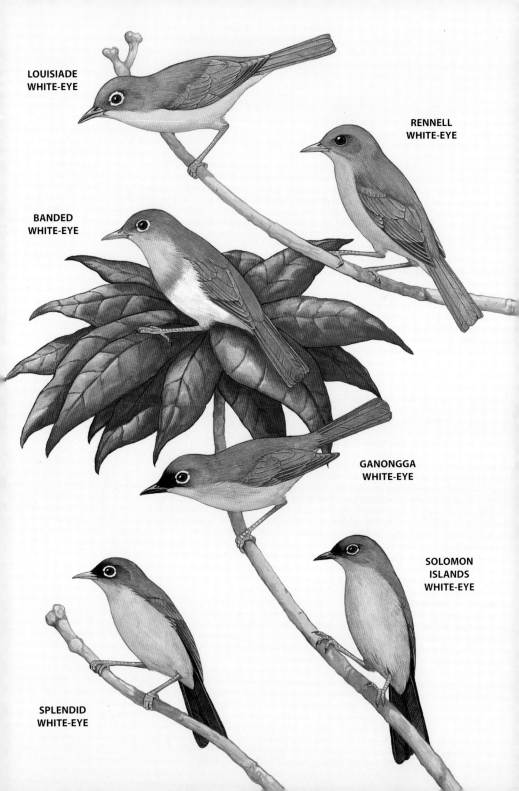

LOUISIADE
WHITE-EYE

RENNELL
WHITE-EYE

BANDED
WHITE-EYE

GANONGGA
WHITE-EYE

SOLOMON
ISLANDS
WHITE-EYE

SPLENDID
WHITE-EYE

KULAMBANGRA WHITE-EYE *Zosterops murphyi* 13–14 cm

Upperparts uniform dark olive-green, slightly yellower below. Has very broad white eyering, black bill with a yellow base, grey legs and feet. Differs from Solomon Islands White-eye by larger size, darker upperparts, much broader eyering, yellow base of bill and grey legs, not yellowish. **SEXES** Alike. **HABITAT** Mossy cloud forest above 900 m. **STATUS** Endemic to Kulambangra Island in the New Georgia group of islands in the central Solomons. Large flocks not uncommon above 900 m. **CALL** A single, rather plaintive note is given when flocks are busy feeding.

YELLOW-THROATED WHITE-EYE *Zosterops metcalfii* 11 cm

Upperparts uniform yellowish olive-green, chin and throat bright yellow, undertail-coverts yellow; remaining underparts white. White eyering, confined to a thin line above and below the eye, or may be absent altogether. Bill black, legs and feet grey. **SEXES** Alike. **HABITAT** Primary forest, forest edge and secondary growth. **STATUS** A common endemic of Buka, Bougainville, the Shortland group, Chouseul, Isabel and the Florida group of islands in the Solomons. **CALL** A loud, high-pitched 'peep'.

GREY-THROATED WHITE-EYE *Zosterops rendovae* 12–13 cm

Upperparts and sides of head dark darkish olive-green with sooty-brown lores sometimes extending to the forehead and around the eyes, narrow, indistinct white eyering. Tail brownish. Chin olive-green, throat and abdomen dark grey with a whitish centre to the abdomen, undertail-coverts yellow; bill blackish with whitish base to lower mandible; legs and feet pale grey. **SEXES** Alike. **HABITAT** Primary forest from sea level to 2000 m, very uncommon below 900 m, but fairly common above this altitude. **STATUS** Endemic to Bougainville, Guadalcanal and Makira Islands in the Solomons. **CALL** A loud, mellow down-slurred 'peeu'.

MALAITA WHITE-EYE *Zosterops stresemanni* 13 cm

Endemic to Malaita Island, where it is the only white-eye. Upperparts uniform olive-green, no eyering; complete underparts very pale yellow; bill has greyish upper and dull orange lower mandible, with a grey tip. **SEXES** Alike. **HABITAT** Primary forest, forest edge and secondary growth, found from sea level to the mountains. **STATUS** Endemic to Malaita Island, where it is abundant. **CALL** Typical *Zosterops* single call, plus a very melodious, thrush-like song.

SANTA CRUZ WHITE-EYE *Zosterops santaecrucis* 12–13 cm

Endemic to the Santa Cruz Islands, where it is the only typical greenish-yellow white-eye. Upperparts uniform dull olive, with a blackish eyering, underparts pale yellowish; bill blackish with a yellow base; legs and feet blue-grey. **SEXES** Alike. **HABITAT** Primary forest, forest edge and secondary growth. **STATUS** Endemic to the Santa Cruz Islands, where it is common. **CALL** Low-pitched, nasal trill.

SILVER-EYE *Zosterops lateralis* 13–14 cm

Head, throat, wings, rump and tail yellowish-olive, mantle, back and abdomen grey. Broad white eyering; bill, legs and feet greyish. **SEXES** Alike. **HABITAT** A bird of the lowlands, occurring along the forest edge, in secondary growth and plantations. **STATUS** A common bird throughout Vanuatu, New Caledonia and the Loyalty Islands. **CALL** High-pitched, drawn-out 'cheew'.

KULAMBANGRA WHITE-EYE

YELLOW-THROATED WHITE-EYE

MALAITA WHITE-EYE

GREY-THROATED WHITE-EYE

SANTA CRUZ WHITE-EYE

SILVER-EYE

LARGE LIFOU WHITE-EYE *Zosterops inornatus* 15 cm

Endemic to Lifou Island, where it is the only white-eye without a white eyering. A large, plump, rather shy bird, with slow, deliberate movements. Head, throat, wings, rump and tail dark olive-green, mantle back and abdomen dark grey. No eyering; bill has greyish upper and flesh-coloured lower mandible; legs and feet also flesh coloured.
SEXES Alike. **HABITAT** Primary forest, forest edge and very occasionally, taller secondary growth. **STATUS** Uncommon endemic of Lifou Island in the Loyalty Islands of New Caledonia. **CALL** A loud, somewhat 'whistler-like' call note.

SMALL LIFOU WHITE-EYE *Zosterops minutus* 10 cm

Endemic to Lifou Island, where it is by far the commonest white-eye. A tiny, greenish-yellow bird with a prominent, broad, white eyering. Differs from Silver-eye and Large Lifou White-eye by smaller size, olive-yellow head, mantle, back and underparts. Lacks grey mantle. Wings and tail are olive-green and underparts are slightly paler on the belly.
SEXES Alike. **HABITAT** Forest edge, secondary growth, scrub and gardens. **STATUS** An abundant endemic on Lifou Island in the Loyalty Islands of New Caledonia. **CALL** Typical *Zosterops* mournful 'tee-oou'.

YELLOW-FRONTED WHITE-EYE *Zosterops flavifrons* 11–12 cm

Endemic to Vanuatu and Banks Islands. Easily identified by small size, bright yellow forehead, prominent white eyering, yellow-green upperparts and bright yelow underparts. Lacks a grey back. Bill has brown upper and pinkish-brown lower mandible; legs and feet, lead-grey.
SEXES Alike. **HABITAT** Occurs from the lowlands to the mountains, in primary forest, secondary growth, plantations and gardens. **STATUS** Endemic to Vanuatu and Banks Islands, where it is common and widespread. **CALL** A short, high-pitched 'tweep-tweep'.

GREEN-BACKED WHITE-EYE *Zosterops xanthochrous* 11 cm

Endemic to New Caledonia and Mare Island in the Loyalty Islands group. Differs from Silver-eye in having dark olive-green forehead and upperparts, lacks the grey back and has the throat, upper breast and undertail-coverts, yellowish-green; abdomen dirty white, bill and legs grey.
SEXES Alike. **HABITAT** Mainly primary forest, from the lowlands to the mountains. **STATUS** Endemic to mainland New Caledonia and Mare Island in the Loyalty Islands group, where it is widespread and common. **CALL** Thin 'see-see-see'.

BARE-EYED WHITE-EYE *Woodfordia superciliosa* 14–15 cm

A large, distinctive bird, endemic to Rennell Island. Upperparts dull olive-brown, top of head, wings and tail, slightly more brownish. Naked black skin on lores and sides of face surrounding the eyes, encircled with white. Underparts greyish-buff; bill long and pinkish at the base, with a dark tip; legs and feet grey.
SEXES Alike. **HABITAT** Primary forest, forest edge and secondary growth. **STATUS** Endemic to Rennell Island in the Solomons, where it is widespread and common. **CALL** A constant 'chip-chip-chip'.

SANFORD'S WHITE-EYE *Woodfordia lacertosa* 16 cm

A large, distinctive bird, endemic to the Santa Cruz Islands. Upperparts pale rufous-brown, the underparts are buffy-ochre. Large, off-white eyering and loral spot; bill and legs straw-yellow.
SEXES Alike. **HABITAT** Primary forest, forest edge and secondary growth. **STATUS** Endemic to the Santa Cruz Islands, where it is fairly common. **CALL** Typical *Zosterops* 'chip' note, uttered frequently when in flocks.

SMALL LIFOU
WHITE-EYE

LARGE LIFOU
WHITE-EYE

GREEN-BACKED
WHITE-EYE

YELLOW-FRONTED
WHITE-EYE

SANDFORD'S
WHITE-EYE

BARE-EYED
WHITE-EYE

SULPHUR-BREASTED WARBLER *Phylloscopus ricketti* 10–11 cm

Upperparts olive-green, with two indistinct yellowish wingbars. Crown blackish with prominent bright yellow crown stripe and eyebrow stripes, and there is a black line through the eye. The complete underparts are bright yellow. Differs from other Phylloscopus *warblers in the region by having a crown stripe, prominent eyebrow stripes and bright yellow underparts.*
SEXES Alike. **HABITAT** Primary and secondary forest. **STATUS** Not yet officially recorded from the region. Breeds in southern China and winters in South-East Asia and the Philippines, so vagrants could easily occur in the northern Solomons. **CALL** Melodious, descending 'sweety-sweety-sweety-swee'.

ISLAND LEAF-WARBLER *Phylloscopus poliocephalus* 9–10 cm

Upperparts dull olive without wingbars. Crown brownish; has an indistinct pale eyebrow stripe and a dark line through the eye, throat whitish, underparts pale greyish-yellow. Differs from all other Phylloscopus *warblers in the region by being much duller, more washed out, especially on the underparts.*
SEXES Alike. **HABITAT** Montane forests above 900 m. **STATUS** Uncommon breeding bird on Bougainville, Isabel, Malaita and Guadalcanal islands in the Solomons. **CALL** A repetitive, high-pitched 'sisse-birredge'.

SAN CRISTOBAL LEAF-WARBLER *Phylloscopus makirensis* 10–11 cm

Upperparts dull olive green, without wingbars, crown brownish, has an indistinct pale eyebrow stripe and a dark line through the eye, throat whitish, underparts rich lemon-yellow. Differs from Island Leaf-Warbler, the only other Phylloscopus *warbler in its range, in having much brighter, rich lemon-yellow underparts.*
SEXES Alike. **HABITAT** Both primary and secondary forest, common in the mountains above 800 m. **STATUS** Endemic to Makira Island in the Solomons. **CALL** A repetitive, high-pitched reeling song.

KULAMBANGRA LEAF-WARBLER *Phylloscopus amoenus* 11–12 cm

Upperparts brownish-olive, without wingbars, crown and face blackish, mottled olive, with indistinct pale eyebrow stripe; underparts dull yellowish-olive, with indistinct but noticeable streaking. Differs from Island Leaf-Warbler, the only other Phylloscopus *in its range, by darker upperparts and dull yellowish-olive, streaked underparts.*
SEXES Alike. **HABITAT** Montane forest above 1000 m. **STATUS** Uncommon endemic of Kulambangra Island in the Solomons. **CALL** A high-pitched warble.

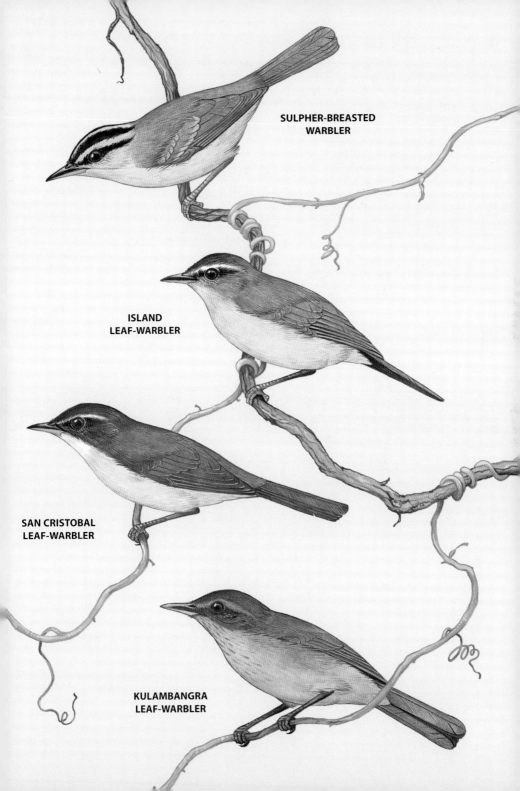

SULPHER-BREASTED
WARBLER

ISLAND
LEAF-WARBLER

SAN CRISTOBAL
LEAF-WARBLER

KULAMBANGRA
LEAF-WARBLER

SHADE WARBLER *Cettia parens* 11–12 cm

A small, nondescript, ground-dwelling warbler. Upperparts uniform dark brown, with an indistinct pale brown eyebrow stripe, throat ochraceous; remainder of underparts brownish-grey. Usually observed foraging amongst the undergrowth but will sometimes sing from cover 2 to 3 metres from the ground.
SEXES Alike. **HABITAT** Montane forest, above 600 m. **STATUS** Fairly common endemic, in the mountains of Makira Island in the Solomons. **CALL** A long sustained whistle, followed by two notes in quick succession, the first rising in pitch, the second dropping in pitch.

AUSTRALIAN REED-WARBLER *Acrocephalus australis* 15–17 cm

A plain, brownish bird of dense reedbeds. Despite rather skulking behaviour, the birds presence is easily detected by its loud, persistent, musical song. Uniform brownish-buff above, with an indistinct pale buff eyebrow stripe; throat and underparts buffy-white, whiter on throat and centre of belly. When singing, clings sideways to reed-stems, puffs up its throat, raises crown feathers and shows bright yellow gape.
SEXES Alike. **HABITAT** Dense reedbeds, over and near water. **STATUS** Common breeding bird throughout the northern Solomons. **CALL** Rich, musical, often repeated 'chutch-chutch-chutch, dect-dect-dect, crotchy-crotchy-crotchy'.

NEW CALEDONIAN GRASSBIRD *Megalurulus mariei* 18 cm

A long-tailed, olive-brown bird which scurries about secretively on or near the ground, in isolated patches of tall blady grass or dense savanna scrub within rainforest. Olive-brown upperparts, slightly darker on the crown, wings and tail. Has a conspicuous, long eyebrow stripe, extending from the base of the bill to the nape. The underparts are creamy white with a pale rufous-buff wash to the sides of the breast and the flanks.
SEXES Alike. **HABITAT** Isolated patches of tall blady grass and dense savanna scrub within rainforest. **STATUS** Endemic to mainland New Caledonia where it is not uncommon, but is very difficult to observe. **CALL** A sharp 'tzik' and a soft kitten-like purring.

BOUGAINVILLE THICKETBIRD *Megalurulus llaneae* 17–18 cm

A large, skulking, ground-dwelling bird, with an upright stance and a relatively short tail, with pointed tips. Geographically separated from the Guadalcanal Thicketbird. Crown and upperparts dark brown with pale edges to the feathers of the wing-coverts; long, broad orangey-rufous eyebrow stripe, bordered below by a blackish line extending from the base of the bill, through the eye and onto the ear-coverts. Sides of face and complete underparts orangey-rufous, darker and browner on sides of breast and flanks.
SEXES Alike. **HABITAT** Frequents the ground and dense ground cover, particularly along the edge of streams in mossy montane forest, rarely below 1200 m, more commonly around 1500 m. **STATUS** A shy, secretive, uncommon endemic of the mountains of Bougainville Island in the Solomons. **CALL** A clear melodic whistle of one or two notes, followed by a much higher-pitched note.

GUADALCANAL THICKETBIRD *Megalurulus whitneyi* 17–18 cm

A large, skulking, ground-dwelling bird, with an upright stance and a relatively short tail, with pointed tips. Geographically separated from the Bougainville Thicketbird. Upperparts rufous-brown, crown, wings and tail dark brown. Long broad ochraceous-rufous eyebrow stripe, bordered below by a blackish-brown line extending from the base of the bill through the eye and onto the ear-coverts. Sides of face and complete underparts ochraceous-rufous, darker and browner on sides of breast and flanks.
SEXES Alike. **HABITAT** Frequents the ground and dense ground cover, particularly along the edge of streams in mossy montane forest, rarely below 700 m, more commonly around 1200 m. **STATUS** A shy, secretive, uncommon endemic of the mountains of Espiritu Santo Island in Vanuatu and Guadalcanal Island in the Solomons. **CALL** A series of piercing, descending notes 'tzwee-zwee-wee-wee'.

SHADE
WARBLER

AUSTRALIAN
REED-WARBLER

NEW CALEDONIAN
GRASSBIRD

GUADALCANAL
THICKETBIRD

OUGAINVILLE
THICKETBIRD

BLUE-FACED PARROTFINCH *Erythrura trichroa* 12 cm

A small emerald-green finch, easily identified by blue face and reddish tail.
ADULT MALE Mainly emerald-green, with forehead and face cobalt-blue, rump and uppertail-coverts dull scarlet, tail olive-brown washed with dark red; bill black. **ADULT FEMALE** Duller, with less blue on the face. **IMM** Dull green, lacking the blue face. **HABITAT** Clearings in forest, forest edge, grassland, farmland and roadside edges. **STATUS** Found on the large islands of Bougainville and Guadalcanal in the Solomons. Patchily distributed throughout Vanuatu, in New Caledonia found in the Loyalty Islands, where it occurs on the islands of Lifu and Mare. Generally rather uncommon throughout the region. **CALL** A short, high-pitched single 'tzee'.

RED-THROATED PARROTFINCH *Erythrura psittacea* 11–12 cm

Mainly grass-green, except for bright red forehead, face, throat and breast; rump and tail are a slightly darker red.
SEXES Alike. **IMM** Dull greenish, without the red. **HABITAT** Grassy openings in forest, forest edge, farmland and roadside edges. **STATUS** A fairly common endemic of New Caledonia. Sporadic sightings of escaped birds in Port Villa, Vanuatu during the 1960s and 1970s, but no recent reports. **CALL** A single or double 'tzeet', often repeated.

COMMON WAXBILL *Estrilda astrild* 12–13 cm

A small, long-tailed finch, pale grey-brown above, a vivid red bill, broad crimson eyebrow and brownish rump. Pale grey underparts finely barred blackish-brown, with slight pinkish wash and small reddish patch on the belly.
SEXES Alike. **IMM** With little or no red, only faint barring and a black bill. **HABITAT** Rank grassland, neglected gardens, often near water. **STATUS** Introduced from Africa to Efate Island in Vanuatu and mainland New Caledonia, where it is fairly common in suitable habitat. **CALL** A soft, nasal 'chewi-chee-chewi-che'.

RED-HEADED PARROTFINCH *Erythrura cyaneovirens* 10 cm

A small green finch with red crown, face, rump and tail. Geographically separated from Royal Parrotfinch.
ADULT MALE Mainly dark green, except for scarlet face and crown, red rump and tail and variable bluish wash on throat and upper breast; bill black. **ADULT FEMALE** Lacks red on the head and bluish wash on the breast. **IMM** similar to adults but duller. **HABITAT** Grassy openings in montane forest and along the forest edge. **STATUS** Uncommon inhabitant of Efate and Aneityum islands in southern Vanuatu. **CALL** A high-pitched 'seep'.

ROYAL PARROTFINCH *Erythrura regia* 11–12 cm

A blue-green finch with bright red head, rump and tail. Geographically separated from Red-headed Parrotfinch.
ADULT MALE Crown and sides of head bright red, back and wings bluish-green, throat and breast blue, remainder of underparts bluish-green, rump bright red, tail rust-red. **ADULT FEMALE** More greenish, much less blue in the plumage. **IMM** Dull blue head, olive-green upperparts and greyish-green underparts, bill bright yellow. **HABITAT** Montane forest. **STATUS** Endemic to islands of northern Vanuatu, where it is uncommon. **CALL** A single 'tzee', given at long intervals when feeding.

RED AVADAVAT *Amandava amandava* 11 cm

Breeding male is red-brown above with a bright red rump, crimson below, with white spotting on wings and flanks.
FEMALE and **NON-BREEDING MALE** Brown above, with a few white spots on the wing, a dark stripe through the eye and a dark red rump. Pale olive-yellow below, darker on the flanks, undertail-coverts creamy-buff. **IMM** Similar, but duller. **HABITAT** Grassland, weeds along the roadside and farmland. **STATUS** A bird of Asian origin observed on Efate Island in Vanuatu in 1988; this small flock probably self-introduced from Fiji, where the bird has become common since being introduced from India. **CALL** A high-pitched twitter.

RED-BROWED FIRETAIL *Neochmia temporalis* 11–12 cm

A small grey and olive finch, with scarlet bill and prominent scarlet eyebrow and rump. Head greyish, back and wings olive-green, olive-yellow patch on side of neck, sides of face, throat and entire underparts grey.
SEXES Alike. **IMM** Black bill, lacks the eyebrow and has slightly duller grey underparts. **HABITAT** Grassland, forest edge and farmland. **STATUS** An Australian species; there was a surprise sighting in 1988 of a small flock at Port Vila, on Efate Island in Vanuatu (origin unknown). **CALL** Piercing, high-pitched 'sseee-seee'.

BLUE-FACED
PARROTFINCH

RED-THROATED
PARROTFINCH

COMMON
WAXBILL

ROYAL
PARROTFINCH

imm

RED-HEADED
PARROTFINCH

RED
AVADAVAT

male

RED-BROWED
FIRETAIL

imm

female,
male non-br

HOUSE SPARROW *Passer domesticus* 14–15 cm

A plump, pugnacious bird, frequenting human habitation.
ADULT MALE Easily recognised by its dark grey crown, chestnut nape, black chin and throat and whitish cheeks. **ADULT FEMALE** and **IMM** Pale brown above and dingy white below, with a narrow off-white eye-stripe and a pale wingbar. **HABITAT** Towns and villages and nearby farmland, never far from human habitation. **STATUS** Introduced from Europe, common in larger towns throughout New Caledonia and well established in the capital city of Port Villa, Vanuatu. **CALL** A variety of harsh chirping notes.

BLACK-HEADED MUNIA *Lonchura malacca* 11 cm

A small, plump bird, with an all-black head, heavy blue-grey bill and short pointed tail. All-black head, rest of upperparts rufous-chestnut, rump darker chestnut. Throat and upper breast black, lower breast, upper belly and flanks chestnut, centre of belly and undertail-coverts black.
SEXES Alike. **IMM** Warm brown above with a chestnut rump, and buff below. **HABITAT** Lowland grasslands and reeds. **STATUS** A native of southern Asia, escaped from captivity in Luganville, Espiritú Santo Island, Vanuatu, in the 1960s and is still present in small numbers around the town. **CALL** A shrill 'peep-peep'.

CHESTNUT-BREASTED MUNIA *Lonchura castaneothorax* 10–11 cm

A small, plump bird, with a black face and diagnostic pale chestnut breast and white abdomen. Black face, grey crown, nape and hindneck with indistinct dark brown streaking, back cinnamon-brown, tail golden yellow; pale chestnut breast separated from white abdomen by a narrow black band.
SEXES Alike. **IMM** Olive-brown above, pale buff below, with brownish-buff breast. **HABITAT** Lowland grasslands. **STATUS** Introduced from Australia to New Caledonia, where now well established throughout the mainland. Escaped from captivity in Luganville on Espiritú Santo Island, Vanuatu and has slowly spread into nearby coastal lowlands. **CALL** A low, bell-like 'teet'.

BISMARCK MUNIA *Lonchura melaena* 10–11 cm

A small, plump bird with an all-black head and a massive, diagnostic black bill. All-black head, rest of upper-parts very dark brown, tinged with chestnut, rump and uppertail-coverts deep reddish chestnut, tail dark brown. Black of upper breast merges into creamy-brown lower breast and belly; flanks are barred with black, vent and undertail-coverts are also black.
SEXES Alike. **IMM** Dark brown above with a chestnut rump, and yellow-buff below. **HABITAT** Rank grasslands, swamps and small forest clearings. **STATUS** An uncommon bird on Buka Island in the northern Solomons. **CALL** A short, high-pitched 'cheep'.

COMMON REDPOLL *Carduelis flammea* 13 cm

A small, heavily streaked brown bird, with short conical bill and slightly forked tail.
ADULT MALE Forehead blackish, forecrown bright crimson, upperparts warm brown with black streaking to centre of feathers, rump reddish, streaked dark brown. Wings and tail dark brown with two buff wing-bars. Sides of face brownish, chin black, throat and breast rose pink, abdomen whitish with dark streaking on the flanks. **ADULT FEMALE** Similar to the male, but lacks red on breast and rump. **IMM** Similar to female but lacks red on the crown and black on the face and is more heavily streaked below. **HABITAT** Woodland and parks and gardens. **STATUS** Introduced to New Zealand from Europe and North America. There is a single specimen from Vanuatu collected in 1961, presumably a vagrant from New Zealand. **CALL** Rapid, sustained twittering.

HOUSE SPARROW

female

male

BLACK-HEADED MUNIA

imm

CHESTNUT-BREASTED MUNIA

imm

BISMARCK MUNIA

imm

COMMON REDPOLL

MIDGET FLOWERPECKER *Dicaeum aeneum* 8 cm

A tiny, stubby bird, with a short bill and a short tail. Male has a diagnostic fiery-red patch on the upper breast.
ADULT MALE Upperparts and wings dark grey with a slight greenish sheen, tail blackish; centre of throat whitish, sides of head, sides of throat, the breast and centre of belly grey, with prominent scarlet patch in the centre of the upper breast. Flanks olive, centre of lower abdomen and undertail-coverts pale buff. **ADULT FEMALE** Similar to male but underparts pale buff, with olive flanks. **HABITAT** Primary forest, forest edge, secondary growth and gardens. **STATUS** A common endemic bird, occurring throughout the northern Solomons, from the lowlands to the mountains. **CALL** A distinctive, repeated 'tik-tik-tik-tik'.

MOTTLED FLOWERPECKER *Dicaeum tristrami* 8–9 cm

A tiny, stubby bird, with a short bill, a short tail and distinctive mottled brown plumage. Upperparts and wings brown, with greyish-white mottling on the forecrown; tail black. Eyebrow and ear patch whitish, cheeks dark brown, throat and upper breast pale brown, faintly mottled whitish, lower abdomen and undertail-coverts whitish.
SEXES Alike. **HABITAT** Primary forest, forest edge and secondary growth. **STATUS** Endemic to Makira Island, where it is an uncommon bird in the lowlands and common in the mountains. **CALL** Repeated, metallic, 'chip-chip-chip'.

OLIVE-BACKED SUNBIRD *Nectarinia jugularis* 11–12 cm

A small, sexually dimorphic bird, with a long, slender, curved bill, short tail and bright yellow underparts.
ADULT MALE Upperparts uniform brownish-olive, with slight yellowish eyebrow, conspicuous dark metallic blue-black gorget, with purple iridescence in the centre; remainder of underparts bright, deep yellow. **ADULT FEMALE** Similar to male, but lacks blue-black gorget. **IMM** Both sexes have duller yellow underparts and males have a narrow metallic blue-black gorget down the centre of the throat. **HABITAT** A bird of coastal lowlands, frequenting mangroves, coastal scrub, secondary growth, forest edge, gardens and coconut plantations. **STATUS** A common bird throughout the Solomons. **CALL** High-pitched 'tzit-tzit' and a rapid, descending trill.

**MIDGET
FLOWERPECKER**

male

female

**MOTTLED
FLOWERPECKER**

**OLIVE-BACKED
SUNBIRD**

male

female

Further Reading

Beehler, B.M., Pratt, H. D., and Zimmerman, D.A. 1986. *Birds of New Guinea*. Princeton University Press, Princeton, N. J.

Bregulla, H.L. 1992. *Birds of Vanuatu*. Anthony Nelson, Oswestry, U.K.

Coates, B.J. 1985. *The Birds of Papua New Guinea*. Dove Publications, Alderley, Australia.

Coates, B.J., Bishop, K.D., and Gardener D. 1997. *A Guide to the Birds of Wallacea*. Dove Publications, Alderley, Australia.

DuPont, J.E. 1976. *South Pacific Birds*. Delaware Museum of Natural History Monograph Series 3.

Falla, R.A,. Sibson, R.B., and Turbott, E.G. 1979. *The New Guide to the Birds of New Zealand and Outlying Islands*. Collins, Auckland and London.

Hadden, D. 1981. *Birds of the North Solomons*. Wau Ecological Institute, Wau, Papua New Guinea.

Hannecart, F., and Letocart, Y. 1980. *Oiseaux de Nlle Caledonie et des Loyautés (Birds of New Caledonia and the Loyalty Islands)*. Les Editions Cardinalis, Nouméa.

Marchant, S., Higgins, P.J., and Davies, J.N. 1990. *Handbook of Australian, New Zealand and Antarctic Birds*. Oxford University Press, Auckland and London.

Mayr, E. 1945. *Birds of the Southwest Pacific*. Macmillan, New York.

Mercer, R. 1966. *A Field Guide to Fiji Birds*. Fiji Museum Special Publications No. 1. Government Press, Suva.

Pratt, H.D., Bruner, P.L., and Berrett D.G. 1987. *A Field Guide to the Birds of Hawaii and the Tropical Pacific*. Princeton University Press, Princeton, N.J.

Simpson, K., and Day, N. 1984. *Field Guide to the Birds of Australia*. Viking O'Neil, Victoria, Australia.

Index of Common English Names

The number refers to the page on which the species account appears.

Albatross
Black-browed 30
Wandering 30
Avadavat
Red 194

Baza
Pacific 54
Bee-eater
Blue-tailed 138
Rainbow 138
Bittern
Australasian 52
Black 52
Yellow 52
Booby
Brown 42
Masked 42
Red-footed 42
Bronze-Cuckoo
Shining 122
Bulbul
Red-vented 182
Bush-hen
Rufous-tailed 70
Buttonquail
Painted 68
Red-backed 68

Cicadabird
Common 170
Cockatoo
Ducorp's 116
Cormorant
Great 28
Little Black 28
Little Pied 28
Coucal
Buff-headed 124
Crake
Spotless 72
White-browed 72
Crested-Tern
Great 92
Lesser 92
Crow
Bougainville 164
New Caledonian 164
White-billed 164

Cuckoo
Brush 122
Fan-tailed 122
Oriental 122
Shining Bronze 122
Cuckoo-Dove
Crested 104
Mackinlay's 104
Cuckoo-shrike
Black-faced 168
Melanesian 170
New Caledonian 170
Solomon 170
White-bellied 168
Yellow-eyed 168
Curlew
Bristle-thighed 74
Far Eastern 74
Little 74

Dollarbird 138
Dove
Bronze Ground 106
Claret-breasted Fruit 110
Cloven-feathered 102
Crested-Cuckoo 104
Emerald 104
Mackinlay's Cuckoo 104
Red-bellied Fruit 108
Santa Cruz Ground 106
Silver-capped Fruit 110
Spotted 104
Stephan's 104
Superb Fruit 108
Tanna Fruit 108
Tanna Ground 106
Thick-billed Ground 106
White-bibbed Ground
106
White-headed Fruit 110
Yellow-bibbed Fruit 110
Drongo
Solomon Islands 164
Duck
Pacific Black 46
Plumed Whistling 44
Wandering Whistling 44
White-eyed 44

Eagle
White-bellied Sea 56
Solomon Sea 56
Egret
Cattle 50
Great 50
Intermediate 50
Little 50
Pacific Reef 50

Falcon
Peregrine 62
Fantail
Brown 152
Dusky 150
Grey 152
Malaita 152
Rennell 152
Rufous 152
Streaked 152
White-winged 150
Firetail
Red-browed 194
Flowerpecker
Midget 198
Mottled 198
Flycatcher
New Caledonian 160
Ochre-headed 160
Steel-blue 160
Vanikoro 160
Friarbird
New Caledonian 140
Frigatebird
Great 40
Lesser 40
Fruit-Dove
Claret-breasted 110
Red-bellied 108
Silver-capped 110
Superb 108
Tanna 108
White-headed 110
Yellow-bibbed 110
Frogmouth
Marbled 128

Gerygone
Fan-tailed 146

Giant Petrel
Antarctic 30
Godwit
Bar-tailed 74
Black-tailed 74
Golden-Plover
Pacific 84
Goshawk
Brown 58
Meyer's 60
Pied 60
Variable 58
White-bellied 58
Goose
Canada 44
Grassbird
New Caledonian 192
Grebe
Australasian 28
Little 28
Greenshank
Common 76
Ground-Dove
Bronze 106
Santa Cruz 106
Tanna 106
Thick-billed 106
White-bibbed 106
Gull
Black-headed 92
Silver 92

Harrier
Swamp 56
Hawk-Owl
Solomon 126
Heron
Rufous Night 52
Striated 52
White-faced 52
Hobby
Oriental 62
Honeyeater
Barred 144
Bougainville 140
Crow 144
Dark-brown 140
Guadalcanal 140
New Hebrides 144

Hornbill
Blyth's 138

Ibis
Australian 50
Glossy 52
Imperial-Pigeon
Baker's 114
Chestnut-bellied 114
Island 112
New Caledonian 114
Pacific 112
Red-knobbed 112

Jaeger
Long-tailed 100
Parasitic 100
Pomarine 100
Junglefowl
Red 15, 68

Kagu 15, 68
Kestrel
Australian 62
Kingfisher
Beach 136
Chestnut-bellied 136
Collared 136
Common 134
Forest 134
Little 134
Moustached 136
Sacred 136
Ultramarine 134
Variable 134
Kite
Brahminy 54
Whistling 54
Koel
Australian 124
Long-tailed 124

Leaf-Warbler
Island 190
Kulambangra 190
San Cristobal 190
Lorikeet
Duchess 120
Meek's 120
New Caledonian 120
Palm 120
Rainbow 118
Red-flanked 120
Lory
Cardinal 118
Yellow-bibbed 118

Magpie
Australasian 166
Mallard 46
Martin
Tree 180
Melidectes
San Cristobal 140
Miner
Noisy 144
Monarch
Black-and-white 158
Black-faced 154
Bougainville 156
Buff-bellied 158
Chestnut-bellied 156
Island 154
Kulambangra 158
Vanikoro 154
White-capped 156
White-collared 158
Moorhen
Dusky 72
San Cristobal 72
Mountain-Pigeon
Pale 114
Munia
Bismarck 196
Black-headed 196
Chestnut-breasted 196
Myna
Common 178
Yellow-faced 178
Myzomela
Black-headed 142
Cardinal 142
New Caledonian 142
Red-bellied 142
Scarlet-naped 142
Sooty 142
Yellow-vented 142

Needletail
White-throated 130
Night-Heron
Rufous 52
Nightjar
New Caledonian Owlet 128
White-throated 128
Noddy
Black 98
Blue-grey 98
Brown 98

Osprey 54
Owl
Australasian Grass 126
Barn 126

Fearful 126
Solomon Hawk 126
Owlet-Nightjar
New Caledonian 128
Oystercatcher
South Island 84

Parakeet
Horned 118
Red-fronted 118
Parrot
Eclectus 116
Finsch's Pygmy 116
Red-breasted Pygmy 116
Singing 116
Parrotfinch
Blue-faced 194
Red-headed 194
Red-throated 194
Royal 194
Pelican
Australian 28
Petrel
Antarctic Giant 30
Beck's 32
Black-bellied Storm 38
Black-winged 34
Bulwer's 32
Collared 34
Gould's 34
Tahiti 32
Herald 32
Kermadec 32
Polynesian Storm 38
Providence 32
White-bellied Storm 38
White-necked 34
Wilson's Storm 38
Phalarope
Red-necked 78
Pigeon
Baker's Imperial 114
Chestnut-bellied Imperial 114
Choiseul 106
Island Imperial 112
Metallic 102
New Caledonian Imperial 114
Nicobar 102
Pacific Imperial 112
Pale Mountain 114
Red-knobbed Imperial 112
Yellow-legged 102
Pintail
Northern 46

Pitta
Black-faced 138
Plover
Double-banded 86
Greater Sand 86
Grey 84
Little Ringed 86
Mongolian 86
Oriental 86
Pacific Golden 84
Pratincole
Oriental 84
Prion
Antarctic 34
Pygmy-Parrot
Finsch's 116
Red-breasted 116

Rail
Buff-banded 70
New Caledonian 70
Roviana 70
Woodford's 70
Redpoll
Common 196
Reed-Warbler
Australian 192
Reef-Egret
Pacific 50
Robin
Scarlet 146
Yellow-bellied 146
Ruff 82

Sanderling 80
Sandpiper
Broad-billed 80
Common 76
Curlew 82
Marsh 76
Pectoral 82
Sharp-tailed 82
Terek 76
Wood 76
Sandplover
Greater 86
Scrubfowl
Melanesian 68
New Hebrides 68
Sea-Eagle
Solomon 56
White-bellied 56
Shearwater
Audubon's 36
Flesh-footed 36
Fluttering 36
Heinroth's 36
Short-tailed 36

Streaked 36
Wedge-tailed 36
Shoveler
Australian 46
Shrikebill
Black-throated 162
Rennell 162
Southern 162
Silver-eye 186
Skua
South Polar 100
Snipe
Swinhoe's 78
Sparrow
House 196
Sparrowhawk
Imitator 60
Spoonbill
Royal 50
Starling
Atoll 176
Brown-winged
174
Common 178
Metallic 176
Mountain 174
Polynesian 178
Rennell 176
San Cristobal 174
Singing 176
Striated 176
Rusty-winged 174
White-eyed 176
Stint
Long-toed 80
Red-necked 80

Storm-Petrel
Black-bellied 38
Polynesian 38
White-bellied 38
Wilson's 38
Sunbird
Olive-backed 198
Swallow
Barn 180
Pacific 180
Swamphen
Purple 72
Swift
Fork-tailed 130
Swiftlet
Glossy 132
Mayr's 132
Uniform 132
White-rumped
132

Tattler
Grey-tailed 78
Wandering 78
Teal
Brown 46
Grey 46
Tern
Black-naped 96
Bridled 98
Common 94
Common White 96
Fairy 96
Great Crested 92
Grey-backed 98
Lesser Crested 92

Little 96
Roseate 94
Sooty 98
Whiskered 94
White-winged 94
Thicketbird
Bougainville 192
Guadalcanal 192
Thick-knee
Beach 11, 84
Thrush
Island 172
New Britain 172
Olive-tailed 172
San Cristobal 172
Song 172
Treeswift
Moustached 130
Triller
Long-tailed 166
Polynesian 166
Tropicbird
Red-tailed 40
White-tailed 40
Turnstone
Ruddy 78

Wagtail
Grey 182
Willie 150
Yellow 182
Warbler
Australian Reed 192
Island Leaf 190
Kulambangra Leaf 190
San Cristobal Leaf 190

Shade 192
Sulphur-breasted 190
Waxbill
Common 194
Whimbrel 74
Whistler
Black-tailed 148
Golden 148
Mountain 148
New Caledonian 148
Rufous 148
Whistling-Duck
Plumed 44
Wandering 44
White-eye
Banded 184
Bare-eyed 188
Ganongga 184
Green-backed 188
Grey-throated 186
Kulambangra 186
Large Lifou 188
Louisiade 184
Malaita 186
Rennell 184
Sandford's 188
Santa Cruz 186
Small Lifou 188
Solomon Islands 184
Splendid 184
Yellow-fronted 188
Yellow-throated 186
White-Tern
Common 96
Woodswallow
White-breasted 166

Index of Scientific Names

The number refers to the page on which the species account appears.

Accipiter
albogularis 60
fasciatus 58
haplochrous 58
hiogaster 58
imitator 60
meyerianus 60
Aceros
plicatus 138
Acridotheres
tristis 178
Acrocephalus
australis 192
Actenoides
bougainvillei 136
Aegotheles
savesi 128
Alcedo
atthis 134
pusilla 134
Amandava
amandava 194
Amaurornis
moluccanus 70
Anas
acuta 46
aucklandica 46
gracilis 46
platyrhynchos 46
rhynchotis 46
superciliosa 46
Anous
minutus 98
stolidus 98
Aplonis
brunneicapilla
176
cantoroides 176
dichroa 174
feadensis 176
grandis 174
insularis 176
metallica 176
santovestris 174
striata 176
tabuensis 178
zelandica 174
Apus
pacificus 130

Arenaria
interpres 78
Artamus
leucorynchus 166
Aviceda
subcristata 54
Aythya
australis 44

Botaurus
poiciloptilus 52
Branta
canadensis 44
Bubulcus
ibis 50
Bulweria
bulwerii 32
Burhinus
giganteus 84
Butorides
striatus 52

Cacatua
ducorpsii 116
Cacomantis
flabelliformis
122
variolosus 122
Calidris
alba 80
acuminata 82
ferruginea 82
melanotos 82
ruficollis 80
subminuta 80
Caloenas
nicobarica 102
Calonectris
leucomelas 36
Carduelis
flammea 196
Casmerodius
albus 50
Catharacta
maccormicki 100
Centropus
milo 124
Cettia
parens 192

Ceyx
lepidus 134
Chalcophaps
indica 104
stephani 104
Chalcopsitta
cardinalis 118
Charadrius
bicinctus 86
dubius 86
leschenaultii 86
mongolus 86
veredus 86
Charmosyna
diadema 120
margarethae 120
meeki 120
palmarum 120
placentis 120
Chlidonias
hybridus 94
leucopterus 94
Chrysococcyx
lucidus 122
Circus
approximans 56
Clytorhynchus
hamlini 162
nigrogularis 162
pachycephaloides 162
Collocalia
esculenta 132
orientalis 132
spodiopygius 132
vanikorensis 132
Columba
pallidiceps 102
vitiensis 102
Coracina
analis 170
caledonica 170
holopolia 170
lineata 168
novaehollandiae
168
papuensis 168
tenuirostris 170
Corvus
moneduloides 164

meeki 164
woodfordi 164
Cuculus
saturatus 122
Cyanoramphus
novaezelandiae
118

Dendrocygna
arcuata 44
eytoni 44
Dicaeum
aeneum 198
tristrami 198
Dicrurus
bracteatus
solomenensis 164
Diomedea
exulans 30
melanophris 30
Drepanoptila
holosericea 102
Ducula
bakeri 114
brenchleyi 114
goliath 114
pacifica 112
pistrinaria 112
rubricera 112

Eclectus
roratus 116
Egretta
garzetta 50
intermedia 50
novaehollandiae 52
sacra 50
Eopsaltria
flaviventris 146
Erythrura
cyaneovirens 194
psittacea 194
regia 194
trichroa 194
Estrilda
astrild 194
Eudynamys
cyanocephala 124
taitensis 124

Eunymphicus
cornutus 118
Eurostopodus
mystacalis 128
Eurystomus
orientalis 138

Falco
cenchroides 62
peregrinus 62
severus 62
Fregata
ariel 40
minor 40
Fregetta
grallaria 38
tropica 38

Gallicolumba
beccarii 106
ferruginea 106
jobiensis 106
salamonis 106
sanctaecrucis 106
Gallinago
megala 78
Gallinula
silvestris 72
tenebrosa 72
Gallirallus
lafresnayanus 70
philippensis 70
rovianae 70
Gallus
gallus 68
Geoffroyus
heteroclitus 116
Gerygone
flavolateralis 146
Glareola
maldivarum 84
Guadalcanaria
inexpectata 140
Gygis
alba 96
Gymnomyza
aubryana 144
Gymnophaps
solomonensis
114
Gymnorhina
tibicen 166

Haematopus
finschi 84
Haliaeetus
leucogaster 56
sanfordi 56

Haliastur
indus 54
sphenurus 54
Hemiprocne
mystacea 130
Hirundapus
caudacautus 130
Hirundo
nigricans 180
rustica 180
tahitica 180

Ixobrychus
flaviocollis 52
sinensis 52

Lalage
leucopyga 166
maculosa 166
Larus
novaehollandiae 92
ridibundus 92
Lichmera
incana 140
Limicola
falcinellus 80
Limosa
lapponica 74
limosa 74
Lonchura
castaneothorax 196
malacca 196
melaena 196
Lorius
chlorocercus 118

Macronectes
giganteus 30
Macropygia
mackinlayi 104
Manorina
melanocephala 144
Mayrornis
schistaceus 154
Megalurulus
llaneae 192
mariei 192
whitneyi 192
Megapodius
eremita 68
layardi 68
Melidectes
sclateri 140
Merops
ornatus 138
philippinus 138
Microgoura
meeki 106

Micropsitta
bruijnii 116
finschii 116
Mino
dumontii 178
Monarcha
barbatus 158
browni 158
castaneiventris 156
cinerascens 154
erythrostictus 156
melanopsis 154
richardsii 156
viduus 158
Motacilla
cinerea 182
flava 182
Myiagra
caledonica 160
cervinicauda 160
ferrocyanea 160
vanikorensis 160
Myzomela
caledonica 142
cardinalis 142
eichhorni 142
lafargei 142
malaitae 142
melanocephala 142
tristrami 142

Nectarinia
jugularis 198
Neochmia
temporalis 194
Neolalage
banksiana 158
Nesasio
solomonensis 126
Nesoclopeus
woodfordi 70
Nesofregetta
fuliginosa 38
Ninox
jacquinoti 126
Numenius
madagascariensis 74
minutus 74
phaeopus 74
tahitiensis 74
Nycticorax
caledonicus 52

Oceanites
oceanicus 38

Pachycephala
caledonica 148

implicata 148
melanura 148
pectoralis 148
rufiventris 148
Pachyptila
desolata 34
Pandion
haliaetus 54
Passer
domesticus 196
Pelecanus
conspicillatus 28
Petroica
multicolor 146
Phaethon
lepturus 40
rubricauda 40
Phalacrocorax
carbo 28
melanoleucos 28
sulcirostris 28
Phalaropus
lobatus 78
Philemon
diemenensis 140
Philomachus
pugnax 82
Phylidonyris
notabilis 144
undulata 144
Phylloscopus
amoenus 190
makirensis 190
poliocephalus 190
ricketti 190
Pitta
anerythra 138
Platalea
regia 50
Plegadis
falcinellus 52
Pluvialis
fulva 84
squatarola 84
Podargus
ocellatus 128
Porphyrio
porphyrio 72
Porzana
cinerea 72
tabuensis 72
Procelsterna
cerulea 98
Pseudobulweria
becki 32
rostrata 32
Pterodroma
brevipes 34

cervicalis 34
heraldica 32
leucoptera 34
neglecta 32
nigripennis 34
solandri 32
Ptilinopus
eugeniae 110
greyii 108
richardsii 110
solomonensis 110
superbus 108
tannensis 108
viridis 110
Puffinus
carneipes 36
gavia 36
heinrothi 36
lherminieri 36
pacificus 36
tenuirostris 36
Pycnonotus
cafer 182

Reinwardtoena
crassirostris 104
Rhipidura
cockerelli 150
drownei 152
fuliginosa 152
leucophrys 150

malaitae 152
rennelliana 152
rufifrons 152
spilodera 152
tenebrosa 150
Rhynochetos
jubatus 68

Stercorarius
longicaudus 100
parasiticus 100
pomarinus 100
Sterna
albifrons 96
anaethetus 98
bengalensis 92
bergii 92
dougallii 94
fuscata 98
hirundo 94
lunata 98
nereis 96
sumatrana 96
Sturnus
vulgaris 178
Stresemannia
bougainvillei 140
Streptopelia
chinensis 104
Sula
dactylatra 42

leucogaster 42
sula 42

Tachybaptus
novaehollandiae 28
ruficollis 28
Threskiornis
molucca 50
Todirhamphus
chloris 136
farquhari 136
leucopygius 134
macleayii 134
sanctus 136
saurophaga 136
Trichoglossus
haematodus 118
Tringa
brevipes 78
cinerea 76
glareola 76
hypoleucos 76
incana 78
nebularia 76
stagnatilis 76
Turdus
philomelos 172
poliocephalus 172
Turnix
maculosa 68
varia 68

Tyto
alba 126
longimembris 126

Woodfordia
lacertosa 188
superciliosa 188

Zoothera
lunulata 172
margaretae 172
talaseae 172
Zosterops
flavifrons 188
griseotinctus 184
inornatus 188
lateralis 186
kulambangrae 184
luteirostris 184
metcalfii 186
minutus 188
murphyi 186
rendovae 186
rennellianus 184
santaecrucis 186
splendidus 184
stresemanni 186
vellalavella 184
xanthochrous 188